¡Listos! 1

Charles Claxton • Tracy Miller • Leanda Reed

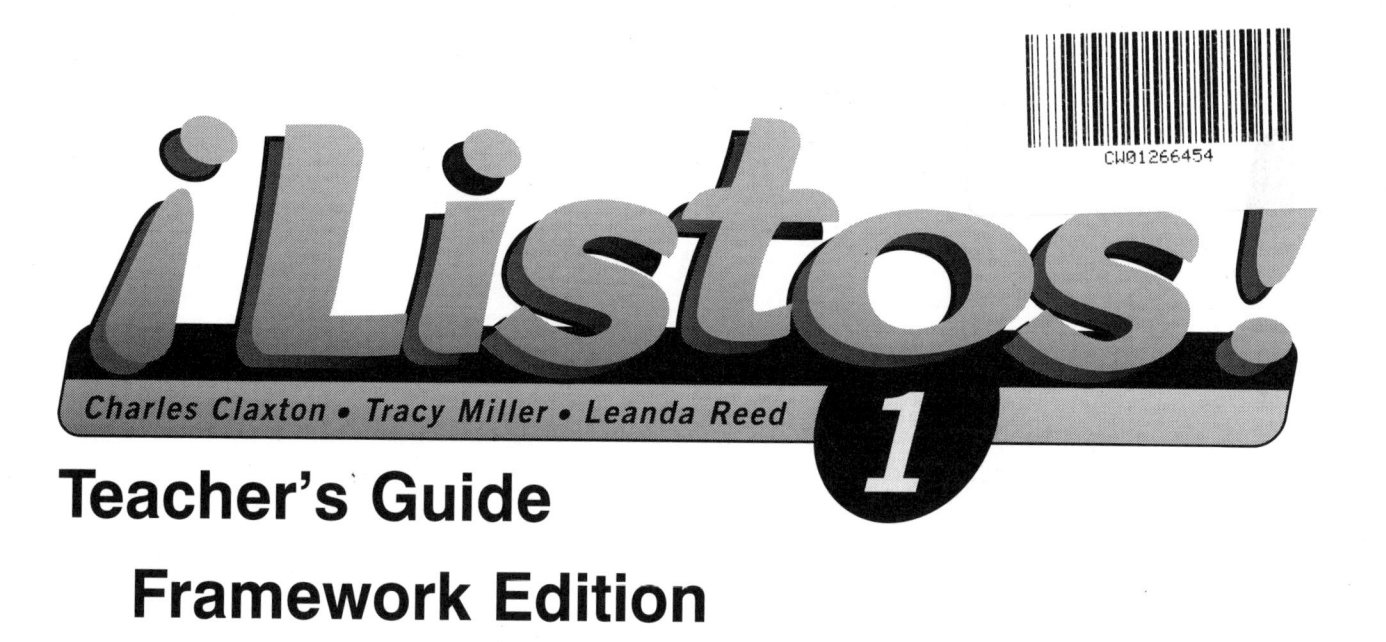

Teacher's Guide
Framework Edition

heinemann.co.uk
✓ Free online support
✓ Useful weblinks
✓ 24-hour online ordering

01865 888058

Heinemann
Inspiring generations

Contents

Introduction	3
Coverage of the MFL Framework Objectives in ¡Listos! 1 and 2	9
Covering the Programmes of Study	11
¡Listos! 1 for Scotland	13
Módulo 1: ¡Bienvenidos!	14
Módulo 2: Tú y yo	47
Módulo 3: ¡Vamos al instituto!	76
Módulo 4: En casa	107
Módulo 5: Mi pueblo	136
Módulo 6: El tiempo libre	164

Heinemann Educational Publishers
Halley Court, Jordan Hill, Oxford OX2 8EJ
Part of Harcourt Education Ltd.

Heinemann is the registered trademark of
Harcourt Education Limited

© Charles Claxton, Tracy Miller and Leanda Reed

First published 2003

07 06 05 04
10 9 8 7 6 5 4

British Library Cataloguing in Publication Data is available
from the British Library on request.

ISBN 0 435 42892 6

Copyright notice
All rights reserved. No part of this publication may be reproduced in any material form (including photocopying or storing it in any medium by electronic means and whether or not transiently or incidentally to some other use of this publication) without the written permission of the copyright owner, except in accordance with the provisions of the Copyright, Designs and Patents Act 1988 or under the terms of a licence issued by the Copyright Licensing Agency, 90 Tottenham Court Road, London W1T 4LP. Applications for the copyright owner's written permission should be addressed to the publisher.

Designed by Ken Vail Graphic Design, Cambridge

Cover design by Hicksdesign

Printed in the UK by Athenaeum Press Ltd.

Cover photograph by Getty Images/Image Bank

Tel: 01865 888058 www.heinemann.co.uk

Introduction

¡Listos! is a lively and easy-to-use Spanish course for pupils aged 11–16 of a wide ability range, which supports Foundation Subjects MFL, including the Framework for teaching MFL. The materials are fully differentiated with parallel Pupil's Books from stage 2.

Teaching Foundation Subjects MFL and the MFL Framework using ¡Listos!

Framework objectives

¡Listos! ensures that there is comprehensive coverage of all five strands of the framework:

- ✓ **Words** – teaching pupils to practise the meaning, spelling and sound of Spanish words together.
- ✓ **Sentences** – teaching pupils how to write simple grammatically correct sentences.
- ✓ **Texts: reading and writing** – teaching pupils how to understand and write more complex text using connectives, pronouns and verbs.
- ✓ **Listening and speaking** – linking listening and speaking to help pupils speak more accurately and authentically.
- ✓ **Cultural knowledge and contact** – giving pupils the opportunity to learn about Spain and other Spanish-speaking countries.

All the **framework objectives** for Year 7 are **launched** and **reinforced** in ¡Listos! 1. The reinforcement of an objective often takes place in a number of units.

Details of where the objectives are launched and reinforced are given:

a) in the Framework Overview grid on pages 9–10 of this Teacher's Guide to help you with your **long-term planning**;
b) in the Teacher's Guide in the overview grids at the beginning of each module (e.g. page 14) to help you with your **medium-term planning**;
c) in the Teacher's Guide in the overview boxes at the start of each teaching unit to help with your **short-term (i.e. lesson) planning**.

In addition, all activities in the Pupil's Book are cross-referenced to the MFL Framework to allow you to launch or reinforce the teaching objectives at different points in the course if you wish. The references are given in the Teacher's Guide at the start of each activity.

Lesson starters

Every unit in the Pupil's Book contains two lesson starters: the first at the beginning of every unit, the second approximately halfway through the unit at the point when a second lesson is likely to begin. All of the starters are described in the Teacher's Guide. Most of them are simple ideas that allow you to recap on previous knowledge or prepare the pupils for new language to be learnt in the unit. They are designed to get the lesson off to a brisk start, focusing the pupils' attention and promoting engagement and challenge. Some of the activities have an accompanying copymaster in the Resource and Assessment File. These copymasters include worksheets, games cards and material which can be photocopied onto overhead transparencies.

Plenaries

Every unit in the Pupil's Book ends with a plenary session. Again, these are simple ideas described in the Teacher's Guide. They aim to draw out the key learning points. Pupils are actively involved and are expected to demonstrate and explain what they have learnt in the unit. They identify links with what the pupils have learnt so far and what they will learn later in the course.

Thinking skills

Modules 3–6 also include a longer Thinking Skills activity, which encourages pupils to engage with language and use their brains in ways that are not traditionally associated with language learning, for example through categorising, lateral thinking and deduction. Worksheets for these Thinking Skills activities are included in the Resource and Assessment File.

The components

¡Listos! 1 consists of:
- Pupil's Book
- Cassettes/CDs
- Workbooks
- Resource and Assessment File
- Teacher's Guide
- Flashcards
- Colour OHT File

Pupil's Book

The Pupil's Book consists of six theme-based modules which are subdivided into seven double-page units (eight in *Módulo* 1). The seventh unit (*¡Extra!*) is a consolidation unit and can be left out if you are short of time or if it is not suitable for your pupils. It contains activities in all four skill areas and is to be used with whole classes in the same way as the other units. The activities tend to be slightly more difficult than in the core units, with longer reading and listening passages, which bring together the language of the module. No new core language is introduced.

¡Extra! is followed by two pages of module word lists (*Palabras*) organised by topic to help with vocabulary learning and revision.

At the end of each module there is a checklist of key functions and structures (*Resumen*) and revision activities that can be used as a practice test (*Prepárate*).

At the back of the Pupil's Book there are three sections of further practice and reference. The *Te toca a ti*

Introduction

section contains self-access differentiated reading and writing activities. *Te toca a ti A* is for lower-ability and *Te toca a ti B* for higher-ability pupils. There is a grammar reference and practice section where all the grammar points introduced in the core units are explained fully and accompanied by practice activities. Finally, there is a comprehensive Spanish–English word list, a shorter English–Spanish word list and a list of instructions covered in the Pupil's Book.

Cassettes/CDs

There are three cassettes/CDs for *¡Listos! 1*. These contain listening material for both presentation and practice. The material includes dialogues, interviews and songs recorded by native speakers. The listening material for all the *Pruebas* (the formal assessment tests in the Resource and Assessment File) can be found on the final CD/cassette.

Workbooks

In *¡Listos! 1* there are two parallel workbooks, one for reinforcement (*Cuaderno A*) and one for extension (*Cuaderno B*). The workbooks provide self-access reading and writing tasks which are designed to be fun. The workbooks are ideal for homework. There is a page of activities for each double-page core unit in the Pupil's Book. There are also two pages of revision material (*¡Extra!*), one or two pages of grammar practice and a self-assessment page at the end of each module (*Resumen*).

Resource and Assessment File Framework Edition

The Resource and Assessment File Framework Edition is organised into modules for ease of use and contains the following photocopiable material.

1. Worksheets/OHT masters to support starters and thinking skills activities.
2. Sheets consisting of pictures with the matching Spanish words/phrases on a corresponding sheet.
3. Speaking sheets for extra practice (e.g. information-gap tasks).
4. Grammar worksheets (*Gramática*) for more practice of grammar points introduced in the Pupil's Book. The Teacher's Guide gives guidance on where these sheets fit into the scheme of work. They can clearly be used at any later point in the scheme (see page 8 for a complete list of grammar worksheets).
5. Skills sheets, practising language learning skills (e.g. dictionary work) introduced in the Pupil's Book.
6. Module word lists (*Vocabulario*): photocopiable versions of the word lists from the Pupil's Book.

And for assessment:

1. *Pruebas*: end-of-module (and end-of-year) tests for formal assessment, together with the teaching notes and the answers for the tests.
2. Target-setting sheet for pupils and pupil-friendly descriptors of the NC Attainment Target Levels.

Teacher's Guide Framework Edition

The Teacher's Guide Framework Edition contains:

- overview grids for each module
- clear teaching notes and full recording transcript
- suggestions for starters and plenaries
- mapping of activities to the Framework, the National Curriculum and 5–14 Guidelines
- guidance on using the materials with pupils of varying abilities
- suggestions for additional differentiated practice
- suggestions for ICT activities
- suggestions for numeracy and literacy activities
- help with using Spanish in the classroom

Flashcards

There are 96 full-colour, single-sided flashcards with the name of the object in Spanish on the reverse for presentation or practice of language. A complete list of flashcards is given on page 7.

OIIT File

There are 16 full-colour transparencies and 16 overlays for presentation or practice of language. The file contains detailed teaching notes on how and where in the course to use the OHTs.

Using ¡Listos! 1 with the full ability range

After initial teacher-led presentation work with the whole class, pupils move on to a range of individual, pair and group activities, which allow them to work at different levels. There is a lot of scope in the core material for differentiation by pace and outcome. Suggestions are provided in the Teacher's Guide. The seventh unit (*¡Extra!*) is an optional extension unit. The activities in the Pupil's Book are supplemented by those in the *Te toca a ti* section at the back of the book. For each module there is a double page of activities: the A page activities are at reinforcement level and the B page activities are at extension level. For ease of use these activities are clearly flagged in the Teacher's Guide. Further differentiation is provided by means of the two parallel workbooks.

For those pupils who are ready to focus on the underlying structure of the language the grammar boxes in the teaching units are backed up by full explanations and practice in the grammar section at the back of the Pupil's Book as well as in the grammar worksheets. These activities can be done at any appropriate point. Although these tasks might be more suitable for higher-ability learners, it is assumed that most pupils will be able to attempt at least some of them during the year.

Introduction

Grammar

The key structures being used in a unit are often presented in a grid on the Pupil's Book page, providing support for speaking and writing activities. A summary of the key structures of each whole module is given in the *Resumen* at the end of each module. Key grammar points are highlighted in *Gramática* boxes on the page and there is a reference and practice section at the back of the Pupil's Book. In addition, there are worksheets which specifically focus on grammar in the Resource and Assessment File.

Progression

There is a clear progression within each module of the Pupil's Book and language is systematically revised and extended throughout the book. Clear objectives are given in the Teacher's Guide at the beginning of each unit to help teachers plan the programme of work which is appropriate for different ability groups.

Assessment for Learning

Revision and self-assessment

¡Listos! 1 encourages learners to revise and check their own progress regularly. At the end of each module there is a *Resumen*, a checklist of key language covered. There is also a version of the *Resumen* in the workbooks, in the form of a page of open-ended writing.

Some starters and plenaries encourage pupils to reflect on their performance and how to improve it. In addition, the target-setting sheet in the Resource and Assessment File Framework Edition allows pupils to record their NC level in each Attainment Target and set themselves improvement targets for the next module. The File also contains the NC level descriptors in pupil-friendly language, to help with their target-setting.

Teacher assessment

The assessment scheme consists of ongoing assessment as well as more formal periodic assessment. The scheme in *¡Listos! 1* focuses on Levels 1–5 in the four National Curriculum Attainment Targets (Levels C to E for the 5–14 Guidelines).

All activities have been matched against National Curriculum levels and the 5–14 Guidelines to assist teachers in carrying out continuous assessment. It must be stressed that performance in an individual activity can only contribute towards evidence that a pupil is achieving that level. Pupils must successfully carry out a range of activities at a particular level in order for the level to be awarded.

The end-of-module (and end-of-year) tests or *Pruebas* in the Resource and Assessment File provide a more formal means of assessment. The *Prepárate* in the Pupil's Book provides activities that will help pupils to prepare for the tests. The tests cover all four skills and can be used with pupils of all abilities. Again, the tasks are matched against NC levels.

The teaching sequence

Lesson starter (see page 3)

Presentation

New language can be presented using the cassettes or CDs, ensuring that pupils have authentic pronunciation models. However, the range of resources in the scheme enables the teacher to vary the way new language is presented.

Flashcards: These can be used in a variety of ways. Ideas for using the flashcards are included in the teaching notes. A list of the flashcards is given on page 7.

Visuals or picture sheets: The Resource and Assessment File contains picture sheets for each module. These can be photocopied and cut up for games or copied onto an overhead transparency and used for presentation work.

Colour overhead transparencies: These can be used for presentation or revision. The Colour OHT File contains detailed teaching notes with suggestions for additional practice.

Practice

Pupils move on to a variety of activities in which they practise the new language, usually in pairs or groups. Many of the practice activities are open-ended, allowing them to work at their own pace and level.

Reinforcement and extension

The units often end with a more extended activity of an open-ended nature. Pupils of all abilities can work on the same basic task and the teacher has an opportunity to work with individuals or small groups.

To cope with the range of ability in a class, additional reinforcement and extension activities are provided in the Pupil's Book (*Te toca a ti*) as well as the differentiated workbooks, already described.

Plenary (see page 3)

Using the target language

Instructions in the first two modules of the Pupil's Book are in Spanish and English. Thereafter they are translated into English the first time they appear. They have been kept as simple and as uniform as possible.

Integrating ICT

Suggestions for ICT activities have been included in the Teacher's Guide. These activities use the following types of software which are likely to be already available in schools.

Word-processing software

The essential difference between word processing

Introduction

and writing with pen and paper is that a word-processed text need never be a final product. Since errors can be corrected and texts can be developed and improved without spoiling the appearance of the work, writers gain the confidence to experiment as well as the motivation to take a more active interest in the language they are using.

Graphics software

Graphics software could take the form of word-processing programs that can import images, desktop publishing programs or graphics programs.

Learners can use this software to produce posters, booklets and leaflets in which they display newly acquired language in an attractive and original way. They can experiment with layout and select from a range of type styles and sizes as well as graphics.

Each module of ¡Listos! 1 contains suggestions for ICT activities.

There are also links to relevant websites in this book. In order to ensure that they are up to date, that the links work and that the sites are not inadvertently linked to sites that could be considered offensive, we have made them available on the Heinemann website at www.heinemann.co.uk/hotlinks
When you access the site, the express code is 3943P.

Games

Card games

The word/picture sheets in the Resource and Assessment File can be used for:

1 Matching pictures and labels.
2 Matching pictures and labels: Set a time limit and see which pair finishes first.
3 Pelmanism or pairs: A series of pairs of cards are laid face down in random order. Pupils match the pictures with the labels. The winner is the person who manages to make the most pairs.
4 Guessing: Each pupil has four or more cards positioned so they can see the cards but their partner can't. Pupils take it in turns to guess their partner's cards using the structures and vocabulary from the unit. First one to guess all correctly is the winner.

Vocabulary games

1 Pupils make own cards to play Pelmanism (drawing pictures and writing their own labels from the unit).
2 Spelling bees: Do these at the end of each unit.
3 Noughts and crosses (in a pair or whole-class team-game played on the board): Almost all vocabulary and structures linked to a unit can be practised playing this game.

Practising vocabulary: as in the Pupil's Book. The vocabulary being introduced is numbered. You/pupils write these numbers on a grid. Pupils guess what the word is for each number to get a nought or a cross (with or without looking in the Pupil's Book, depending on how difficult you want to make it).

4 Wordsearches: These are used throughout the book; however as an extension activity you could ask pupils to make up their own wordsearches.
5 'I went to market and I bought …' Each pupil repeats the previous word and adds their own. This can be adapted for different topics.
6 Cracking codes: Get pupils to write their own code for partners to crack. Use the symbol function on a computer to make up a code.
7 Telephones: Write a variety of made-up telephone numbers on pieces of paper (keep a list of these numbers). Hand out to pupils. The first pupil reads out a number and carries out a conversation with the person whose number it is, e.g. ¡Hola! ¿Cómo te llamas? etc. Keep the pace fast. To make it more difficult pupils could ask how the name is spelt and write it down.

Number games

Once pupils have learnt numbers 1–20 there are lots of number games for them to practise.

1 Mexican wave: Pupils stand up as they say their number and then sit down.
2 Lotto/bingo:
   a quick lotto (use as a lesson starter): Ask pupils to choose seven numbers from, for example, 1 to 20. Pupils tick off their numbers as they are called out. First one to tick all numbers shouts out 'lotto'.
   b bingo: Same as lotto, except pupils draw a grid of, for example, 12 boxes and write the numbers in the boxes.
3 Buzz: Pupils all stand up and count from, for example, 1 to 20, and leave out multiples of, for example, five. Instead of saying this they must say 'buzz' or 'vaya'. If they forget and say the multiple of five they are out and must sit down.
4 Counting with a soft toy: Count round the class throwing a soft toy.
5 Rub out the number on the board: Divide the board in half. Write the same numbers but in a different place on each half of the board. One member from each team stands in front of the board with chalk or a boardmarker and tries to be the first to cross out the number called out. Keep a tally showing which team has scored the most points.

Introduction

List of flashcards

1. las ciencias
2. la tecnología
3. la educación física
4. el francés
5. la geografía
6. la historia
7. la informática
8. el inglés
9. las matemáticas
10. la música
11. la religión
12. el español
13. un bocadillo
14. una hamburguesa
15. una ensalada
16. unas patatas fritas
17. unos espaguetis
18. fruta
19. una naranjada
20. una limonada
21. un agua mineral
22. un zumo de naranja
23. en autobús
24. en bici
25. en coche
26. en metro
27. en moto
28. en tren
29. a pie
30. un piso en un bloque moderno
31. un piso en un bloque antiguo
32. una casa
33. un chalet
34. una granja
35. la cocina
36. el salón
37. el comedor
38. el (cuarto de) baño
39. el dormitorio
40. el despacho
41. el aseo
42. la escalera
43. el garaje
44. el jardín
45. me despierto
46. me levanto
47. me ducho
48. me visto
49. me peino
50. desayuno
51. me lavo los dientes
52. el centro comercial
53. el cine
54. el parque
55. la plaza de toros
56. el polideportivo
57. la tienda de regalos
58. el estadio
59. la playa
60. la estación de autobuses
61. la estación de trenes/de RENFE
62. la piscina
63. el instituto
64. la oficina de turismo
65. el mercado
66. el café de Internet
67. un aeropuerto
68. un castillo
69. un monumento
70. un museo
71. un palacio
72. un parque nacional
73. un puerto
74. una catedral
75. una fábrica
76. hace sol
77. hace fresco
78. hace calor
79. hace viento
80. hace frío
81. hace mal tiempo
82. hace buen tiempo
83. llueve
84. nieva
85. hay niebla
86. hay tormenta
87. hacer mis deberes
88. arreglar mi dormitorio
89. ir de compras
90. pasar la aspiradora
91. sacar la basura
92. poner la mesa
93. quitar(se) la mesa
94. fregar los platos
95. lavar el coche
96. planchar mi uniforme

Symbols used in the teaching notes

+ Extension material/suggestion for extending an activity for the more able

R Reinforcement material/suggestion for simplifying an activity for the less able

▦ Game

🖱 ICT activity

Introduction

Answers to *Gramática* activities (Pupil's Book pages 128–136)

1 Nouns (p.128)
1. bolígrafos
2. reglas
3. profesores
4. conversaciones
5. peces

2.1 Definite articles (p.129)
1. la regla
2. el cuaderno
3. la mochila
4. el libro
5. los bolígrafos
6. los lápices
7. el estuche
8. la agenda (f)
9. la carpeta
10. el diccionario

2.2 Indefinite articles (p.129)
1. un perro
2. un agenda (f)
3. un gato
4. una cobaya
5. unas gomas
6. unos bolígrafos
7. un pájaro
8. un sacapuntas
9. una mochila
10. unos lápices
11. un ordenador
12. unos peces
13. unos hermanos
14. una hermana

3 Pronunciation (p.129)

ll, ñ, rr

4.1 Cardinal numbers (p.130)

tres, siete, once, trece, dieciocho, veintidós, veintinueve, treinta, treinta y uno, cuarenta, cincuenta, sesenta, setenta, ochenta, noventa

5 Dates (p.131)

mil novecientos noventa y ocho;
dos mil uno;
dos mil cuatro.

6.3 Seasons (p.131)
1. febrero
2. julio
3. noviembre
4. martes
5. sábado
6. verano, invierno

7 Adjectives (p.132)
1. mexicana
2. galés
3. paquistaní
4. escocés
5. canadiense
1. francés
2. inglés
3. español
4. canadiense

12.2 The polite form (p.133)
1. Hablo, ¿Qué idiomas habláis?
2. como, ¿Coméis en casa a mediodía?
3. Vivo, ¿Dónde vivís?

13 Verbs (2): irregular (p.134)
1. tengo
2. hace
3. salimos
4. tiene
5. voy
6. tienen
7. vamos
8. salgo
9. hacen
10. tienes

14 Verbs (3): *ser* and *estar* (p.134)
1. eres
2. Soy
3. Es
4. es
5. Está
6. estás

16 Verbs (5): reflexive verbs (p.135)
1. Me acuesto, I go to bed
2. Te diviertes, You enjoy yourself
3. Me llamo, I am called
4. Nos divertimos, We enjoy ourselves
5. Te acuestas, You go to bed
6. Te llamas, You are called

Grammar

List of grammar worksheets (*Gramática*) in the Resource and Assessment File

Resource and Assessment File	Grammar	Teacher's Guide
Módulo 1 Grammar 1 p.6	Masculine, feminine, singular and plural	22
Módulo 1 Grammar 2 p.7	Some useful verbs	39
Módulo 2 Grammar p.27	Adjective endings	63
Módulo 3 Grammar p.52	Gustar	84
Módulo 4 Grammar p.71	Reflexive verbs	125
Módulo 5 Grammar p.90	How to say 'to'	147
Módulo 6 Grammar 1 p.113	Verbs	185
Módulo 6 Grammar 2 p.114	Practising verbs	185

Coverage of the MFL Framework Objectives in ¡Listos! 1 and 2

The following charts show coverage of the Framework Objectives in *¡Listos! 1* and *2*.

The charts indicate where an objective is launched and reinforced. The reinforcement of an objective often takes place in a number of units and the reference here is just an example.

Year 7 Objectives

Objective	Launch	Reinforcement	Objective	Launch	Reinforcement	Objective	Launch	Reinforcement	Objective	Launch	Reinforcement	Objective	Launch	Reinforcement
7W1	1.1	4.4	7S1	1.8	5.3	7T1	2.6	5.3	7L1	1.1	4.5	7C1	2.7	5.5
7W2	1.5	5.2	7S2	1.5	6.3	7T2	1.6	4.2	7L2	2.3	5.3	7C2	3.7	5.7
7W3	1.2	1.7	7S3	1.3	2.5	7T3	2.6	4.6	7L3	2.3	3.1	7C3	3.3	5.5
7W4	1.2	2.1	7S4	1.1	2.3	7T4	3.3	4.6	7L4	2.1	6.4	7C4	2.4	5.5
7W5	1.3 (present) 4.3 (preterite)	5.1	7S5	1.2	1.8	7T5	2.6	3.5	7L5	3.6	4.3	7C5	1.1	5.3
7W6	1.6	3.5	7S6	3.1	5.5	7T6	3.3	3.4	7L6	1.5	4.6			
7W7	4.3	5.2	7S7	3.4 (present) 5.6 (preterite) 6.5 (imm. future)	3.7	7T7	3.2	5.6						
7W8	1.4	5.7	7S8	1.2	2.3									
			7S9	1.6	5.1									

References are to *¡Listos! 1*
1.2 = Módulo 1, Unit 2

Introduction

Year 8 Objectives

Objective	Launch	Reinforcement	Objective	Launch	Reinforcement	Objective	Launch	Reinforcement	Objective	Launch	Reinforcement	Objective	Launch	Reinforcement
8W1	2.1r 2.2v	5.2	8S1	3.1	4.3r 6.4v	8T1	2.5r 4.1v	6.4r 4.3v	8L1	1.4r 2.4v	2.5r 3.3v	8C1	*	*
8W2	2.1r 2.2v	5.2	8S2	3.6r 3.5v	5S.r 4.3v	8T2	4.3r 4.4v	4.5r 5.4v	8L2	6.4	6.6	8C2	1.1	1 *Te toca a ti*
8W3	*	*	8S3	4.1r 3.6v	6.5r 6.3v	8T3	1.6	5.7r 2.7v	8L3	1.5r 2.3v	4.2	8C3	1.7	3.5
8W4	1.1	3.2r 1.3v	8S4	1.1	6.6r 5.1v	8T4	1.6	4.7r 2.1v	8L4	2.2	5.2r 4.4v	8C4	6.1r 2.7v	6.1v
8W5	1.2r 2.5r 4.3r 1.5v 3.4v 4.4v	2.6r 3.4r 4.4r 2.6v 3.6v 4.5v	8S5	1.4	2.6	8T5	5.6r 4.1v	6.2r 4.3v	8L5	5.2	*	8C5	2.5	5.4 5.1v
8W6	4s		8S6	1.1	5.2r 6.2v	8T6	1.6	4.3r 3.5v	8L6	5.1	5.4			
8W7	2.7r 3.7v	4.7r 4.6v	8S7	1.1r 3.4r 4.3r 1.1v 3.4v 4.4v	4.5r 5.5v	8T7	all	all						
8W8	3.6r 4.1v	6.4	8S8	3.6r 4.6v	4.1r 6.6v									

References are to ¡Listos! 2
r = *rojo*
v = *verde*
References without r or v apply to both books.
S = skills sheet

Year 9 Objectives

Objective	Launch	Reinforcement	Objective	Launch	Reinforcement	Objective	Launch	Reinforcement	Objective	Launch	Reinforcement	Objective	Launch	Reinforcement
9W1	5.2		9S1	*		9T1	1.7	All 'Extra' 2.7	9L1	3.3r	5.1r	9C1	*	*
9W2	5.6r	5.7r	9S2	3.6r	'Extra' 3.7r	9T2	1.7	4.3r	9L2	3.4r	6.6r	9C2	1 *Te toca a ti*	
9W3	*		9S3	4.3r	4.7r	9T3	1.7	All 'Extra'	9L3	4.7r	5.4r	9C3	3.7	5.2
9W4	3.4r	4.4r	9S4	5.4	6.6r	9T4	All 'Extra' 1.6	All 'Extra' 6.1r	9L4	2.7r	6.6r	9C4	2 *Te toca a ti* r 4.6v	4.1r
9W5	1.7	4.5r	9S5	*	*	9T5	5.3	6.6r	9L5	5.2r		9C5	4.1	5.4
9W6	1.2r		9S6	5.6r	5.7r	9T6	6.5r		9L6	6.1r 6.3v	6.3r			
9W7	4s		9S7	5.6r	6.6r	9T7	Throughout	Throughout						
9W8	All 'Extra' 1.7	All 'Extra' 2.7	9S8	4.7r										

References are to ¡Listos! 2 rojo.
'Extra' = Extension spreads at end of each Módulo.
Prep. = *Prepárate* (practice test)
Te toca a ti = self-access reading and writing section

Covering the Programmes of Study

The table below indicates where in ¡Listos! 1 pupils have the opportunity to develop the skills and understanding prescribed in the National Curriculum Programmes of Study. For each area we have indicated where these appear in the core units of the Pupil's Book. There are further opportunities both in the Pupil's Book and the supplementary components. More detail is provided in the grids at the beginning of each module in this Teacher's Guide. Some skills are more appropriate or are practised more easily at later stages of language learning. Where this is the case we have indicated at what stage of ¡Listos! pupils will encounter these. Some opportunities, especially in section four, are beyond the scope of a coursebook. We have used the symbol *** to denote these.

1 Acquiring knowledge and understanding of the target language – pupils should be taught:	
a the principles and relationships of sounds and writing in the target language	Mod. 1 Unit 1, Mod. 3 Unit 1, Mod. 5 Unit 4, Mod. 6 Unit 1
b the grammar of the target language and how to apply it	Mod. 1 Unit 2, Mod. 2 Unit 1, Mod. 3 Unit 2, Mod. 4 Unit 1, Mod. 5 Unit 1, Mod. 6 Unit 2
c how to express themselves using a range of vocabulary and structures	Mod. 1 Unit 1, Mod. 2 Unit 1, Mod. 3, Unit 3, Mod. 4 Unit 1, Mod. 5 Unit 1, Mod. 6 Unit 1

2 Developing language skills – pupils should be taught:	
a how to listen carefully for gist and detail	Mod. 1 Extra, Mod. 2 Unit 3, Mod. 3 Unit 3, Mod. 4 Unit 1, Mod. 6 Unit 6
b correct pronunciation and intonation	Mod. 1 Unit 1, Mod. 2 Unit 3
c how to ask and answer questions	Mod. 1 Unit 1, Mod. 2 Unit 1, Mod. 3 Unit 1, Mod. 4 Unit 1, Mod. 5 Unit 1, Mod. 6 Unit 1
d how to initiate and develop conversations	Mod. 1 Unit 1, Mod. 4 Unit 5, Mod. 6 Unit 4
e how to vary the target language to suit context, audience and purpose	Mod. 5 Unit 1
f how to adapt language they already know for different contexts	Mod. 1 Extra, Mod. 2 Unit 2, Mod. 3 Unit 4, Mod. 6 Unit 3
g strategies for dealing with the unpredictable	Mod. 3 Extra
h techniques for skimming and for scanning written texts for information, including those from ICT-based sources	Mod. 3 Unit 5, Mod. 4 Resumen, Mod. 5 Extra, Mod. 6 Unit 4
i how to summarise and report the main points of spoken or written texts, using notes where appropriate	Mod. 5 Unit 6
j how to redraft their writing to improve its accuracy and presentation, including the use of ICT	¡Listos! 2 onwards

3 Developing language-learning skills – pupils should be taught:	
a techniques for memorising words, phrases and short extracts	Mod. 1 Unit 2, Mod. 2 Unit 1, Mod. 3 Resumen, Mod. 4 Unit 3, Mod. 5 Unit 4, Mod. 6 Resumen
b how to use context and other clues to interpret meaning	Mod. 5 Unit 5
c to use their knowledge of English or another language when learning the target language	Mod. 2 Resumen, Mod. 3 Unit 3, Mod. 4 Resumen, Mod. 5 Resumen, Mod. 6 Resumen
d how to use dictionaries and other reference materials appropriately and effectively	Mod. 1 Resumen, Mod. 2 Resumen, Mod. 3 Resumen
e how to develop their independence in learning and using the target language	Mod. 1 Unit 2, Mod. 2 Resumen, Mod. 3 Resumen, Mod. 4 Resumen, Mod. 5 Resumen, Mod. 6 Resumen

Covering the Programmes of Study

4 Developing cultural awareness – pupils should be taught about different countries and cultures by:	
a working with authentic materials in the target language, including some from ICT-based sources	***
b communicating with native speakers	***
c considering their own culture and comparing it with the cultures of the countries and communities where the target language is spoken	Mod. 3 Unit 3, Mod. 4 Unit 3, Mod. 6 Extra
d considering the experiences and perspectives of people in these countries and communities	Mod. 3 Unit 3, Mod. 5 Extra, Mod. 6 Extra
5 Breadth of study – during key stages 3 and 4, pupils should be taught the knowledge, skills and understanding through:	
a communicating in the target language in pairs and groups, and with their teacher	Mod. 1 Unit 1, Mod. 2 Unit 5, Mod. 4 Unit 1, Mod. 5 Unit 3, Mod. 6 Unit 6
b using everyday classroom events as an opportunity for spontaneous speech	Mod. 1 Unit 5
c expressing and discussing personal feelings and opinions	Mod. 3 Unit 1, Mod. 4 Unit 2, Mod. 6 Unit 2
d producing and responding to different types of spoken and written language, including texts produced using ICT	Mod. 6 Te toca a ti
e how to use a range of resources, including ICT, for accessing and communicating information	Mod. 3 Unit 3
f using the target language creatively and imaginatively	Mod. 2 Unit 6, Mod. 4 Unit 4
g listening, reading or viewing for personal interest and enjoyment, as well as for information	Mod. 1 Unit 2, Mod. 2 Unit 4, Mod 4. Unit 4, Mod 6. Unit 6
h using the target language for real purposes	Mod. 6 Unit 4
i working in a variety of contexts, including everyday activities, personal and social life, the world around us, the world of work and the international world	All modules

¡Listos! 1 for Scotland

All the activities in the ¡Listos! 1 Pupil's Book are matched to the 5–14 Guidelines. The information on which levels are assessed in each activity is contained in the Teacher's Guide. The following table shows where the Strands can be assessed in ¡Listos! 1. It does not show every single assessment opportunity, but is designed to illustrate the range of such opportunities in ¡Listos! 1. There are additional opportunities throughout the book which are clearly marked in this Teacher's Guide.

More formal assessment is available in the Resource & Assessment File which contains end-of-module tests and an end-of-year test.

Strand	Module 1	Module 2	Module 3	Module 4	Module 5	Module 6
Listening for information and instructions	Unit 3, ex. 4	Unit 5, ex. 2a	Unit 3, ex. 5	Unit 2, ex. 2a	Unit 5, ex. 2a	Unit 2, ex. 3a
Listening and reacting to others						
Listening for enjoyment	Unit 2, ex. 3	Unit 4, ex. 7		Unit 4, ex. 4a	Unit 5, ex. 4	Unit 6, ex. 3a
Speaking to convey information	Unit 2, ex. 1b	Unit 3, ex. 7b	Unit 5, ex. 2d	Unit 1, ex. 2c	Unit 3, ex. 3c	
Speaking and interacting with others	Unit 4, ex. 11a	Unit 6, ex. 3	Unit 3, ex. 6	Unit 3, ex. 2b	Unit 3, ex. 2	Unit 4, ex. 3b
Speaking about experiences, feelings and opinions			Unit 2, ex. 4			
Reading for information and instructions	Unit 4, ex. 7a	Unit 5, ex. 4	Unit 2, ex. 3b	Unit 2, ex. 3b	Unit 5, ex. 1a	Unit 4, ex. 4a
Reading aloud						
Reading for enjoyment				Unit 4, ex. 3a		
Writing to exchange information and ideas	Unit 4, ex. 11b	Unit 3, ex. 7a	Unit 6, ex. 3b		Unit 3, ex. 5b	Unit 4, ex. 4b
Writing to establish and maintain personal contact	Unit 7, ex. 5	Unit 4, ex. 8	Unit 1, ex. 6	Unit 1, ex. 3b	Unit 4, ex. 4	Unit 5, ex. 3c
Writing imaginatively/ to entertain	Unit 6, ex. 4					

módulo 1 ¡Bienvenidos!

(Pupil's Book pages 6–25)

Unit/topics	Key Framework Objectives	PoS	Key language and Grammar
1 ¡Hola! (pp. 6–7) Asking a friend's name Giving your name Greeting someone Asking how someone is	7W1 Everyday words (L) 7S4 Basic questions (L) 7L1 Sound patterns (L) 7C5 Social conventions (L)	1a sounds and writing 1c how to express themselves 2b correct pronunciation/ intonation 2c ask/answer questions 2d initiate/develop conversations 5a communicating in the target language	¡Hola! ¿Cómo te llamas? Me llamo Neus. ¿Y tú? ¡Adiós! ¡Hasta luego! ¿Qué tal? ¿Cómo está usted? Bien. Mal. Regular. Fatal.
2 En la mochila (pp. 8–9) Saying what you have in your rucksack Naming classroom items Saying what you need	7W3 Classroom words (L) 7W4 Gender/plural (L) 7S5 Basic negatives (L) 7S8 Punctuation (L)	1b grammar and how to apply it 3a memorising 3e develop their independence 5a communicating in the target language	Numbers 1–10 Gender Indefinite article ¿Tienes un cuaderno? No tengo una regla.
3 ¿Cuántos años tienes? (pp. 10–11) Saying how old you are Asking someone their age	7W5 Verbs present (Part-L) 7S3 Adapting sentences (L)	2d initiate/develop conversations 5a communicating in the target language	Numbers 11–20 ¿Cuántos años tienes? Tengo quince años. Luis tiene 14 años.
4 ¡Feliz cumpleaños! (pp. 12–13) Talking about dates Saying when your birthday is Months	7W8 Finding meanings (L) 7W1 Everyday words (R)	1a sounds and writing 1b grammar and how to apply it 2c ask/answer questions	Numbers 21–31 ¿Cuándo es tu cumpleaños? Mi cumpleaños es el trece de julio. El cumpleaños de Marcus es el siete de marzo.
5 En clase (pp. 14–15) Classroom instructions Classroom objects Days of the week	7W2 High-frequency words (L) 7S2 Sentence gist (L) 7L6 Improving speech (L)	1a sounds and writing 1b grammar and how to apply it 5a communicating in the target language 5b spontaneous speech	Definite article, singular and plural la pizarra la puerta el ordenador Abrid los libros. Mirad la pizarra. Sentaos. Levantaos.
6 ¿Cómo se escribe? (pp. 16–17) The Spanish alphabet Spelling your name More classroom phrases	7W6 Letters and sounds (L) 7S9 Simple sentences (L) 7T2 Reading aloud (L)	1a sounds and writing 2c ask/answer questions 5a communicating in the target language	¿Cómo se escribe tu nombre? No comprendo. ¿Puede repetir? Déjame un libro, por favor. Me hace falta. Necesito.
7 ¡Conéctate! (pp. 18–19) Naming parts of a computer Phrases for using a computer	7W8 Finding meanings (L) 7W3 Classroom words (R)	1b grammar and how to apply it 1c how to express themselves 5i working in a variety of contexts	el ratón la pantalla Busca en la red. Entra al sistema. Salva el trabajo.
Resumen y Prepárate (pp. 20–21) Pupils' checklist and practice test	7W1 Everyday words (R) 7W3 Classroom words (R) 7S4 Basic questions (R) 7S9 Simple sentences (R)	3a memorising 3d use reference materials 3e develop their independence	
¡Extra! 8 Se llama Neus (pp. 22–23) Optional extension unit: A school photo story	7S1 Word order (L) 7W2 High-frequency words (R) 7S4 Basic questions (R) 7S5 Basic negatives (R)	2a listen for gist/detail 2f adapt language for different contexts	
Te toca a ti (pp. 116–117) Self-access reading and writing at two levels		2f adapt language for different contexts	

módulo 1

1 ¡Hola!
(Pupil's Book pages 6–7)

Main topics
- Asking a friend's name
- Giving your name
- Greeting someone
- Asking how someone is

Key Framework Objectives
- Everyday words 7W1 (Launch)
- Basic questions 7S4 (Launch)
- Sound patterns 7L1 (Launch)
- Social conventions 7C5 (Launch)

Other aims
- Pronunciation practice: *ci, ca*

Key language
¡Hola! ¿Cómo te llamas?
Me llamo Neus.
¿Y tú?
¡Adiós!
¡Hasta luego!
¿Qué tal?
¿Cómo está usted?
¿Cómo estás?

Bien.
Mal.
Regular.
Fatal.
Buenos días.
Buenas tardes.
Buenas noches.

Resources
Cassette A, side 1
CD 1, track 2
Cuaderno A and B, page 2
Starter 2, Resource and Assessment File, page 10

Starter 1: Find the meaning [W1,2; S4,9; C5]

Aims: To introduce pupils to the layout of the textbook and make them aware of different techniques for deducing the meaning of unfamiliar language. (Timing: 5 minutes)

Pairwork activity. Ask pupils to look at pages 6 and 7 and to write down any Spanish words which they may know already (stop them after one minute). Ask pupils how they know these words (from films, trips to Spain, Spanish friends/relatives etc). Then tell pupils they have two minutes to look at the same pages and write down any words in Spanish for which they can work out the meaning in English. You could give an example on the board: the word *escucha* must mean 'listen' if you compare the English/Spanish instructions for exercises 1a, 2a and 2b. Ask pupils to justify their answers. Did they guess, look at the English, look at pictures etc? It is important to keep to strict timings and to maintain the pace of the activity.

Suggestion

Introduce ¡Hola! ¿Cómo te llamas? Me llamo … using puppets or dolls in a variety of different voices. Some pupils who are already familiar with these structures may like to 'meet' the puppets and be asked their name.

All pupils can be given an opportunity to greet the rest of the class and introduce themselves by 'chaining' this structure around the classroom: this activity will work best if pupils are seated or standing in a horseshoe or circle.

1 Escucha y lee. (AT1/1, AT3/1) [W6; L1; C2]

Listening for information and instructions – Level C

Listening/Reading. Pupils listen to the recording and read the dialogue between Neus and Eduard. Teachers may wish to invite pupils to read the dialogue in pairs after listening.

Tapescript
– ¡Hola! ¿Cómo te llamas?
– ¡Hola! Me llamo Neus.
– ¿Y tú?
– Me llamo Eduard.
– ¡Adiós!
– ¡Adiós! ¡Hasta luego!

2a Escucha y lee. Elige tus nombres favoritos. (AT1/1, AT3/1) [W6; L1; C2]

Listening for enjoyment

Listening/Reading. Pupils listen to the recording and practise pronouncing the names. Refer to the *¡OJO!* box to make pupils aware of the pronunciation of *ci* and *ca*. Teachers may wish to use this opportunity to discuss cultural differences between Spanish names and those of their pupils.

Tapescript
1 – Alicia
2 – Andres
3 – Camila
4 – Carlos
5 – Carmen
6 – Elena
7 – Eva
8 – Francisco
9 – Javier
10 – Lucía
11 – Jorge
12 – Luis
13 – Patricia
14 – Raúl
15 – Sergio
16 – Sol

módulo 1 ¡Bienvenidos!

2b Escucha y escribe los números de los nombres. (1–10) (AT1/1) [L1]

✶ *Knowing about language*

Listening. Pupils listen to the recording and write down who is speaking.

Answers

13, 4, 12, 16, 15, 6, 14, 10, 2, 3

Tapescript

– Hola, me llamo Patricia.

– Hola, me llamo Carlos.

– ¿Cómo te llamas?
– Me llamo Luis. ¿Y tú?
– Me llamo Sol.

– Hola, ¿cómo te llamas?
– Me llamo Sergio. ¿Y tú, cómo te llamas?
– Me llamo Elena.
– ¿Cómo te llamas?
– Me llamo Raúl. ¿Y tú?
– Me llamo Lucía.

– ¿Cómo te llamas?
– Me llamo Andrés.

– ¿Cómo te llamas?
– Me llamo Camila.
– Adiós, Camila. Hasta mañana.
– Adiós, hasta mañana.

3a Con tu compañero/a, elige un nombre español. (AT2/2) [W1,2; S4,9; C5]

✶ *Speaking and interacting with others – Level C*

Speaking. Working in pairs, pupils choose a Spanish name and practise the conversation on page 6 of the Pupil's Book with their partner. Before attempting this activity, teachers may prefer to 'chain' this dialogue round the class, with each pupil saying *Hola. Me llamo … ¿Y tú?*

3b Escribe tu diálogo. (AT4/2) [W1; S4,9; T5,6; C5]

✶ *Writing to exchange information and ideas – Level C*

Writing. Pupils write up their dialogue from activity **3a**.

> **Starter 2: Letter strings [W6; L1; C2]**
>
> *Aims:* To develop cultural awareness of different Spanish names. To make links between the spelling and pronunciation of words. (Timing: 5 minutes)
>
> *Resources:* Resource and Assessment File, page 10 (Starter 2)

Activity: Explain to pupils that you will read out a list of Spanish names, some of which they have heard previously, and a few new ones, and they must try to write down the name using the letter strings on the OHT. Pupils could use mini whiteboards or complete the whole exercise in their books.
Text to read: Alicia, Paco, Francisco, Patricia, Jorge, María, Sergio, Raúl, Andrés, Monica, Carmen, Pepe, Javier, José, Ángela

R For lower-ability pupils, you can correct the names one by one and cross off the ending to the words so they have less choice for the next name.
+ For pupils with good literacy skills, you could cut out the letter strings and mix the two columns placing them randomly on the projector.

4 Escucha y lee. Empareja las preguntas con las respuestas. (AT1/2, AT3/2) [W1; S4,9; C5]

✶ *Listening for information and instructions – Level C*

Listening/Reading. Before attempting this activity, the teacher should make sure that pupils have read the *Gramática* box and understood how to say 'you' in Spanish. Pupils match up the questions with the appropriate responses.

Answers

a 3	b 2	c 4	d 1

Tapescript

1 – ¡Hola, Sergio! ¿Qué tal?
– Mal.

2 – ¡Jorge! ¡Hola! ¿Qué tal?
– Bien. ¿Y tú?

3 – ¡Hola, Señora Martínez! ¿Cómo está usted?
– Regular. ¿Y usted?

4 – ¿Cómo estás, Patricia?
– ¡Fatal!

5 Con tu compañero/a, lee los diálogos en **4**. (AT2/2) [W1; S4,9; T2; C5]

✶ *Speaking and interacting with others – Level C*

Speaking. Using the answers from activity **4**, pupils act out the conversations in pairs.

6a Escucha y repite. (AT1/1, AT2/1, AT3/1) [W1; L1; C5]

✶ *Knowing about language*

Listening/Speaking. Pupils read and listen to the greetings, and repeat them.

¡Bienvenidos!

módulo 1

Tapescript

1
– Buenos días.
– Buenos días.

2
– Buenas tardes.
– Buenas tardes.

3
– Buenas noches.
– Buenas noches.

6b Indica un número en **6a**. Tu compañero/a dice el saludo apropiado. (AT1/1, AT2/1, AT3/1) [7W1; 7C5]

✠ *Knowing about language*

Listening/Speaking/Writing. Pupils practise the pronunciation of the greetings in activity **6a** in pairs, with one partner pointing to a greeting and the other partner pronouncing it correctly. This activity can be varied by one partner saying a greeting and seeing if the other partner can identify it correctly in the book. Pupils can be further extended if the teacher tells them to cover the text of the greetings and use only the pictures in activity **6a**.

7 Escribe un diálogo. Cambia las palabras subrayadas. (AT4/2) [W1;S3,4,9;T6;C5]

✠ *Writing to exchange information and ideas – Level C*

Writing. Pupils write their own dialogue by copying the one in activity **7** and changing the underlined words. Pupils can be further extended by adding *¿Cómo te llamas?* to the dialogue.

Plenary

Ask pupils in groups to prepare three questions on what they have learnt in the module to test other groups. Try to encourage a variety of questions that look at pronunciation, punctuation or spelling, as well as meaning. Pupils then take turns to ask different groups a question each. Reward interesting and inventive questions with points.

En casa [W1; T5; C5]

Personal dossier. This can be an ongoing project throughout the book. Pupils compile information about themselves using what they have learnt when they reach the end of each unit or module. Pupils collect information and put it in a separate folder. For this unit, pupils could draw or find a photo of themselves and write down a greeting and their name, for example *¡Hola! Me llamo Patricia*.

Some pupils may prefer to use a word-processing or desk-top publishing package to create a disk of personal information. Teachers may find a presentation package such as *PowerPoint* is ideal for work at this level, and it allows pupils to add to and edit a presentation which can subsequently be used as stimulus for oral work.

Cuaderno A, page 2

1 Elige las frases apropiadas para los globos. (AT3/2) [W1; S4,9; C5]

✠ *Knowing about language*

Reading. Pupils choose the correct sentences for the speech bubbles.

Answers

1	f	Me llamo Tomás. ¿Y tú?
2	c	¿Qué tal?
3	e	Bien. ¿Y tú?
4	a	Adiós.
5	b	¿Cómo te llamas?
6	d	¡Hola!

2 Escribe *buenos días, buenas tardes,* o *buenas noches*. (AT4/1) [W1; C5]

✠ *Knowing about language*

Writing. Pupils write the appropriate greeting according to whether it is morning, afternoon or night.

Answers

1 buenas noches	2 buenos días
3 buenas tardes	4 buenos días
5 buenas noches	6 buenos días

Cuaderno B, page 2

1 Elige las frases apropiadas para los globos. (AT3/2) [W1; S4,9; C5]

✠ *Knowing about language*

Reading. Pupils choose the correct sentences for the speech bubbles.

Answers

1	f	Me llamo Tomás. ¿Y tú?
2	c	¿Qué tal?
3	e	Bien. ¿Y tú?
4	a	Adiós.
5	b	¿Cómo te llamas?
6	d	¡Hola!

módulo 1 ¡Bienvenidos!

2 Escribe *buenos días, buenas tardes* o *buenas noches*. (AT4/1) [W1; C5]

✉ *Knowing about language*

Writing. Pupils write the appropriate greeting according to whether it is morning, afternoon or night.

Answers

1 buenas noches	2 buenos días
3 buenas tardes	4 buenos días
5 buenas noches	6 buenos días

3 Pon las frases en el orden correcto. (AT3/2) [W1; S4,9; C5]

✉ *Reading – knowledge about language*

Reading. Pupils number the phrases in the correct order.

Answers

| a 5 | b 6 | c 1/2 | d 7 | e 3 | f 8 | g 9/10 | h 2/1 | i 4 | j 10/9 |

módulo 1

2 En la mochila
(Pupil's Book pages 8–9)

Main topics
- Saying what you have in your rucksack
- Naming classroom items
- Saying what you need

Key Framework Objectives
- Classroom words 7W3 (Launch)
- Gender/plural 7W4 (Launch)
- Basic negatives 7S5 (Launch)
- Punctuation 7S8 (Launch)

Grammar
- Masculine and feminine words
- Indefinite article

Key language
¿Tienes un cuaderno?
No tengo una regla.

En mi mochila, tengo …
una agenda
un bolígrafo
una carpeta
un cuaderno
un diccionario
un estuche
una goma
un lápiz
un libro
una pluma
una regla
un sacapuntas
dos/unos cuadernos
tres/unas gomas

Numbers 1–10: *uno, dos, tres, cuatro, cinco, seis, siete, ocho, nueve, diez*

Resources
Cassette A, side 1
CD 1, track 3
Cuaderno A and B, page 3
Starter 2, Resource and Assessment File, page 10
Grammar 1, Resource and Assessment File, page 6
OHTs 1 and 2: indefinite article

Starter 1: **Squashed sentences** [S1,8;T2;L6]

Aims: To write simple sentences accurately and to reinforce knowledge of punctuation and spelling. (Timing: 10 minutes)

Pairwork activity: Write up sentences a–d from exercise 4 on page 7 of the Pupil's Book on the board or projector with no punctuation or spacing. e.g.
holasergioquetal; jorgeholaquetal; holasenoramartinezcomoestausted; comoestaspatricia
You could also invent a couple more using language from pages 6–7. Give pupils two minutes with their partner to say the sentences to each other. Ask different pupils to read aloud the sentences to the class. Pupils write down the sentences. Remind them about question and exclamation marks in Spanish. Pupils then compare their punctuation with the text on page 7 of the Pupil's Book followed by a class discussion on the differences that may arise (e.g. use of exclamation marks, accents, etc).

Suggestion
The teacher could take to the lesson a bag containing all the items mentioned in activity **1a**. The words are introduced to the class using the structure *Tengo un/una …*

Alternatively, the items could be introduced using pictures (either flashcards or on OHP) which could be grouped according to gender (*un/una*) with all the items which go with *un* on one side of the board, and those which go with *una* on the other.

1a Mira la foto, escucha y repite. Pon atención a la pronunciación. (AT1/1, AT2/1) [W3,4,6; L1]

✉ *Knowing about language*

Listening/Speaking. Pupils listen to the recording and repeat.

Point out the difference between *un* and *una*. See if pupils can make up the rule for themselves before reading the ***Gramática*** box.

R This grammar point can be further reinforced by the pupils arranging the words in activity **1a** into two columns headed *un* and *una*. This can be done in a variety of ways: the teacher can make cards of the words, which the pupils can arrange into *un* and *una* columns in pairs or small groups (this also works well on the OHP with volunteers); alternatively, pupils could write out the words in two columns in their exercise books, under the headings *un* and *una*.

Tapescript
Tengo una mochila, un cuaderno, un libro, un bolígrafo, un lápiz, un sacapuntas, una goma, una pluma, una regla, un diccionario, un estuche, una agenda y una carpeta.

1b Juega al juego de la memoria. (AT2/1) [W3,4]

✉ *Speaking to convey information – Level D*

Speaking. This game can be played in pairs, small groups, or as a whole-class activity. Pupils repeat the original phrase and then keep on adding one item round the group.

1 Kim's game. This is where the bag from the start of the lesson comes in useful. Pupils are given 30 seconds to memorise all the contents shown on the teacher's table. These are then covered up and volunteers are

módulo 1 ¡Bienvenidos!

invited to tell the rest of the class the contents from memory. This can also be played in pairs.

The same game can also be played using the OHP. To vary this activity, take one item away, and see if pupils can guess which item is missing (this is also a good way to introduce the difference between *tengo* and *no tengo*).

2 What's in the bag? Volunteers are invited to dip their hands into the teacher's bag and guess the contents by feeling them.

1c ¿Qué tiene Neus en su mochila? Qué le hace falta? (AT1/2) [W3,4; S9; L3]

Listening for information and instructions – Level D

Listening. Prepare pupils before this activity by practising *tengo* and introducing *no tengo*.

Answers

Neus has: a book, an exercise book, some biros, some pencils, a diary, a dictionary
She needs: a file, a pencil sharpener, a rubber, a ruler, a fountain pen — *pencil case* —

Tapescript

- ¿Qué tienes en tu mochila?
- A ver, en mi mochila tengo un libro y tengo un cuaderno pero no tengo una carpeta. Necesito una carpeta.
- ¿Tienes bolígrafos?
- Sí, tengo unos bolígrafos y unos lápices pero no tengo ni sacapuntas ni goma. Me hacen falta un sacapuntas y una goma.
- ¿Tienes una agenda?
- Sí, tengo una agenda y un diccionario pero no tengo una regla. Necesito una regla …
- ¿Tienes un estuche?
- No, no tengo estuche ni pluma. Necesito una pluma.

2 Con tu compañero/a, pregunta y contesta. (AT2/1) [W3,4; S4,5,9]

Speaking and interacting with others – Level D

Speaking. Working in pairs, pupils take it in turns to say what they haven't got in their pencil cases or school bags, and ask their partner if they have the things. Teachers may want to produce a prompt sheet for pupils who have everything in their school bags!

Starter 2: **Odd one out [W4]**
Aims: To reinforce the understanding and knowledge of gender with classroom objects (*un bolígrafo, un lápiz, un sacapuntas, un estuche, un libro, una agenda, un diccionario, una pluma, una mochila*) and to use thinking skills. (Timing: 10 minutes)

Resources: Resource and Assessment File page 10 (Starter 2)

Pairwork activity: Make an OHT using the sheet provided. Pupils must locate the odd one out in each row. Encourage use of the target language by giving an example and putting keywords on the board (*masculino, femenino, número tres es la excepción porque …*) but allow pupils to communicate in English for more complex ideas. Pairs feed back to the whole class and justify their decision (in English). Accept all valid suggestions. Repeat the process using columns instead of rows.

3 Escucha y canta los números del uno al diez. (AT1/1, AT2/1) [W6; L1; C4]

Listening for enjoyment

Listening/Speaking. Pupils listen to the recording and sing the song.

¡Loto! Pupils draw a blank grid of four squares, and write a number from 1–10 in each of the squares, or the teacher may prefer to use pre-prepared grids. The teacher calls out numbers from 1–10 in a random order, and pupils tick off the numbers appearing on their grids. The first pupil to have all four numbers ticked off calls out *¡Loto!*

Tapescript

uno, dos, tres, cuatro, cinco, seis, siete, ocho, nueve, diez
uno, dos, tres, cuatro, cinco, seis, siete, ocho, nueve, diez
uno, dos, tres, cuatro, cinco, seis, siete, ocho, nueve, diez

4 Escucha y suma o sustrae los números. (1–10) (AT1/1) [L1]

Listening for information and instructions – Level D

Listening. Pupils listen to the sums on the recording and write down the totals. Pupils could also be asked to write down the sums.

R Before attempting this activity, the teacher should make sure that all pupils understand the terms *más, menos* and *son*. Pupils could practise some sums as a class before starting.

National Numeracy Strategy

Note: This type of activity is excellent evidence for a numeracy policy, as it is very similar to 'mental maths'. If the department does not already have one, the teacher should talk to their school's numeracy coordinator.

Answers

1 siete	2 nueve	3 tres	4 diez	5 diez
6 uno	7 seis	8 ocho	9 dos	10 nueve

¡Bienvenidos! módulo 1

Tapescript

Ejemplo
  ¿Uno más uno son?
  Dos.
1 ¿Tres más cuatro son? 7
2 ¿Cuatro más cinco son? 9
3 ¿Seis menos tres son? 3
4 ¿Nueve más uno son? 10
5 ¿Ocho más dos son? 10
6 ¿Siete menos cinco son? 2
7 ¿Diez menos cuatro son? 6
8 ¿Dos más seis son? 8
9 ¿Cinco menos tres son? 2
10 ¿Uno más ocho son? 9

¡OJO!

The recording contains a short additional pronunciation activity (which does not appear in the Pupil's Book), focusing on the letters *g* and *j*.

Tapescript

Gema, Javier, Sergio, Juan
Gema, Sergio, Jaime, José, Juan

5 Mira los dibujos y lee las notas. ¿Cuáles son las mochilas de Neus y Eduard? (AT3/2) [W3; T1]

✕ *Reading for information and instructions – Level D*

Reading. Pupils read the two descriptions and decide which of the rucksacks (a–c) belongs to Neus and which to Eduard.

This activity contains examples of plural items which can be exploited using the writing frame and *Gramática* box at the bottom of page 9 of the Pupil's Book.

Answers

| Neus: rucksack b | Eduard: rucksack a |

6 Escribe una lista de las cosas que tienes en tu mochila. (AT4/2) [W3,4; T5]

✕ *Knowledge about language – Level D*

Writing. Pupils write a list of things they have in their own rucksack.

Literacy activity

Shared writing. This technique is one of many suggested in the National Literacy Strategy. Teachers should check that their department has a copy. Shared writing is a good way of developing pupil autonomy for extended writing. The picture of the contents of rucksack **c** could be used as a stimulus, and pupils asked to suggest phrases, which the teacher 'edits' and writes on the board. The final resulting draft could act as a stimulus for the pupils' own writing for activity **6**.

💿 ICT activities

There are a number of ICT activities that could be attempted using software loaded on most school networks.

MS Word. Pupils can word-process a description of their school bag. If the department does not have a Spanish dictionary and spellchecker loaded on the network, these can be purchased relatively inexpensively and make a tremendous difference to the accuracy of pupils' work, as well as raising confidence in writing.

MS PowerPoint. Pupils could produce a presentation of what they do and don't have in their school bag, which could then be presented to the rest of the class if access to an interactive whiteboard is possible. Pupils should be encouraged to add graphics and animation. They could even add recordings of their own voices.

MS Excel. Pupils could carry out a class survey on the contents of school bags, enter the results into *Excel* (label the heading of each column with the names of the items in activity **1a**), and use the chart wizard to produce a pie chart or bar chart of the most and least common items in school bags. This is another good numeracy activity.

Plenary

Spot the mistake. Write out or say different sentences on the topic. Pupils have to spot the mistakes (gender, singular or plural, etc.), e.g. *Tengo una cuaderno; En mi mochila hay dos libro.* Then ask pupils, in pairs, to write one incorrect sentence and one correct sentence. These are then read aloud to the class, who have to spot the incorrect sentence and explain why it is incorrect.

Cuaderno A, page 3

1 Empareja las palabras con las cosas en la foto. (AT3/1) [W1,2,3]

✕ *Knowing about language*

Reading. Pupils match up the words with the items in the photo.

Answers

| 1 a | 2 k | 3 b | 4 c | 5 d | 6 e | 7 f | 8 m | 9 g | 10 i | 11 l | 12 j |

2 Escribe una frase para cada dibujo. (AT4/2) [W3; S5,9]

✕ *Knowing about language*

Writing. Pupils write a sentence for each picture, using *tengo/no tengo*.

Answers

1 No tengo un cuaderno.	6 Tengo un diccionario.
2 Tengo un bolígrafo.	7 No tengo un libro.
3 Tengo un estuche.	8 Tengo una agenda.
4 No tengo una carpeta.	9 Tengo una regla.
5 Tengo un sacapuntas.	10 No tengo una mochila.

módulo 1 ¡Bienvenidos!

Cuaderno B, page 3

1 Empareja las palabras con las cosas en la foto. (AT3/1) [W1,2,3]

✗ *Knowing about language*

Reading. Match the words with the items in the photo.

Answers

| 1 a | 2 k | 3 b | 4 c | 5 d | 6 e | 7 f | 8 m | 9 g | 10 i | 11 l | 12 j |

2 Escribe una frase para cada dibujo. (AT4/2) [W3; S5,9]

✗ *Knowing about language*

Writing. Pupils write an appropriate sentence for each picture, using *tengo/no tengo*.

Answers

1 No tengo un cuaderno.	5 Tengo un sacapuntas.
2 Tengo un bolígrafo.	6 Tengo un diccionario.
3 Tengo un estuche.	7 No tengo un libro.
4 No tengo una carpeta.	8 Tengo una agenda.

3 Mira el dibujo y completa las frases. (AT4/2) [W3; T5]

✗ *Knowing about language*

Writing. Pupils complete the sentences based on what does and does not appear in the picture.

Answers

En mi mochila tengo unos bolígrafos, un libro, una carpeta, un estuche, una regla, una goma, un sacapuntas. No tengo un cuaderno, unos lápices, una pluma, un diccionario, una agenda …

Grammar 1, Resource and Assessment File, page 6

A matching activity to practise classroom item vocabulary and to identify the items as masculine/feminine, singular/plural. [W1,3,4]

Answers

a una agenda, f, s	h un lápiz, m, s
b un sacapuntas, m, s	i unos libros, m, pl
c unos lápices, m, p	j una carpeta, f, s
d un bolígrafo, m, s	k una goma, f, s
e un cuaderno, m, s	l un diccionario, m, s
f una regla, f, s	m un estuche, m, s
g unas plumas, f, pl	

módulo 1

3 ¿Cuántos años tienes?

(Pupil's Book pages 10–11)

Main topics
- Saying how old you are
- Asking someone their age
- Numbers 11–20

Key Framework Objectives
- Verbs present 7W5 (Part-launch. See also 4.3)
- Adapting sentences 7S3 (Launch)

Other aims
- Pronunciation practice: c + e/i
   c + a/u/o

Grammar
- *tener: tengo, tienes, tiene*

Key language
¿Cuántos años tienes?
Tengo quince años.
Luis tiene catorce años.
Numbers 11–20: *once, doce, trece, catorce, quince, dieciséis, diecisiete, dieciocho, diecinueve, veinte*

Resources
Cassette A, side 1
CD 1, track 4
Cuaderno A and B, page 4
Starter 2, Resource and Assessment File, page 11

Starter 1: Match up [W4; S3,4; T1]

Aims: To reinforce the understanding of gender and sentence structure (*Tengo, No tengo, Necesito ... un libro, una mochila, un cuaderno, tres lápices, una regla,* etc.). (Timing: 5 minutes)

Activity: Write up the following sentence halves on the board or OHP in two columns: (Column 1): *Tengo una No tengo dos En mi estuche tengo Necesito un*; (Column 2): *gomas mochila cuaderno tres lápices y una regla*. Pupils must match up the sentence halves. Correct the sentences and ask for justification of their answers. Pupils then have three minutes to change one detail in each sentence. This could be a grammatical detail (i.e. from singular to plural), or a meaning. Pupils then read out sentences to the class.

Suggestion
Before introducing the new numbers 11–20, recap the numbers 1–10, and see if any pupils already know, or can deduce, any of the new numbers.

1 Escucha y repite. (AT1/1, AT2/1) [W1; L1]

✉ *Knowing about language*

Listening/Speaking. Pupils listen to the recording and repeat the numbers.

Tapescript

once, doce, trece, catorce, quince, dieciséis, diecisiete, dieciocho, diecinueve, veinte

¡OJO!
The recording contains a short additional pronunciation activity, focusing on the combinations *c + e/i* and *c + a/u/o*.

Tapescript

cinco, once, doce, trece
catorce, cuatro, cinco

Teachers may wish to highlight a common difficulty encountered by learners of Spanish, mixing *dos* and *tres* with *doce* and *trece*.

2 Con tu compañero/a, di los números. (AT2/1) [W1; L1]

✉ *Speaking and interacting with others – Level C*

Speaking. Pupils say the numbers to their partner.

3 Con tu compañero/a, juega al bingo. Haz un cuadro de seis números. (AT2/1) [W1; L1]

✉ *Speaking to convey information – Level C*

Speaking. Pupils copy the grid from the Pupil's Book and play bingo in pairs. Teachers may wish to start with a whole-class game of bingo, including numbers from 1–20. To make the activity more difficult, the number of squares in the grid can be reduced.

4 Escucha. ¿Cuántas cosas tiene Neus y cuántas tiene Eduard? (AT1/2) [W1,3; L1]

✉ *Listening for information and instructions – Level D*

Listening. Pupils copy the grid and fill in the details from the recording. Depending on the ability of the pupils, the teacher may play the recording non-stop to make this activity more challenging, or pause after each item on the grid if support is needed.

	lápices	bolígrafos	cuadernos	sacapuntas	gomas
Neus	15	11	14	1	19
Eduard	20	17	12	18	16

módulo 1 ¡Bienvenidos!

Tapescript

– Neus, ¿Cuántos lápices tienes?
– Tengo quince. ¿Y tú?
– Tengo veinte. ¿Cuántos bolígrafos tienes?
– Tengo once.
– Yo tengo diecisiete, de diferentes colores.
– Ah. Y, ¿cuántos cuadernos tienes?
– Tengo doce. ¿Y tú?
– Catorce. Tengo catorce cuadernos. De matemáticas, historia, geografía, muchos.
– ¿Cuántos sacapuntas tienes?
– Sólo uno. ¿Y tú?
– Tengo dieciocho.
– ¡Dieciocho!
– Sí, todos diferentes, los colecciono.
– Yo tengo una colección de gomas.
– ¿Cuántas gomas tienes?
– Tengo diecinueve.
– Yo sólo tengo dieciséis.

5 Escucha las conversaciones. ¿Cuántos años tienen los jóvenes? (1–5) (AT1/2) [W1,5; S4; L1]

✖ *Listening for information and instructions – Level D*

Listening. Teachers should make sure that pupils understand that they need to write down two ages for each answer.

Before attempting this activity, teachers should introduce the structures ¿Cuántos años tienes? Tengo … años? ¿Y tú?

Answers

| 1 13, 14 | 2 12, 15 | 3 12, 13 | 4 13, 15 | 5 20, 19 |

Tapescript

1 – ¿Cuántos años tienes?
   – Tengo trece años. ¿Y tú?
   – Tengo catorce años.
2 – ¿Cuántos años tienes?
   – Tengo doce años. ¿Y tú?
   – Tengo quince años.
3 – ¿Cuántos años tienes?
   – Tengo doce años. ¿Y tú?
   – Tengo trece años.
4 – ¿Cuántos años tienes?
   – Tengo trece años. ¿Y tú?
   – Tengo quince años.
5 – ¿Cuántos años tiene usted?
   – Tengo veinte años. ¿Y usted?
   – Tengo diecinueve años.

Starter 2: Snakey card game [W1,2; L1,4] (any time after numbers 11–20 have been introduced)

Aims: To practise numbers 1–20 (as well as use of *más* and *menos*) and to develop general numeracy. (Timing: 10 minutes)

Resources: Resource and Assessment File, page 11 (Starter 2)

Activity: Make sets of cards using the sheet provided. Check that pupils understand and can say 'more than' (*más*) and 'less/fewer than' (*menos*), which are needed for this exercise. Pupils work in groups of three or four. Each group is given a set of cards and pupils deal the cards within their groups. The person with a card with 'P' (*principio*) starts by reading aloud the sum on the card. The others listen and the person with the answer to the sum reads it aloud in Spanish, followed by the sum underneath. Pupils continue in this way until all the cards have been used and they reach the card marked 'F' (*fin*).

➕ For very able students, you could use words and phrases instead of numbers, making a new template.

6a Haz un sondeo. Pregunta a tus compañeros/as de clase. (AT2/2) [W1,5; S4,9]

✖ *Speaking and interacting with others – Level C*

Speaking. Pupils prepare a grid for the survey, using the model in activity **6b**. They interview their classmates to find out their ages. Pupils could be allocated different ages, so they don't all say *doce*.

6b Copia y rellena el cuadro con la información del sondeo en **6a**. (AT4/1) [W1,3]

✖ *Writing to exchange information and ideas – Level C*

Writing. Teachers may find that it is easiest for pupils to fill in the grid while they are doing the survey.

🖱 **ICT/numeracy activity using MS Excel**

Pupils could enter the results into *Excel* (label the heading of each column with the ages of classmates), and use the chart wizard to produce a pie chart or bar chart of the average class age.

7 Escucha. ¿Cuántos años tienen los jóvenes? (1–6) (AT1/1) [W1,5; L3]

✖ *Listening for information and instructions – Level D*

Listening. Pupils listen to the recording and write down the ages of the six young people.

¡Bienvenidos! módulo 1

Answers

1 Miguel tiene quince años.
2 Sara tiene catorce años.
3 Juan tiene dieciocho años.
4 Aurora tiene dieciséis años.
5 Antonio tiene trece años.
6 Margarita tiene quince años.

Tapescript

1 – ¿Cuántos años tienes, Miguel?
  – Tengo 15 años.
2 – ¿Y tú, Sara, cuántos años tienes?
  – Tengo 14 años.
3 – ¿Cuántos años tienes, Juan?
  – Pues, tengo 18 años.
4 – Aurora, ¿cuántos años tienes?
  – 16, tengo 16.
5 – Y tú, Antonio, ¿cuántos años tienes?
  – Tengo 13 años.
6 – ¿Cuántos años tienes, Margarita?
  – Tengo 15 años.

The new structure *tiene* should be exploited before activity **8** is attempted. Pupils should already be confident with *tengo* and *tienes*: make the link to *tener* explicit now by referring to the **Gramática** box. Teachers may wish to refer back to the young people in activity **7** to practise *tiene* by asking ¿Cuántos años tiene Miguel? etc.

8 Mira las fechas de nacimiento de estos jóvenes. ¿Cuántos años tienen? Completa las frases. (AT4/2) [W1,5]

✳ *Writing to exchange information and ideas – Level C*

Writing. Pupils copy and complete the sentences, filling in the correct age of each person according to their date of birth.

This is another good **numeracy activity**, as it involves pupils working out ages based on dates of birth.

Answers

Answers will change according to when the activity is done: dates of birth only given here. Answers to be of the type 'José tiene … años.'

1 José 1.11.90
2 Merceditas 6.6.87
3 Fernando 15.10.91
4 Ágata 20.8.89
5 Luis 28.2.96

Plenary

Throw-and-catch game using a soft ball or object. Throw it to a student, asking a question in Spanish from those introduced so far. Students answer and throw the ball back to you. For example: ¿Cómo te llamas? ¿Qué tal? ¿Cómo estás? ¿Qué tienes en tu mochila? ¿Cuántos años tienes? When you have asked the questions a number of times, a student can replace you and throw the ball and ask the questions. Eventually the ball can be thrown to a student who will answer a question and then pose another question, throwing the ball to another student.

Cuaderno A, page 4

1a Busca los números. (AT3/1) [W1,7]

✳ *Knowing about language*

Reading. Pupils find the numbers in the grid.

Answers

d	i	e	c	i	n	u	e	v	e	d	q	f	q	a	d	v
n	h	x	k	q	s	n	l	o	n	i	s	u	c	t	f	e
u	t	r	e	s	m	o	h	t	a	e	d	t	i	p	y	i
e	a	p	x	i	q	c	w	r	w	c	e	o	n	n	v	n
v	d	o	c	e	o	o	c	h	o	i	t	n	c	f	c	t
e	o	e	r	i	e	a	k	a	j	s	e	c	o	d	q	e
s	s	d	c	t	r	e	c	e	o	é	i	e	y	h	s	g
d	g	e	o	l	z	d	i	e	c	i	s	i	e	t	e	f
l	i	u	c	u	a	t	r	o	u	s	i	v	g	b	i	h
d	a	c	a	t	o	r	c	e	s	f	d	i	e	z	s	y

1b Escribe los números en el orden correcto. (AT4/1) [W1]

✳ *Knowing about language*

Writing. Pupils write out the numbers from the grid in the correct order.

Answers

uno, dos, tres, cuatro, cinco, seis, siete, ocho, nueve, diez, once, doce, trece, catorce, quince, dieciséis, diecisiete, dieciocho, diecinueve, veinte

2 Empareja las frases con los números. (AT3/1) [W1,5; S9]

✳ *Knowing about language*

Reading. Pupils match up the sentences with the numbers.

Answers

| 1 11 | 2 19 | 3 14 | 4 13 | 5 12 | 6 15 | 7 16 | 8 8 | 9 5 | 10 10 |

módulo 1 ¡Bienvenidos!

Cuaderno B, page 4

1a Busca los números. (AT3/1) [W1,7]

✂ *Knowing about language*

Reading. Pupils find the numbers in the grid.

Answers

d	i	e	c	i	n	u	e	v	e	d	q	f	q	a	d	v
n	h	x	k	q	s	n	l	o	n	i	s	u	c	t	f	e
u	t	r	e	s	m	o	h	t	a	e	d	t	i	p	y	i
e	a	p	x	i	q	c	w	r	w	c	e	o	n	n	v	n
v	d	o	c	e	o	o	c	h	o	i	t	n	c	f	c	t
e	o	e	r	i	e	a	k	a	j	s	e	c	o	d	q	e
s	s	d	c	t	r	e	c	e	o	é	i	e	y	h	s	g
d	g	e	o	l	z	d	i	e	c	i	s	i	e	t	e	f
l	i	u	c	u	a	t	r	o	u	s	i	v	g	b	i	h
d	a	c	a	t	o	r	c	e	s	f	d	i	e	z	s	y

1b Escribe los números en el orden correcto. (AT4/1) [W1]

✂ *Knowing about language*

Writing. Pupils write out the numbers from the grid in the correct order.

Answers

uno, dos, tres, cuatro, cinco, seis, siete, ocho, nueve, diez, once, doce, trece, catorce, quince, dieciséis, diecisiete, dieciocho, diecinueve, veinte

2 Empareja las frases con los números. (AT3/1) [W1,5; S9]

✂ *Knowing about language*

Reading. Pupils match up the sentences with the numbers.

Answers

| **1** 11 | **2** 19 | **3** 14 | **4** 13 | **5** 12 | **6** 15 |

3 Completa las frases. (AT4/1) [W1,5; S9]

✂ *Knowing about language*

Writing. Pupils complete the sentences with the correct number.

Answers

1 Tengo dieciocho años.
2 Tengo diez años.
3 Tengo veinte años.
4 Tengo dieciséis años.
5 Tengo nueve años.
6 Tengo diecisiete años.

módulo 1

4 ¡Feliz cumpleaños!
(Pupil's Book pages 12–13)

Main topics
- Talking about dates
- Saying when your birthday is
- Numbers 21–31

Key Framework Objectives
- Finding meanings 7W8 (Launch)
- Everyday words 7W1 (Reinforcement)

Grammar
- mine/yours/his, hers, its: *mi, tu, su*

Key language
¿Cuándo es tu cumpleaños?
Mi cumpleaños es el trece de julio.
El cumpleaños de Marcus es el siete de marzo.
The months: *enero, febrero, marzo, abril, mayo, junio, julio, agosto, septiembre, octubre, noviembre, diciembre*
Numbers 21–31: *veintiuno, veintidós, veintitrés, veinticuatro, veinticinco, veintiséis, veintisiete, veintiocho, veintinueve, treinta, treinta y uno*

Resources
Cassette A, side 1
CD 1, track 5
Cuaderno A and B, pages 5–6
Hoja de trabajo 1, Resource and Assessment File, page 4

Starter 1: Cognates [W1,8]

Aims: To show pupils that there are many words in Spanish that are very similar to English – for example, the months of the year (*enero, febrero, marzo, abril, mayo, junio, julio, agosto, septiembre, octubre, noviembre, diciembre*) – and to build confidence in their learning. (Timing: 5 minutes)

Activity: Write out the months of the year on a transparency and jumble them up (or write them out on a template to cut out and give to the pupils). Working in groups, pupils then have to race against the clock to put the months in the correct order. The class can then check their answers on page 12 of the Pupil's Book and listen to the correct pronunciation.

1 Escucha y lee. (AT1/1, AT3/1) [W1,7; L1]

✉ *Knowing about language*

Listening/Reading. Pupils listen to the recording and read the months.

Tapescript
enero, febrero, marzo, abril, mayo, junio, julio, agosto, septiembre, octubre, noviembre, diciembre

2 Con tu compañero/a, haz un rap para presentar los meses. (AT2/1) [W1,7; L1]

✉ *Speaking to convey information – Level D*

Speaking. In pairs, pupils make up a rap in Spanish to present the months.

3 Escucha la canción. ¿Qué meses oyes? (AT1/2) [W1,7; L1, C2,4]

✉ *Listening for enjoyment – Level D*

Listening. Pupils pick out the months mentioned in the song. They may need to hear the recording more than once.

Answers

| January, February, March, April, May, June, July |

Tapescript
Uno de enero
Dos de febrero
Tres de marzo
Cuatro de abril
Cinco de mayo
Seis de junio
Siete de julio, San Fermín.
A Pamplona, hemos de ir
Con una media, con una media.
A Pamplona, hemos de ir, con una media y un calcetín.

Cultural note Teachers may want to explain the origins of this popular song which refers to the 7th of July, the start of the famous bullfights in Pamplona, Spain.

4 Escucha y lee. (AT1/1, AT3/1) [W1,6; L1]

✉ *Knowing about language*

Listening/Reading. Pupils listen to the recording and read the numbers from 20–31.

Tapescript
veinte, veintiuno, veintidós, veintitrés, veinticuatro, veinticinco, veintiséis, veintisiete, veintiocho, veintinueve, treinta, treinta y uno

5 Con tu compañero/a, repite los números. (AT2/1) [W1,6; L1]

✉ *Knowing about language – Level C*

módulo 1 ¡Bienvenidos!

Speaking. Pupils repeat the numbers in pairs. Encourage more confident pupils to test one another once they have repeated the numbers using the Pupil's Book.

6 Escribe seis números del 21 al 31. Escucha y subraya los números que oyes. (AT1/1) [W1; L1]

✄ *Listening for information and instructions – Level C*

Listening. This is a variation on bingo, where the pupils write down any six numbers between 21 and 31. Teachers may still want pupils to call out *¡Loto!* if they have underlined all six numbers.

Answers

21, 23, 31, 25, 29, 30

Tapescript

veintiuno, veintitrés, treinta y uno, veinticinco, veintinueve, treinta

---

Starter 2: Word classification [W1] (after introduction of numbers 20–31)

Aims: To revise numbers, months and classroom objects (Timing: 10 minutes)

Activity: Write up the following list of 20 words on the board or on a transparency: *enero, veinte, una agenda, Sergio, once, un sacapuntas, mayo, treinta y uno, diciembre, quince, Raúl, un estuche, diecinueve, abril, Andrés, un bolígrafo, Antonio, cuatro, Miguel, una mochila.* Give pupils the four headings: *Números, Nombres, Meses, Objetos.* Then give pupils three minutes to classify the 20 words. Follow the activity with a discussion on the quickest way to do this. Ask questions such as: How were the names/objects easy to spot?

7a Empareja las fechas. (AT3/1) [W1,2,6]

✄ *Reading for information and instructions – Level C*

Reading. Pupils match up the dates.

Before attempting this activity, teachers may wish to explain how dates are written in Spanish.

Answers

1 c	2 f	3 b	4 g	5 j	6 i	7 a	8 e	9 d	10 h

7b Dos meses faltan. ¿Cuáles son? (AT3/1) [W1]

✄ *Reading for information and instructions – Level C*

Reading. Pupils find the two months not mentioned in activity **7a**. This is best done as an extension activity for those pupils who complete activity **7a** quickly.

Answers

julio, noviembre

8 Escribe seis fechas. Tu compañero/a dice las fechas. (AT2/1) [W1,2]

✄ *Speaking and interacting with others – Level D*

Speaking. First practise saying dates as a whole-class activity by writing a date on the board, e.g. 14/10, and asking a volunteer to say the date. Pupils should then have the confidence to attempt this activity in pairs.

9 Escucha y escribe las fechas. (1–6) (AT1/2) [W1; L3]

✄ *Listening for information and instructions – Level D*

Listening. Pupils write down the dates of the birthdays mentioned on the recording.

Before starting the activity, pupils should read through the *Gramática* box for an explanation of *mi, tu* and *su*.

Answers

1 19th March	2 5th May	3 21st June
4 2nd November	5 16th April	6 14th October

Tapescript

1 – ¿Cuándo es tu cumpleaños?
 – Mi cumpleaños es el diecinueve de marzo.
2 – ¿Cuándo es tu cumpleaños?
 – Mi cumpleaños es el cinco de mayo.
3 – ¿Cuándo es tu cumpleaños?
 – Mi cumpleaños es el veintiuno de junio.
4 – ¿Cuándo es tu cumpleaños?
 – Mi cumpleaños es el dos de noviembre.
5 – ¿Cuándo es tu cumpleaños?
 – Mi cumpleaños es el dieciséis de abril.
6 – ¿Cuándo es tu cumpleaños?
 – Mi cumpleaños es el catorce de octubre.
 – ¿Qué día es hoy?
 – Hoy es el catorce de octubre.
 – ¡Feliz cumpleaños!

✚ As an extension activity, pupils could write out the dates in full sentences.

10 Escribe tu cumpleaños. Completa la frase: Mi cumpleaños es … (AT4/2) [W1; S3]

✄ *Writing to establish and maintain personal contact – Level C*

Writing. Pupils copy and complete the sentence, saying when their own birthday is.

Once pupils have completed this activity, ask volunteers *¿Cuándo es tu cumpleaños?* Encourage pupils to answer using the full sentence that they have written down.

¡Bienvenidos! módulo 1

11a Haz un sondeo. Pregunta a cinco compañeros/as de clase. Copia y rellena el cuadro. (AT2/2) [W1,2; S4,9]

✉ *Speaking and interacting with others – Level D*

Speaking. Pupils copy the grid and carry out a survey of the class, filling in names and birthdays. They should ask at least five classmates.

11b Escribe cinco frases. (AT4/2) [S3]

✉ *Writing to exchange information and ideas – Level D*

Writing. Teachers should make sure that pupils understand the structure *El cumpleaños de … es …* Pupils write sentences giving the birthdays of five classmates.

➕ 1 Teach the class to sing 'Happy Birthday' in Spanish:

Cumpleaños feliz,
Cumpleaños feliz,
Te lo deseamos todos,
Cumpleaños feliz.

➕ 2 Use the pairwork cards from *Hoja de trabajo 1* to prepare an extended role-play (AT2/3) which could be videoed or tape-recorded.

💿 ICT activity

There are a number of websites offering 'virtual' birthday cards. Pupils could send one another birthday cards in Spanish. If access to the Internet is limited, it is possible to make attractive birthday cards using the templates on *MS Publisher*.

Plenary

A discussion on listening skills. There are five listening activities on pages 12–13 of the Pupil's Book and pupils have now completed a whole range of these. Ask pupils to decide what is hard or easy about listening exercises, why they are important and any ideas for improving listening skills. If there is time, ask pupils to close their eyes for 30 seconds and ask about the noises/sounds/words, etc. they heard during that time.

Cuaderno A, pages 5–6

1a Mira la clave y descifra los nombres. (AT3/1) [W1]

✉ *Reading for enjoyment*

Reading. Pupils use the code to work out the names.

Answers

1 Jennifer López	2 Lisa Simpson
3 Harry Potter	4 Antonio Banderas
5 Robbie Williams	6 Victoria Beckham

1b Escribe otros nombres famosos utilizando la clave. (AT4/1) [W1]

✉ *Writing imaginatively/to entertain – Level C/D*

Writing. Pupils choose other famous names to write out using the code. They could then see if their classmates, or even the teacher, can crack the code.

2 Mira el calendario en la página seis. ¿Cuándo son los cumpleaños de las personas? (AT3/2) [W1]

✉ *Writing to exchange information and ideas – Level D*

Reading/Writing. Pupils use a different context (the calendar is on the next page of the workbook) to work out the birthdays of famous people and complete the sentences.

Answers

1 El cumpleaños de Mel C es el 12 de enero.
2 El cumpleaños de Tiger Woods es el 30 de diciembre.
3 El cumpleaños de Jennifer Aniston es el 11 de febrero.
4 El cumpleaños de Prince William es el 21 de junio.
5 El cumpleaños de Kylie Minogue es el 28 de mayo.
6 El cumpleaños de Tom Hanks es el 9 de julio.

Cuaderno B, pages 5–6

1a Mira la clave y descifra los nombres. (AT3/1) [W1]

✉ *Reading for enjoyment*

Reading. Pupils use the code to work out the names.

Answers

1 Jennifer López	2 Lisa Simpson
3 Harry Potter	4 Antonio Banderas
5 Robbie Williams	6 Victoria Beckham

1b Escribe otros nombres famosos utilizando la clave. (AT4/1) [W1]

✉ *Writing imaginatively/to entertain – Level C/D*

Writing. Pupils choose other famous names to write out using the code. They could then see if their classmates, or even the teacher, can crack the code.

módulo 1 ¡Bienvenidos!

2a Mira el calendario en la página seis. ¿Cuándo son los cumpleaños de las personas? (AT3/2) [W1]

✉ *Writing to exchange information and ideas – Level D*

Reading/Writing. Pupils use a different context (the calendar is on the next page of the workbook) to work out the birthdays of famous people and complete the sentences.

Answers

1 El cumpleaños de Mel C es el 12 de enero.
2 El cumpleaños de Tiger Woods es el 30 de diciembre.
3 El cumpleaños de Jennifer Aniston es el 11 de febrero.
4 El cumpleaños de Prince William es el 21 de junio.
5 El cumpleaños de Kylie Minogue es el 28 de mayo.
6 El cumpleaños de Tom Hanks es el 9 de julio.

2b Contesta a las preguntas. (AT3/2, AT4/2) [W1,2]

✉ *Reading for information and instructions – Level D*

Reading/Writing. Pupils answer the questions and write the answers. Teachers should encourage them to write in full sentences in order to work towards a higher level, e.g. *El cumpleaños de Cameron Diaz es el treinta de agosto.*

Answers

1 el treinta de agosto
2 el diecisiete de enero
3 el tres de marzo
4 el diecisiete de junio
5 el catorce de octubre
6 el dos de septiembre
7 el once de noviembre

Hoja de trabajo 1, page 4 [T6]

Cards for pairwork which can be used for practising:

¿Cómo te llamas?
¿Cómo se escribe?
¿Cuántos años tienes?
¿Cuándo es tu cumpleaños?

módulo 1

5 En clase
(Pupil's Book pages 14–15)

Main topics
- Understanding classroom instructions
- Naming things in the classroom
- Days of the week

Key Framework Objectives
- High-frequency words 7W2 (Launch)
- Sentence gist 7S2 (Launch)
- Improving speech 7L6 (Launch)

Grammar
- Definite article: el/la, los/las

Key language
la mesa
la puerta
la ventana
la pizarra
la silla
el ordenador

Voy a pasar lista.
Escuchad la cinta.
Sentaos.
¡Silencio, por favor!
Escribid en los cuadernos.
Mirad la página 10.
Trabajad en el ordenador.
Abrid los libros.
Mirad la pizarra.
Levantaos.
lunes, martes, miércoles, jueves, viernes, sábado, domingo

Resources
Cassette A, side 1
CD 1, track 6
Cuaderno A and B, page 7
Hoja de trabajo 2, Resource and Assessment File, page 5
Skills 1, Resource and Assessment File, page 8
OHTs 3 and 4: definite article

Starter 1: Unjumble the sentences [W3; W2,4]

Aims: To understand a typical sentence's word order and to use familiar words and cognates to work out the meaning. (Timing: 5 minutes)

Pairwork activity: Choose four classroom instruction sentences from the following list, which students will have heard you use: *Mirad la pizarra, Voy a pasar lista, Abrid los libros, ¡Silencio por favor!, Escuchad la cinta, Tira el chicle en la papelera, Escribid en los cuadernos, Mirad la página 10, Trabajad en el ordenador*, and write them on the board with the words jumbled up, e.g. *los en escribid cuadernos*. Explain that the sentences are all classroom instructions and ask pupils in pairs to write the sentences with the words in the correct order. If pupils are having difficulties, give them the meaning in English or help them work out what individual words mean. Pupils can check their answers on page 14 of the Pupil's Book.

1a Escucha. ¿Qué dibujo es? (1–12) (AT1/1) [W3; S9]

✎ *Knowing about language*

Listening. Pupils write the letters of the pictures in the order that they are mentioned on the recording.

Answers

| 1 e | 2 b | 3 g | 4 c | 5 d | 6 k | 7 i | 8 h | 9 a | 10 f | 11 j | 12 l |

Tapescript

1 – ¡Silencio, por favor!
2 – ¡Sentaos!
3 – ¡Por favor, tira el chicle en la papelera!
4 – Voy a pasar lista.
5 – Abrid los libros.
6 – Trabajad en el ordenador.
7 – Mirad la página 10.
8 – Escribid en los cuadernos.
9 – Mirad la pizarra.
10 – Escuchad la cinta.
11 – Levantaos.
12 – Los deberes.

1b Busca una frase en inglés para cada dibujo en **1a**. (AT3/2) [W3; S2]

✎ *Reading for information and instructions – Level D*

Reading. Pupils match the English and Spanish phrases for classroom commands.

Answers

| a 3 | b 6 | c 8 | d 12 | e 4 | f 2 | g 11 | h 10 | i 9 | j 7 | k 1 | l 5 |

2 Indica un dibujo en **1a**. Tu compañero/a dice la frase apropiada. (AT2/1) [W3; L1]

✎ *Speaking to convey information – Level C*

Speaking. Working in pairs, pupils pronounce the phrases their partner points to.

Teachers should agree mimes for each classroom command with the pupils, and practise giving the commands with pupils responding by acting out the mime. Many pupils will find that this kinaesthetic (or 'total physical response', TPR) way of learning works best for them. This could lead to a 'Simon says …' game, with the teacher giving the instruction, and the pupils only performing the mime if it is preceded by *El profesor/la profesora dice …*

módulo 1 ¡Bienvenidos!

Starter 2: **Back-to-front sentences** [W3; S9; L1,6]

Aims: To develop reading skills by focusing closely on the text. (Timing: 5 minutes)

Pairwork activity: Write the following sentences on a transparency: *Mirad la pizarra, Voy a pasar lista, Abrid los libros, ¡Silencio por favor!, Escuchad la cinta, Tira el chicle en la papelera, Escribid en los cuadernos, Mirad la página 10, Trabajad en el ordenador.* Position the transparency on the projector with the text back-to-front and ask pupils to read the sentences in pairs. One person reads the sentence and the other listens and corrects any errors in pronunciation.

3 Escucha y escribe las cosas en el orden correcto. (1–11) (AT1/1) [W2,3,4]

✄ *Listening for information and instructions – Level C*

Listening. Pupils put the classroom items into the order in which they hear them.

Answers

| 1 g | 2 a | 3 f | 4 e | 5 h | 6 d | 7 j | 8 c | 9 i | 10 k | 11 b |

Tapescript

1 – la ventana
2 – la pizarra
3 – la mesa
4 – la silla
5 – la mesa del profesor
6 – el libro
7 – los libros
8 – el cuaderno
9 – los cuadernos
10 – el ordenador
11 – la puerta

Teachers should point out the difference between *el, la, los* and *las*. See if pupils can make up the rule for themselves before reading the *Gramática* box.

R This grammar point can be further reinforced by the pupils arranging the words in activity 1a into four columns: *el, la, los* and *las*. This can be done in a variety of ways: the teacher can make cards of the words, or use *Hoja de trabajo 2*, which the pupils can arrange into *el, la, los* and *las* columns, in pairs or small groups (this also works well on the OHP with volunteers); alternatively, pupils could write out the words in two columns in their exercise books, under the headings *el, la, los* and *las*.

4 Indica una letra en **3**. Tu compañero/a dice el nombre de la cosa apropiada. (AT2/1) [W2,3,4]

✄ *Speaking to convey information – Level C*

Speaking. Pupils take it in turns to say the names of classroom items.

5 Escucha y repite. (AT1/1, AT2/1) [W1; L1]

✄ *Knowing about language*

Listening/Speaking. Pupils listen and repeat the days of the week.

Tapescript

lunes, martes, miércoles, jueves, viernes, sábado, domingo
lunes, martes, miércoles, jueves, viernes, sábado, domingo
lunes, martes, miércoles, jueves, viernes, sábado, domingo

6a Escribe el nombre de tu programa favorito de televisión para cada día. (AT4/1) [W1]

✄ *Writing to exchange information and ideas – Level C*

Writing. Pupils write the name of their favourite television programme alongside each day of the week.

6b Escribe una frase para cada día de la semana. (AT4/2) [W1,2,5; S3]

✄ *Writing to exchange information and ideas – Level C*

Writing. Pupils can be extended by writing a full sentence about their favourite television programme for each day of the week.

Plenary

Ask pupils to write down five nouns they have learned in the lesson. Individuals reveal their answers and the rest of the class judges by giving a thumbs up or thumbs down, depending on whether the words they have chosen are, indeed, nouns. Narrow down the search and ask pupils to identify two masculine singular nouns and two masculine plural nouns and then the same with the feminine.

Cuaderno A, page 7

1 Completa el crucigrama. (AT4/1) [W1,3]

✄ *Knowing about language*

Writing. Pupils do the crossword.

¡Bienvenidos!

módulo 1

Answers

							¹P
							I
				²L			Z
	³P			⁴S	I	L	L	A
	U		⁵C		B			R
	E	⁶V		U		R		R
⁷O	R	D	E	N	A	D	O	R	A
	T		N		D			
	A		T		E			
			A		R			
			N		N			
⁸M	E	S	A		O			

2 Empareja las frases con los dibujos apropiados. (AT3/2) [W1,3,5; S9]

✂ *Knowing about language*

Reading. Pupils match up the sentences to the correct pictures.

Answers

| a 2 | b 4 | c 5 | d 1 | e 3 | f 6 |

Cuaderno B, page 7

1 Completa el crucigrama. (AT4/1) [W1,3]

✂ *Knowing about language*

Writing. Pupils do the crossword.

Answers

(crossword as above)

2 Completa las frases. (AT3/2) [W1,3,5; S9]

✂ *Knowing about language*

Reading. Pupils join together the sentence halves.

Answers

| 1 g | 2 f | 3 h | 4 e | 5 d | 6 b | 7 c | 8 a |

3 Elige una frase de **2** para cada dibujo. Escribe la frase en el globo apropiado. (AT4/2) [W1,3,5; S9]

✂ *Knowing about language*

Writing. Pupils write the appropriate classroom command for each picture.

Answers

1 Escuchad la cinta.
2 Tira el chicle en la papelera.
3 Trabajad en los ordenadores.
4 Mirad la pizarra.

Hoja de trabajo 2, page 5

Cards for pairwork featuring classroom items: pupils match picture to correct word.

Skills 1, Resource and Assessment File, page 8 [W3; S9]

Pupils match the beginnings and endings of sentences to practise classroom instructions.

módulo 1

6 ¿Cómo se escribe?

(Pupil's Book pages 16–17)

Main topics
- The alphabet in Spanish
- Spelling your name
- More classroom phrases

Key Framework Objectives
- Letters and sounds 7W6 (Launch)
- Simple sentences 7S9 (Launch)
- Reading aloud 7T2 (Launch)

Key language
¿Cómo se escribe tu nombre?
¿Cómo se dice 'biro' en español?
No comprendo.
¿Puede repetir?
Me hace falta papel.
Necesito un bolígrafo.
Déjame un libro, por favor.

Resources
Cassette A, side 1
CD 1, track 7
Cuaderno A and B, page 8
Starter 1, Resource and Assessment File, page 11
Skills 2, Resource and Assessment File, page 9

Starter 1: Letter strings [W6; L1]

Aims: To make links between the spelling and pronunciation of Spanish cities, thereby building on cultural awareness, and to prepare for learning the alphabet (*Barcelona, Madrid, Alicante, Sevilla, Bilbao, Toledo, Ceuta, Almería*). (Timing: 5 minutes)

Resources: Resource and Assessment File, page 11 (Starter 1)

Activity: Make an OHT using the sheet provided. Explain to pupils that this is a preparation for the alphabet, which they will learn subsequently. Read out the cities listed above. Pupils write the correct spelling by using the letter strings. Follow with a discussion on letters that are pronounced differently in Spanish than in English. Pupils can look at how individual letters sound in Spanish on page 16 of the Pupil's Book. Pupils can also try to locate the cities on a map of Spain in the classroom.

1 Escucha y canta el alfabeto. (AT1/1, AT2/1) [W6; C4]

✉ *Listening for enjoyment*

Listening/Speaking. Pupils listen to and sing the alphabet song.

Tapescript
A – ah, B – beh, C – theh, Ch – cheh, D – deh, E – eh,
F – efeh, G – heh, H – acheh, I – ee, J – hota, K – kah,
L – eleh, Ll – elyeh, M – emeh, N – eneh, Ñ – enyeh, O – oh,
P – peh, Q – cuh, R – ere, Rr – erre, S – eseh, T – teh,
U – uuh, V – uuveh, W – uuveh dobleh, X – ekis,
Y – ee griegah, Z – theta

2 Con tu compañero/a, di cómo se escribe tu nombre. (AT2/1) [W1,6; S4; L4]

✉ *Speaking and interacting with others – Level D*

Speaking. Pupils work in pairs to ask and spell out their names.

✚ Teachers may wish to practise this activity with the whole class first. Most pupils would respond well to an extension of this activity (AT2/2) where their partner asks *¿Cómo te llamas?* before asking *¿Cómo se escribe?*

3a Escucha y escribe los nombres de estas personas. (1–5) (AT1/1) [W6; L1]

✉ *Listening for information and instructions – Level D*

Listening. Pupils write down the names they hear being spelt out.

Answers
1 Salma Hayek
2 Raúl
3 Príncipe Felipe
4 Enrique Iglesias
5 Conchita Martínez

Tapescript
1 S-A-L-M-A H-A-Y-E-K
2 R-A-Ú (con acento)-L
3 P-R-Í (con acento) N-C-I-P-E F-E-L-I-P-E
4 E-N-R-I Q-U-E I-G-L-E-S-I-A-S
5 C-O-N-C-H-I-T-A M-A-R-T-Í (con acento)-N-E-Z

3b Con tu compañero/a, imagina que eres una persona famosa. (AT2/2) [W1,6; S4; L4]

✉ *Speaking to convey information – Level D*

Speaking. In pairs, pupils play this guessing game using the names of famous people.

4 Haz un alfabeto de palabras españolas. (AT4/1) [W1,6]

✉ *Writing imaginatively/to entertain – Level D*

¡Bienvenidos! módulo 1

Writing. Pupils make up an alphabet of Spanish words. This will require some teacher assistance in the use of the glossary at the back of the Pupil's Book, or a dictionary.

ICT activity

Teachers may wish to ask pupils to word-process their alphabet of Spanish words.

Starter 2: Alphabet practice [W6] (after introduction of the alphabet)

Aims: To practise spelling and recognition of the alphabet. (Timing: 5–10 minutes)

Pairwork activity: Pupils take it in turns to choose a word or phrase from each section of vocabulary on pages 24–25 of the Pupil's Book (other than '*El ordenador*', which they have yet to study). They spell out this word and their partner has to write it down in Spanish and write its English equivalent, if they know it. Both students then check the spelling and award points to each other for spelling and writing down the meaning.

➕ Encourage higher-ability students to choose phrases over words.

5 Escucha las frases útiles para la clase. (AT1/2) [W3,6; S4,9; L5]

✉ *Knowing about language*

Listening/Reading. Pupils read and listen to the four short dialogues containing useful classroom phrases.

Tapescript

1 – ¿Cómo se dice 'paper' en español?
 – Papel.
 – No comprendo. ¿Puede repetir?
 – Papel. P-A-P-E-L.
2 – Señorita, necesito un bolígrafo. Déjame un bolígrafo, por favor.
 – Toma.
 – Gracias.
3 – Me hace falta un libro. Déjame un libro, por favor.
 – Tome.
 – Gracias.
4 – He terminado. ¿Qué hago ahora?

6a Con tu compañero/a, pregunta y contesta. (AT2/2) [W3; S4; L4,5]

✉ *Speaking and interacting with others – Level C*

Speaking. In pairs, pupils practise the structure *¿Cómo se dice … en español?*

6b Con tu compañero/a, pide las cosas en **6a**. (AT2/2) [W1,2,3; S9; L5]

✉ *Speaking and interacting with others – Level D*

Speaking. In pairs, pupils practise the structures *Me hace falta*, *Déjame* and *Necesito*.

Teachers should now insist that pupils use these useful phrases in class. Pupils could make posters of the phrases to help them remember them.

7 Con tu compañero/a, di estas frases en tono muy bajo. Tu compañero/a tiene que adivinarlas y utilizar 'No comprendo' o '¿Puedes repetir?' (AT2/2) [W1,3; S4,9; T2; L4,5]

✉ *Speaking to convey information – Level D*

Speaking. In pairs, pupils take turns to whisper the phrases. This is also very effective as a whole-class activity. If pupils need the phrases to be repeated, teachers should insist on the use of *No comprendo. ¿Puedes repetir?*

Plenary

From the language introduced on page 17 of the Pupil's Book, say and spell out words and phrases to pupils. They must stand up if they spot a deliberate mistake or stay seated if you have spelled words correctly. Then select pupils randomly to tell you the meaning of the words/phrases in English. If time allows, pupils can then do this together in groups or pairs.

Cuaderno A, page 8

1 Completa los globos con las palabras apropiadas. (AT3/2) [W1,3; S4,9]

✉ *Knowing about language*

Reading/Writing. Pupils choose the correct words for the speech bubbles.

Answers

1 f, escribe, g, repetir	**2** b, dice
3 h, falta, i, Déjame, d, Gracias	**4** a, hago
5 c, No, e, libro	

2 Completa las frases. (AT3/2) [W1,3; S4,9]

✉ *Knowing about language*

Reading. Pupils match up the sentence halves.

Answers

1 f	**2** e	**3** g	**4** c	**5** d	**6** a	**7** b

Cuaderno B, page 8

1 Elige las frases apropiadas para los globos. (AT3/2) [W1,3; S4,9]

Knowing about language

Reading. Pupils choose the correct phrases for the speech bubbles.

Answers

1 e, f	**2** b	**3** g, a	**4** c	**5** d

2 Utiliza las frases para escribir un diálogo. (AT4/2) [W1,3; S4,9, T5]

Knowing about language

Writing. Pupils use the sentences to write a dialogue.

Skills 2, Resource and Assessment File, page 9 [W6; L1]

Pupils make a list of Spanish words beginning with each letter of the alphabet to reinforce their understanding of the sounds of the different letters.

módulo 1

7 ¡Conéctate!

(Pupil's Book pages 18–19)

Main topics

- Naming parts of a computer
- Phrases for using a computer

Key Framework Objectives

- Finding meanings 7W8 (Reinforcement)
- Classroom words 7W3 (Reinforcement)

Grammar

- *ser: es, son*

Key language

los auriculares
la contraseña
el disquete
el botón
el disco compacto
el micrófono
el número de identidad
la pantalla
la tecla
Busca en la red.
Sal del sistema.
Mete el disco compacto/el disquete.
Salva el trabajo.
Imprime el trabajo.
Escribe la dirección.
Envía un correo electrónico.
el ordenador
el ratón
el teclado
Entra al sistema.

Resources

Cassette A, side 1
CD 1, track 8
Cuaderno A and B, page 9
Starter 2, Resource and Assessment File, page 12
Grammar 2, Resource and Assessment File, page 7

Suggestion

Teachers could use the *Say IT in Spanish* brochure, available from BECTa, to help develop pupils' confidence when using Spanish in the IT room.

Starter 1: Cognates [W8,3]

Aims: To show pupils that there are many words in Spanish that are very similar to English, and build confidence in their learning. (Timing: 5–10 minutes)

Activity: Explain to pupils that they are going to be learning the language for using a computer. Write out the following ICT language on the board or on a transparency: *el ratón, el disco compacto, el micrófono, el ordenador, los auriculares, el número de identidad, la contraseña, la pantalla, la tecla, el teclado, el disquete, el botón*. Pupils work in groups to brainstorm the words in English that they will need for this topic and then look at the words on the board or OHT and see if they can work out their meaning. The class can then complete a general brainstorm on the board and ask the teacher for the remaining words or look them up in a dictionary, if there is time.

1 Mira el dibujo, escucha y repite. Pon atención a la pronunciación. (AT1/1, AT3/1) [W1,3; L1]

✉ *Knowing about language*

Listening/Reading. Pupils listen to the recording, find the words mentioned, and repeat them.

Tapescript

– ¿Qué es **a**?
– **a** es el ratón.
– ¿Qué es **b**?
– **b** es el disco compacto.
– ¿Qué son **c** y **d**?
– **c** es el micrófono y **d** es el ordenador.
– ¿Qué es **e**?
– **e** son los auriculares.
– ¿Qué es **f**?
– **f** es el número de identidad.
– ¿Qué son **g** y **h**?
– **g** es la contraseña y **h** es la pantalla.
– ¿Qué es **i**?
– **i** es la tecla.
– ¿Qué es **j**?
– **j** es el teclado.
– ¿Qué son **k** y **l**?
– Son el disquete y el botón.

2 Con tu compañero/a, juega al tres en raya. Pon una letra del dibujo en **1** en cada cuadro. Indica el cuadro que quieres y di el nombre. (AT2/1) [W3,5]

✉ *Speaking to convey information – Level C*

Speaking. Pupils play noughts and crosses in pairs using the letters and words from activity 1.

R Teachers may wish to consolidate the new vocabulary items further by asking *¿Qué es …?, ¿Qué son …?* See if pupils can work out the difference between *es* and *son* by emphasising the *el, la* and *los, las* difference in the question, before reading through the *Gramática* box.

3 Descifra los anagramas. (AT4/1) [W3,6]

✉ *Knowing about language*

Writing. Pupils work out the anagrams.

Answers

1 disquete	2 ratón	3 auriculares
4 botón	5 ordenador	6 disco compacto
7 tecla	8 pantalla	9 teclado
10 contraseña	11 micrófono	12 número de identidad

módulo 1 ¡Bienvenidos!

Starter 2: **Odd one out** [W4]

Aims: To reinforce the understanding and knowledge of gender with computer language (*el botón, el disquete, el micrófono, el ordenador, el teclado, los auriculares, la contraseña, la pantalla, la tecla*) and to use thinking skills. (Timing: 10 minutes)

Resources: Resource and Assessment File, page 12 (Starter 2).

Pairwork activity: Pupils must locate the odd one out in each row. Encourage use of the target language by giving an example and putting keywords on the board (*masculino, femenino, diferente, número tres es la excepción porque ...*), but allow pupils to communicate in English for more complex ideas. Pairs feed back to the whole class and justify their decision (in English). Accept all valid suggestions. Repeat the process using the columns instead of rows.

4a Empareja las frases. (AT3/2) [W1,3; S9]

✳ *Reading for information and instructions – Level D*

Reading. Pupils match up the Spanish and English sentences.

Answers

| 1 b | 2 f | 3 d | 4 c | 5 a | 6 h | 7 e | 8 g |

4b Escucha y empareja las frases con los dibujos. (1–8) (AT1/2) [W1,3; L1]

✳ *Listening for information and instructions – Level D*

Listening. Pupils listen and match up the sentences with the pictures.

Answers

| 1 c | 2 d | 3 h | 4 b | 5 a | 6 e | 7 f | 8 g |

Tapescript

1 – Busca en la red.
2 – Mete el disco compacto.
3 – Entra al sistema.
4 – Escribe la dirección.
5 – Sal del sistema.
6 – Salva el trabajo.
7 – Imprime el trabajo.
8 – Escribe un correo electrónico.

5 Envía un correo electrónico a un/a amigo/a. (AT4/3) [W1; S3; T6]

✳ *Writing to establish and maintain personal contact – Level D*

Writing. Pupils adapt the model to write an e-mail to a Spanish-speaking friend.

🖱 ICT activities

1 Use a word-processing or desk-top publishing package to produce a Spanish users' guide for the school computers.

2 Use e-mail to send the message prepared for activity 5 to a Spanish-speaking friend. Most schools now have e-mail addresses for their pupils: teachers should see the school's IT co-ordinator if they are not sure. If the school does not have a partner school in a Spanish-speaking country, the best starting place is the Windows on the World website which can be accessed through www.heinemann.co.uk/hotlinks which will help teachers to find a partner school, as well as case studies and advice on funding.

Plenary

At the beginning of the lesson explain to two students (of similar ability) that you will be asking them to summarise the main points of the lesson at the end of the class. They take it in turns to cover what has been learned, using the board or an OHP. The rest of the class discusses the summary, corrects any mistakes and adds any information that was omitted.

Cuaderno A, page 9

1 Busca diez palabras. (AT3/1) [W1,2,3,7]

✳ *Reading for enjoyment*

Reading. Pupils find ten words in the word snake.

Answers

contraseña, ratón, auriculares, botón, micrófono, ordenador, disquete, pantalla, teclado, tecla

2 Empareja las palabras con los dibujos. (AT3/1) [W1,2,3]

✳ *Knowing about language*

Reading/Writing. Pupils match up the words with the pictures.

¡Bienvenidos!

módulo 1

Answers

a la pantalla	b los auriculares
c el botón	d el ratón
e el disco compacto	f el disquete
g el número de identidad	h el ordenador
i la contraseña	j el teclado
k la tecla	l el micrófono

Cuaderno B, page 9

1 Empareja las palabras con los dibujos. (AT3/1) [W1,2,3]

✥ *Knowing about language*

Reading. Pupils match up the words with the pictures.

Answers

a la pantalla	b los auriculares
c el botón	d la tecla
e el ratón	f el teclado
g el número de identidad	h la contraseña
i el micrófono	j el ordenador
k el disco compacto	l el disquete

2 Empareja las frases con los dibujos. (AT3/2) [W1,2,3; S9]

✥ *Knowing about language*

Reading/Writing. Pupils match up the sentences with the pictures.

Answers

| a 8 | b 1 | c 2 | d 3 | e 4 | f 7 | g 6 | h 5 |

Grammar 2, Resource and Assessment File, page 7 [W5; C5]

Pupils complete the grid by supplying the correct forms of the verb *llamarse, ser* and *tener* in the singular.

Activity to practise which form of 'you' (*tú/usted*) to use in a range of contexts.

1 Answers

	llamarse *to be called*	ser *to be*	tener *to have*
I	me llamo	soy	tengo
You	te llamas	eres	tienes
He	se llama	es	tiene
She	se llama	es	tiene
It	se llama	es	tiene

2 Answers

| a usted | b tú | c tú | d usted | e tú |

módulo 1

Resumen y Prepárate

(Pupil's Book pages 20–21)

Resumen

This is a checklist of language covered in Module 1. There is a comprehensive **Resumen** list for Module 1 in the Pupil's Book (page 20) and a **Resumen** test sheet in Cuaderno A and B (page 14).

Key Framework Objectives

- Everyday words 7W1 (Reinforcement)
- Classroom words 7W3 (Reinforcement)
- Basic questions 7S4 (Reinforcement)
- Simple sentences 7S9 (Reinforcement)

Prepárate

A revision test to give practice for the test itself at the end of the module.

Resources

Cassette A, side 1
CD 1, track 9
Cuaderno A and B, Repaso (previously ¡Extra!) pages 10–11; Gramática pages 12–13

---

1 Escucha y escribe los números que oyes. (AT1/1) [W1; L1]

Listening for information and instructions – Level C

Listening. Pupils listen and write down the 10 numbers that they hear.

Answers

2, 10, 31, 19, 14, 23, 28, 30, 15, 11

Tapescript

dos, diez, treinta y uno, diecinueve, catorce, veintitrés, veintiocho, treinta, quince, once

---

2 Escucha y escribe los artículos en el orden correcto. (AT1/1) [W1,3]

Listening for information and instructions – Level C

Listening. Pupils listen and write the numbers of the articles in the order they hear them.

Answers

3, 4, 8, 6, 2, 7, 1, 5

Tapescript

una mochila, un bolígrafo, una carpeta, un libro, un cuaderno, una hoja de papel, un lápiz, un estuche

---

3 Con tu compañero/a, empareja las preguntas con las respuestas. (AT2/2, AT3/2) [W1,6; S9; C5]

Speaking to convey information – Level C

Speaking/Reading. In pairs, pupils match up the questions and answers.

Answers

1 b	**2** e	**3** d	**4** c	**5** a

---

4 Pregunta y contesta para ti. (AT2/2) [W1,6; S9; C5]

Speaking and interacting with others – Level D

Speaking. In pairs, pupils ask and answer the questions from activity 3 with information about themselves.

---

5 Empareja las preguntas con las respuestas. (AT3/2) [W1,3; C5]

Knowing about language

Reading. Pupils match up the questions and answers.

Answers

a 5	**b** 1	**c** 3	**d** 6	**e** 4	**f** 2

---

6 Copia y completa las frases con la palabra apropiada. (AT4/1) [W1,3; S2,4,9]

Knowing about language

Writing. Pupils complete the sentences with the correct word.

Answers

1 Hasta	**2** pizarra	**3** Cuántos	**4** Cómo	**5** cumpleaños

---

Cuaderno A, pages 10–11

Repaso (previously ¡Extra!)

1 Busca los días y los meses. (AT3/1) [W1,7]

Reading for enjoyment

Reading. Pupils find the days and months in the wordsearch.

¡Bienvenidos!

módulo 1

Answers

```
o y a m k s o q a v s w n
r m l b h v i e r n e s o
e d s u p o y g x l k v
n a o q n b j u n i o p i
e r d h k e q z g r c m e
e m a r t e s g m b r u m
j a b a b r w b z a é e b
u r á d o m i n g o i r r
e z s y j u l i o k m b e
v o q a g o s t o x j u m
e z a o r e r b e f e t f
s e p t i e m b r e j c d
v e r b m e i c i d w o k
```

2 ¿Verdad (✓) or mentira (✗)? (AT3/2) [W1]

✖ *Reading for information and instructions – Level C*

Reading. Pupils read the sums and decide if they are true (*verdad*) or false (*mentira*).

Answers

| a ✗ | b ✓ | c ✗ | d ✗ | e ✓ | f ✓ | g ✓ | h ✗ |

3 Completa las calculaciones. (AT3/2) [W1]

✖ *Knowing about language*

Reading/Writing. Pupils do the sums.

Answers

| a veintitrés | b veinticinco | c veintidós |
| d diecisiete | e cinco | f treinta y uno |

4 Escribe los diálogos en los globos apropiados. (AT3/2, AT4/2) [W1,2; S4; T5; C5]

✖ *Knowing about language*

Reading/Writing. Pupils put the phrases in the correct speech bubbles to make a dialogue for each picture.

Answers

1 c	1st speaker: Hasta luego, Cristina.
	2nd speaker: Adiós, Fernando.
2 a	1st speaker: Hola. ¿Cómo te llamas?
	2nd speaker: Me llamo Javier. ¿Y tú?
	1st speaker: Me llamo Alejandra.
3 e	2nd speaker: ¿Cuántos años tienes?
	1st speaker: Tengo cinco años.
4 d	1st speaker: Déjame una regla.
	2nd speaker: Toma.
5 f	1st speaker: ¿Cuándo es tu cumpleaños?
	2nd speaker: Es el seis de enero.
6 b	2nd speaker: ¿Qué hago ahora?
	1st speaker: Mira la página cuatro.

Cuaderno B, pages 10–11

Repaso (previously ¡Extra!)

1 Busca los días y los meses. (AT3/1) [W1,7]

✖ *Reading for enjoyment*

Reading. Pupils find the days and months in the wordsearch.

Answers

```
o y a m k s o q a v s w n
r m l b h v i e r n e s o
e d s u p o y g x l k v
n a o q n b j u n i o p i
e r d h k e q z g r c m e
e m a r t e s g m b r u m
j a b a b r w b z a é e b
u r á d o m i n g o i r r
e z s y j u l i o k m b e
v o q a g o s t o x j u m
e z a o r e r b e f e t f
s e p t i e m b r e j c d
v e r b m e i c i d w o k
```

2a ¿Verdad (✓) or mentira (✗)? (AT3/2) [W1]

✖ *Reading for information and instructions – Level C*

Reading. Pupils read the sums and decide if they are true (*verdad*) or false (*mentira*).

Answers

| a ✗ | b ✓ | c ✗ | d ✗ | e ✓ | f ✓ | g ✓ | h ✗ |

2b Corrige las sumas falsas. (AT3/2) [W1]

✖ *Knowing about language*

Reading/Writing. Pupils write the correct answers to the sums in activity **2a** which are wrong.

Answers

| a quince | c catorce | d cinco | h uno |

3 Completa las sumas. (AT3/2) [W1]

✖ *Knowing about language*

Reading/Writing. Pupils do the sums.

Answers

| a veintitrés | b quince | c ocho | d nueve | e cinco | f ocho |

módulo 1 ¡Bienvenidos!

4 Escribe los diálogos en los globos apropiados. (AT3/2, AT4/2) [W1,2; S4; T5; C5]

✸ *Knowing about language*

Reading/Writing. Pupils put the phrases in the correct speech bubbles to make a dialogue for each picture.

Answers

1 d	1st speaker:	Hola. ¿Cómo te llamas?
	2nd speaker:	Me llamo Javier. ¿Y tú?
	1st speaker:	Me llamo Alejandra.
2 e	2nd speaker:	¿Cuántos años tienes?
	1st speaker:	Tengo cinco años.
3 b	1st speaker:	Déjame una regla.
	2nd speaker:	Toma
4 a	1st speaker:	¿Cuándo es tu cumpleaños?
	2nd speaker:	Es el seis de enero.
5 f	1st speaker:	¿Qué tal?
	2nd speaker:	Fatal.
6 c	1st speaker:	¿Cómo se escribe 'lápiz'?
	2nd speaker:	Se escribe L-Á-P-I-Z.

5 Escribe un diálogo similar. Cambia las palabras subrayadas. (AT4/2–3) [W1,2; S3,4; T6; C5]

✸ *Writing to exchange information and ideas – Level D/E*

Writing. Pupils write their own dialogues, changing the words which are underlined in activity 4.

Cuaderno A, pages 12–13

Gramática

1 Completa las preguntas con las palabras apropiadas. (AT3/2, AT4/1) [W1,2; S4]

✸ *Knowing about language*

Reading/Writing. Pupils write in the correct question words to complete the sentences.

Answers

a Qué	b Cómo	c Cómo	d Cómo	e Cuántos	f Cuándo

2 Completa las frases con la forma apropiada de los verbos. (AT3/2, AT4/1) [W5]

✸ *Knowing about language*

Reading/Writing. Pupils complete the sentences with the correct form of the verbs.

Answers

a llamo	b te llamas	c se llama
d tienes	e Tengo	f tiene

3 Escribe el plural de las palabras. (AT4/1) [W4]

✸ *Knowing about language*

Writing. Pupils write the plural form of the words.

Answers

a pizarras	b botones	c auriculares	d estuches
e lápices	f mesas	g ordenadores	h disquetes

4 Escribe *el, la, los* o *las*. (AT4/1) [W2,4]

✸ *Knowing about language*

Writing. Pupils write the correct definite article.

Answers

a la	b el	c el	d los	e las	f la

5 Escribe *un, una, unos* o *unas*. (AT4/1) [W2,4]

✸ *Knowing about language*

Writing. Pupils write the correct indefinite article.

Answers

a una	b un	c un	d unos	e unas	f una

Cuaderno B, page 12–13

Gramática

1 Completa las preguntas con las palabras apropiadas. (AT3/2, AT4/1) [W1,2; S4]

✸ *Knowing about language*

Reading/Writing. Pupils write in the correct question words to complete the sentences.

Answers

a Qué	b Cómo	c Cómo	d Cómo	e Cuántos	f Cuándo

2 Completa las frases con la forma apropiada de los verbos. (AT3/2, AT4/1) [W5]

✸ *Knowing about language*

Reading/Writing. Pupils complete the sentences with the correct form of the verbs.

Answers

a llamo	b te llamas	c se llama
d tienes	e Tengo	f tiene

3 Escribe el plural de las palabras. (AT4/1) [W4]

✸ *Knowing about language*

Writing. Pupils write the plural form of the words.

¡Bienvenidos! módulo 1

Answers

a pizarras	b botones	c auriculares	d estuches
e lápices	f mesas	g ordenadores	h disquetes

4 Escribe *el, la, los* o *las*. (AT4/1) [W2,4]

✠ *Knowing about language*

Writing. Pupils write the correct definite article.

Answers

a la	b el	c el	d los	e las	f la

5 Escribe *un, una, unos* o *unas*. (AT4/1) [W2,4]

✠ *Knowing about language*

Writing. Pupils write the correct indefinite article.

Answers

a una	b un	c un	d unos	e unas	f una

módulo 1

¡Extra! 8 Se llama Neus

(Pupil's Book pages 22–23)

Main topics

This is an optional unit which reviews some of the key language of the module: it consists of a photo story set in a school.

Key Framework Objectives

- Word order 7S1 (Launch)
- High-frequency words 7W2 (Reinforcement)
- Basic questions 7S4 (Reinforcement)
- Basic negatives 7S5 (Reinforcement)

Resources

Cassette A, Side 1
CD 1, track 10
Starter 1, Resource and Assessment File, page 12
Starter 2, Resource and Assessment File, page 13

Starter 1: Stepping stones [W5; S1,9]

Aims: To consolidate pupils' knowledge of *llamarse* and *tener* in the present tense (*me llamo/se llama Señor/Señora Moreno/Rodriguez, yo tengo/ Maribel/Gustavo tiene doce años/un ordenador/una mochila, ¿Cómo te llamas?*). (Timing: 5–10 minutes)

Resources: Resource and Assessment File, page 12 (Starter 1)

Activity: Make an OHT using the sheet provided. Pupils must use the stepping stones to create accurate, meaningful sentences, using either a copy of the transparency, paper or mini-whiteboards. Pupils must then justify their choices and may come to the projector to show how their chosen sentences are formed using the stepping stones. Write any incorrect sentences given by pupils on the board and ask the class to explain the error(s).

1a Escucha y lee. (AT1/2, AT3/2) [W1,2,3; S9; T1; L3; C5]

✖ *Knowing about language*

Listening/Reading. Pupils listen to the recording and follow the dialogue in their books.

Tapescript

1 – ¡Hola, Eduard! ¿Qué tal?
   – Mal … terrible … No tengo los deberes … No tengo la carpeta …
2 – Buenos días.
3 – ¡Silencio, por favor! Sentaos y abrid los libros.
4 – No tengo el libro.
5 – Toma.
   – Gracias.
6 – Escribid en los cuadernos.
7 – ¿Tienes un bolígrafo?
   – Sí, toma.
8 – ¡Hola!
   – Tenemos una alumna nueva.
9 – ¡Hola, Eduard! ¿Qué tal?
   – ¡Bien … fenomenal!
10 – Bueno, los deberes: ejercicio tres en la página 26.
11 – Hola, me llamo Miguel. ¿Cómo te llamas?
12 – Se llama Neus.

1b Elige las palabras apropiadas para los espacios. (AT3/2) [W1,2,3; S9; T1; C5]

✖ *Knowing about language*

Reading. Pupils choose the correct words from the list for the spaces a–i in the photo story dialogue.

Answers

a ¿Qué tal?	b Buenos días	c por favor
d tengo	e los	f bolígrafo
g ¡Hola!	h Bien	i me llamo

2a Escribe las palabras en el orden correcto. (AT4/2) [W1,2,3; S1,5]

✖ *Knowing about language*

Writing. Pupils write the words in the correct order in the phrases.

Answers

1 No tengo los deberes.	2 Sentaos y abrid los libros.
3 ¿Tienes un bolígrafo?	4 ¡Hola, Eduard! ¿Qué tal?
5 ¿Cómo te llamas?	6 Se llama Neus.

2b ¿Quién dice cada frase en **2a**? (AT3/2) [W1,3; S2]

✖ *Reading for information and instructions – Level D*

Reading. Pupils use the dialogue to decide who says each of the phrases in activity **2a**.

Answers

1 Eduard	2 Teacher	3 Eduard
4 Friend/Neus	5 Miguel	6 Eduard

¡Bienvenidos! módulo 1

Starter 2: **Reordering text [T1,5] (any time after reading the photo story)**

Aims: To develop memory, reading and prediction skills (missing words: *Buenos días, por favor, tengo, los, bolígrafo, ¡Hola!, Bien, me llamo*). As this is a longer activity, it could be used instead of or in addition to *Leer* 2a and 2b. (Timing: 15 minutes)

Resources: Resource and Assessment File, page 13 (Starter 2)

Activity: Make sets of cards using the sheet provided. Pupils read the photo story on page 22 of the Pupil's Book. It is important to set a time limit of two minutes. Give pupils a set of cards and in groups or pairs they must try to order the conversation. Some parts are numbered in order to make the exercise possible. When pupils have finished, ask them to check their answers and discuss what made the exercise difficult or easy.

3 ¿Cuáles de estas cosas se mencionan en la fotonovela? Escribe las frases en que se mencionan. (AT3/2) [W3; T1]

✕ *Reading for information and instructions – Level D*

Reading. Pupils reread the photo story dialogue to find out which of the items pictured are mentioned in it. They write down the sentences in which the items are mentioned.

Answers

| Escribid en los cuadernos. |
| No tengo la carpeta. |
| ¿Tienes un bolígrafo? |

4 ¿Verdad (✓) o mentira (✗)? (AT3/2) [W3,5; S2,5]

✕ *Reading for information and instructions – Level D*

Reading. Pupils decide if the statements are true (*verdad*) or false (*mentira*).

Answers

| a ✓ | b ✗ | c ✗ | d ✗ | e ✓ |

5 En grupos de cuatro, actúa el diálogo de la fotonovela para la clase. (AT2/3) [W3,5; S4,5; T2; L1]

✕ *Speaking and interacting with others – Level C/D*

Speaking. Pupils practise and act out the dialogue in groups of four.

6 Escribe un diálogo similar. Cambia los nombres y otras palabras. (AT4/3) [W3,5; S3,4,5; T6]

✕ *Writing to exchange information and ideas – Level D/E*

Writing. Pupils make up a similar dialogue based on the photo story, changing key words and names.

Plenary

Ask pupils to use the ***Resumen*** section on page 20 of the Pupil's Book to test each other on the language that has been introduced during the module. Pupils can award each other a point for each correct answer. Pupils with the most points after three minutes can take up the challenge of the 'hot seat', where they have to accurately answer questions asked by the teacher and/or other students in order to stay in the seat.

módulo 1

Te toca a ti
(Pupil's Book pages 116–117)

- Self-access reading and writing at two levels

A Reinforcement

1 Pon las frases del diálogo en el orden correcto. (AT3/2) [W1; S9]

✉ *Knowing about language*

Reading. Pupils put the sentences into the correct order to make a dialogue.

Answers

c, i, f, b, g, d, a, j, h, e

2 Empareja los números. (AT3/1) [W1]

✉ *Knowing about language*

Reading. Pupils match up the numbers with the words.

Answers

12 doce, 2 dos, 22 veintidós, 31 treinta y uno, 13 trece, 3 tres, 7 siete, 27 veintisiete, 17 diecisiete, 5 cinco, 15 quince, 25 veinticinco

3 Empareja las palabras con los dibujos. (AT3/1) [W1,3]

✉ *Knowing about language*

Reading. Pupils match up the pictures of items in their school bags with the correct words.

Answers

1 e	2 i	3 c	4 b	5 g	6 h	7 f	8 d	9 a

4 Copia y rellena los espacios en blanco con las palabras apropiadas. (AT4/2) [W3,4,5; S2]

✉ *Knowing about language*

Writing. Pupils copy the text and fill in the blanks using the words in the box.

Answers

mochila, carpeta, libros, cuaderno, un, tengo, una, No, unos

B Extension

1 Empareja las frases. (AT3/2) [W1,2,4; S4,9]

✉ *Knowing about language*

Reading. Pupils match up the sentence halves.

Answers

1 j	2 i	3 g	4 k	5 f	6 h	7 c	8 e	9 d	10 a	11 b

2a Copia y rellena el cuadro. (AT3/3) [W1; T1]

✉ *Reading for information and instructions – Level D*

Reading. Pupils copy the grid and fill in the information for the five young people pictured.

Answers

	Nombre	Edad	Cumpleaños
1	Jaime	14	15/11
2	Susana	16	6/6
3	Vicente	15	7/1
4	Ángela	16	19/10
5	José Carlos	14	25/8

2b Escribe un texto similar sobre ti. (AT4/3) [W1; T6]

✉ *Writing to establish and maintain personal contact – Level D/E*

Writing. Pupils adapt the texts in activity **2a** to write a similar description of themselves.

módulo 2 — *Tú y yo*
(Pupil's Book pages 26–43)

Unit/topics	Key Framework Objectives	PoS	Key language and Grammar
1 ¿De dónde eres? (pp. 26–27) Country names / Saying your nationality / Saying where you are from	7L4 Classroom talk (L) 7W4 Gender/plural (R) 7W5 Verbs present (R)	1b grammar and how to apply it 1c how to express themselves 2c ask/answer questions 3a memorising	Country names Nationalities, masculine and feminine singular *¿De dónde eres?* *Soy de (Escocia/Madrid).* *¿Cuál es tu nacionalidad?* *Soy (escocés/escocesa).*
2 ¿Dónde vives? (pp. 28–29) Saying where you live / Saying what languages you speak	7W5 Verbs present (R) 7L4 Classroom talk (R)	2c ask/answer questions 2f adapt language for different contexts	*¿Dónde vives?* *Vivo en Barcelona.* *¿Qué idiomas hablas?* *Hablo español e inglés.*
3 ¿Tienes hermanos? (pp. 30–31) Talking about your family	7L2 Following speech (L) 7L3 Gist and detail (L) 7S4 Basic questions (R) 7S8 Punctuation (R)	1b grammar and how to apply it 2a listen for gist/detail 2c ask/answer questions 2f adapt language for different contexts	*¿Tienes hermanos?* *Sí, tengo un hermano y dos hermanas.* *No, no tengo hermanos. Soy hija única/hijo único.* *¿Cómo se llama/se llaman?* *Mi madre se llama Clara.* *Mi padre se llama Rafael.* *Mi hermana tiene 5 años.*
4 ¿Tienes un animal en casa? (pp. 32–33) Talking about pets	7C4 Stories and songs (L) 7W4 Gender/plural (R) 7W6 Letters and sounds (R) 7L1 Sound patterns (R)	1b grammar and how to apply it 2f adapt language for different contexts	Vocabulary for pets Colours, with agreement *¿Tienes un animal en casa?* *Sí, tengo un perro/dos gatos.* *No, no tengo un animal.* *¿De qué color es/son?*
5 Los ojos y el pelo (pp. 34–35) Describing your eyes and hair	7W4 Gender/plural (R) 7S1 Word order (R) 7S3 Adapting sentences (R)	1b grammar and how to apply it 1c how to express themselves 2f adapt language for different contexts 5a communicating in the target language	Vocabulary to describe hair and eyes *¿De qué color son tus ojos?* *¿De qué color es tu pelo?* *Tengo los ojos marrones y el pelo castaño.* *Tengo el pelo largo y liso.* *Tengo pecas.* *Llevo barba y bigote.* *Llevo gafas.*
6 ¿Cómo eres? (pp. 36–37) Describing your size / Describing your colouring	7T1 Reading using cues (L) 7T3 Checking before reading (L) 7T5 Assembling text (L) 7W4 Gender/plural (R)	1b grammar and how to apply it 2f adapt language for different contexts 5f using the TL creatively and imaginatively	*¿Cómo eres?* *Soy/Es alto/a.* *Soy/Es bajo/a.* *Soy/Es de talla mediana.* *Soy/Es moreno/a.*
Resumen y Prepárate (pp. 38–39) Pupils' checklist and practice test	7S4 Basic questions (R) 7T1 Reading using cues (R) 7L3 Gist and detail (R)	3a memorising 3d use reference materials 3e develop their independence	
¡Extra! Se habla español (pp. 40–41) Optional extension unit: A map showing Spanish-speaking countries across the world	7C1 Geographical facts (L)	5i working in a variety of contexts	
Te toca a ti (pp. 118–119) Self-access reading and writing at two levels		2f adapt language for different contexts	

módulo 2

1 ¿De dónde eres?

(Pupil's Book pages 26–27)

Main topics

- Country names
- Saying your nationality
- Saying where you are from

Key Framework Objectives

- Classroom talk 7L4 (Launch)
- Gender/plural 7W4 (Reinforcement)
- Verbs present 7W5 (Reinforcement)

Grammar

- *ser: soy, eres, es*
- Adjective agreement: *australiano/a, español/española*

Key language

¿De dónde eres?
Soy de (Escocia/Madrid).

¿Cuál es tu nacionalidad?
Soy (escocés/escocesa).

Australia	australiano/a
Escocia	escocés/escocesa
España	español/española
Estados Unidos	estadounidense
Gales	galés/galesa
Inglaterra	inglés/inglesa
Irlanda	irlandés/irlandesa
Jamaica	jamaicano/a
México	mexicano/a
Nigeria	nigeriano/a
Paquistán	paquistaní

Resources

Cassette A, Side 2
CD 1, track 11
Cuaderno A and B, page 15
OHTs 5 and 6: Countries, nationalities

Suggestion

The TLF initiative (Teaching and Learning Foundation subjects) will have a significant impact on the relationship between MFL and humanities subjects. This topic is an ideal opportunity to reinforce links between Spanish and Geography in your school. Do not overestimate your pupils' ability to name countries, much less say where they are on a map. It would be a good idea to find out from the Geography department what countries your pupils will be familiar with and use these as a starting point. You may even be able to work together on delivering a cultural awareness unit: a number of case studies will be available. CILT and Canning House, as well as the embassies of Hispanic countries, are able to provide a wide variety of information. Better still, use the Internet!

You may wish to introduce your students to the Spanish-speaking world using the **¡Extra! Se habla español** section on pages 40–41.

¡Starter 1: Alphabetic order race [W1,8]

Aims: To expose pupils to countries in Spanish and to build on their dictionary skills. (Timing: 5–10 minutes)

Activity: Write up the following countries on the board or on a transparency: *Australia, Escocia, España, Estados Unidos, Gales, Inglaterra, Irlanda, Jamaica, México, Nigeria, Paquistán.* Ask pupils to work out their English equivalents. Pupils must race to put the countries in alphabetical order. You can build on this activity by holding a discussion on where in the world the countries are located and what language(s) they speak.

R For less-able students, copy the words onto a card that can be cut out so that it becomes a more kinaesthetic activity.

1 Escucha y mira el mapa. Empareja los números con los países. (AT1/1, AT3/1) [L1]

✂ *Listening for information and instructions – Level C*

Listening/Reading. Pupils match up the numbers with the countries.

It is best to introduce the names of the countries first and, if one is available, show their location on a wall map or OHP. Pupils can then predict the names of the countries 1–11 on the map, and then listen to the recording to check their answers.

Answers

1 Estados Unidos	2 México	3 Jamaica
4 Irlanda	5 Escocia	6 Gales
7 Inglaterra	8 España	9 Nigeria
10 Paquistán	11 Australia	

Tapescript

– Uno: Estados Unidos
– Dos: México
– Tres: Jamaica
– Cuatro: Irlanda
– Cinco: Escocia
– Seis: Gales
– Siete: Inglaterra
– Ocho: España
– Nueve: Nigeria
– Diez: Paquistán
– Once: Australia

2 Con tu compañero/a, practica los países. (AT2/1) [L1]

✂ *Speaking and interacting with others – Level C*

Tú y yo — módulo 2

Speaking. In pairs, pupils practise saying the names of the countries.

3a Escucha las entrevistas. Elige la nacionalidad apropiada de cada persona. (1–5) (AT1/2) [W4; L1,3]

✠ *Listening for information and instructions – Level D*

Listening. Pupils choose the correct nationality for each of the five speakers.

It is best to introduce the nationalities first, using the vocabulary in the *Gramática* box.

Answers

| 1 b | 2 a | 3 e | 4 c | 5 d |

Tapescript

1. – Hola, ¿cómo te llamas?
   – Me llamo Kristy.
   – ¿De dónde eres?
   – Soy de Estados Unidos.
   – ¿Cuál es tu nacionalidad?
   – Soy estadounidense.
2. – ¿Cómo te llamas?
   – Me llamo Declan.
   – ¿De dónde eres?
   – Soy de Irlanda. Soy irlandés.
3. – Hola, ¿cómo te llamas?
   – Me llamo Chanelle.
   – ¿De dónde eres, Chanelle?
   – Soy de Jamaica. Soy jamaicana.
4. – Hola, me llamo Antonio.
   – ¿Cuál es tu nacionalidad?
   – Soy español.
5. – Hola, me llamo Lizzie. Soy de Edimburgo en Escocia. Soy escocesa.

3b Con tu compañero/a, pregunta y contesta. (AT2/2) [W2,4,5; S4; L4]

✠ *Speaking and interacting with others – Level D*

Speaking. Working in pairs, pupils ask and answer questions about where they are from and their nationality.

Before attempting this activity, teachers may wish to use activity **3b** as a model for whole-class speaking, asking volunteers the questions, until all the pupils are confident with the new structures and vocabulary. Look at the verb *ser* in the *Gramática* box before starting.

Starter 2: What nationality? [W4; L1,6]

Aims: To revise nationalities, including gender, pronunciation, spelling and meaning. (Timing: 10 minutes)

Activity: Write the words *chico* and *chica* on the board with stick-figure symbols. Read out a country from the following list, followed by either the word *chico* or *chica*: Australia, Escocia, España, Estados Unidos, Gales, Inglaterra, Irlanda, Jamaica, México, Nigeria, Paquistán. Pupils must write down the correct nationality, e.g. teacher says *Inglaterra, chico*; pupils write *inglés*. (*Australiano/a, escocés/a, español/a, estadounidense, galés/a, inglés/a, irlandés/a, jamaicano/a, mexicano/a, nigeriano/a, paquistaní*).

4a Con tu compañero/a, empareja la persona con la nacionalidad apropiada. (AT2/2) [W4]

✠ *Speaking and interacting with others – Level D*

Speaking. Working in pairs, pupils take turns to match up the famous people with their nationality, taking care with masculine and feminine adjective endings.

Answers

| Kylie Minogue es australiana. |
| Ronan Keating es irlandés. |
| Catherine Zeta Jones es galesa. |
| Ewan McGregor es escocés. |
| Cameron Diaz es estadounidense. |
| Enrique Iglesias es español. |
| Ryan Giggs es galés. |
| Denise Lewis es inglesa. |
| David Beckham es inglés. |
| Penélope Cruz es española. |
| Waqar Younis es paquistaní. |

4b Escribe las frases en **4a**. (AT4/2) [W4,5]

✠ *Writing to exchange information and ideas – Level C*

Writing. Pupils write out the sentences from activity **4a**.

4c Elige una persona de la lista en **4a**. Tu compañero/a te hace preguntas para adivinar quién eres. (AT2/2) [W4,5; S4; L4]

✠ *Speaking and interacting with others – Level D/E*

Speaking. Pupils play this guessing game in pairs, choosing a celebrity from activity **4a**. They have to answer their partner's questions about their country of origin and nationality in order for their partner to guess who they are.

5 Lee y escribe la información. (AT3/3) [W4; T1]

✠ *Reading for information and instructions – Level D*

Reading. Pupils copy the grid and fill in the name, country of origin and nationality of the seven young people.

módulo 2 Tú y yo

Answers

Nombre	País	Nacionalidad
Mariana	España	española
Robert	Inglaterra	inglés
Callum	Escocia	escocés
Sinead	Irlanda	irlandesa
Jorge	España	español
Anwen	Gales	galesa
Meha	Inglaterra	inglesa

6 Escribe tu nombre, país y nacionalidad. (AT4/3) [W4,5; T6]

✠ *Writing to establish and maintain personal contact – Level C*

Writing. Pupils write a short paragraph about themselves in Spanish, giving their name, country of origin and nationality.

R Teachers may wish to exploit the descriptions in activity **5** further before pupils attempt activity **6**:

1 Consolidate the key questions *¿Cómo te llamas? ¿De dónde eres? ¿Cuál es tu nacionalidad?* by asking about the young people in the descriptions.

2 Use shared writing techniques from the National Literacy Strategy to construct a model answer based on a pupil from the class.

Plenary

Pupils work in groups to list what they have learned during the lessons on countries/nationalities. Then ask pupils to feed back to the class. It is likely that pupils will only list new words in Spanish that they have learned, so ask them to repeat the exercise, thinking about the following headings: Instruction language (e.g. *mira el mapa*, etc.); Grammar; Geography and Famous People.

Cuaderno A, page 15

1 Escribe los nombres de los países. (AT3/1, AT4/1) [W1]

✠ *Knowing about language*

Reading/Writing. Pupils match up the labelled countries on the map with their names.

Answers

a Escocia	b Jamaica	c Estados Unidos
d Paquistán	e España	f Inglaterra
g Irlanda	h Nigeria	i Gales
j México	k Australia	

2 Escribe los países apropiados. (AT4/1) [W1]

✠ *Knowing about language*

Writing. Pupils write the names of the countries that correspond to the nationalities listed. Teachers should remind pupils that the correct spellings appear next to the map in activity **1**.

Answers

España, Paquistán, Estados Unidos, Nigeria, Irlanda, Gales

3 Completa las frases con la nacionalidad apropiada. (AT3/2, AT4/1) [W1,2,4,5]

✠ *Knowing about language*

Reading/Writing. Pupils complete the descriptions using the correct nationality. Teachers should remind pupils to choose the correct adjective ending.

Answers

a escocesa	b galés	c española
d inglés	e estadounidense	f jamaicano

Cuaderno B, page 15

1 Escribe los nombres de los países. (AT3/1, AT4/1) [W1]

✠ *Knowing about language*

Reading/Writing. Pupils match up the labelled countries on the map with their names.

Answers

a Escocia	b Jamaica	c Estados Unidos
d Paquistán	e España	f Inglaterra
g Irlanda	h Nigeria	i Gales
j México	k Australia	

2a Completa las frases con la nacionalidad apropiada. (AT3/2, AT4/1) [W1,2,4,5]

✠ *Knowing about language*

Reading/Writing. Pupils complete the descriptions using the correct nationality. Teachers should remind pupils to choose the correct adjective ending.

Answers

a escocesa	b galés	c española
d inglés	e estadounidense	f jamaicano

2b ¿Verdad (✓) o mentira (✗)? (AT3/2) [W1,4,5]

✠ *Knowing about language*

Reading. Pupils decide if the sentences based on activity **2a** are true (*verdad*) or false (*mentira*).

Answers

| a ✗ | b ✓ | c ✗ | d ✗ | e ✓ | f ✗ |

Tú y yo — módulo 2

3 Escribe cinco frases similares. (AT4/2) [W4,5]

✖ *Knowing about language*

Writing. Pupils use activity **2b** as a model to write their own sentences giving the nationality of five celebrities of their own choice.

módulo 2

2 ¿Dónde vives?

(Pupil's Book pages 28–29)

Main topics

- Saying where you live
- Saying what languages you speak

Key Framework Objectives

- Verbs present 7W5 (Reinforcement)
- Classroom talk 7L4 (Reinforcement)

Grammar

- *vivir: vivo, vives, vive*
- *hablar: hablo, hablas, habla*

Key language

¿Dónde vives?
Vivo en Barcelona.
¿Qué idiomas hablas?
Hablo español e inglés.

el idioma	el francés
el alemán	el galés
el catalán	el inglés
el español	el italiano

Resources

Cassette A, Side 2
CD 1, track 12
Cuaderno A and B, page 16
Starter 1, Resource and Assessment File, page 30
Starter 2, Resource and Assessment File, page 31

Starter 1: **Spanish quiz** [C1,2]

Aims: To encourage pupils to think about the cultural differences between Spain and England and to focus on their knowledge about each country. (Timing: 5–10 minutes)

Resources: Resource and Assessment File, page 30 (Starter 1)

Pairwork activity: Make worksheets using the master provided. Pupils complete the worksheet that tests their cultural and geographical knowledge of Spain in order to find out how much they know, or need to learn, about Spain. Correct any wrong answers and discuss any questions or comments that arise.

Suggestion

A map of Spain can be used to introduce the principal cities highlighted on page 28. Teachers may wish to talk to their pupils about the cultural diversity of Spain, as well as the policy of regionalism, which since the death of Franco and the dawn of democracy in the last 30 years, has seen the encouragement of regional autonomy and a rebirth of languages such as Basque and Catalan. It is also worth pointing out to pupils that Spain covers an area twice the size of Great Britain, and therefore these cities are very far apart, and have completely different climates. Seville in the south has a dry, hot Mediterranean climate, and, as in all of Andalucía, has evidence of its links with North Africa in the architecture, food, place names and music. Bilbao, on the other hand, is on the Atlantic coast, with a wet climate more similar to Britain.

1 Escucha y lee. Escribe el orden en que se menciona cada ciudad. (1–5) (AT1/1, AT3/1) [L1]

✴ *Knowing about language*

Listening/Reading. Pupils listen to the recording and look at the map. They write down the names of the cities in the order in which they are mentioned.

Answers

| 1 Madrid | 2 Sevilla | 3 Bilbao | 4 Barcelona | 5 Valencia |

Tapescript

1 – ¿Dónde vives?
 – Vivo en Madrid.
2 – ¿Dónde vives?
 – Vivo en ~~Sevilla~~. Valencia
3 – ¿Dónde vives?
 – Vivo en ~~Bilbao~~. BCN
4 – ¿Dónde vives?
 – Vivo en ~~Barcelona~~. Bilbao
5 – ¿Dónde vive Ud?
 – Vivo en ~~Valencia~~. Sevilla

2 Con tu compañero/a, pregunta y contesta. (AT2/2) [W1,2,5; S4]

✴ *Speaking and interacting with others – Level C*

Speaking. In pairs, pupils ask and answer questions about where they live. Teachers may want them to pretend that they live in one of the cities mentioned on the map, in order to further practise pronunciation.

3a Escucha a los jóvenes y lee las frases. ¿Verdad (✓) o mentira (✗)? (AT1/2, AT3/2) [W2,5; L3]

✴ *Listening for information and instructions – Level C*

Listening/Reading. Pupils listen to the recording and read the sentences, indicating if the sentences are true (*verdad*) or false (*mentira*). Teachers may wish pupils to correct the sentences that are false.

Tú y yo — módulo 2

Answers

| 1 ✗ (Vive en Bilbao.) | 2 ✓ | 3 ✓ | 4 ✗ (Vive en ~~Valencia~~ Sevilla.) |

Tapescript

– ¡Hola! Me llamo Mateo. Vivo en Bilbao.
– Me llamo Juan. Vivo en Barcelona.
– Me llamo Arturo. Vivo con mi hermana Susana en Barcelona.
– Me llamo Ana. Vivo en Sevilla.

3b Con tu compañero/a, pregunta y contesta. (AT2/2) [W2,5; L4]

✉ *Speaking and interacting with others – Level D*

Speaking. In pairs, pupils ask and answer questions on where the people from activity **3a** live.

Before attempting this activity, read the *Gramática* box to familiarise pupils with the parts of the verb *vivir*.

> **Starter 2:** Verb revision [W5; S3] (after introducing verb *hablar*)
>
> *Aims:* To revise the first, second and third person singular of the present tense verbs *ser, tener, vivir* and *hablar* (Hablo muy bien el español, Vive en México, Tiene once años, ¿Eres de España?, No hablo alemán, Es paquistaní). (Timing: 5 minutes)
>
> *Resources:* Resource and Assessment File, page 31 (Starter 2)
>
> *Pairwork activity:* Make an OHT using the sheet provided. Give pupils three minutes to write down the correct Spanish versions corresponding to the English sentences, using the correct person of the verb. When correcting the exercise, ask pupils to justify their answers.

4a Lee los datos. ¿Puedes adivinar qué idiomas habla cada persona? (AT3/2) [T1; C1]

✉ *Reading for information and instructions – Level C*

Reading. Students read the personal information tags and guess which languages each person speaks. Teachers should remember not to mark the predictions, as the answers are contained in activity **4b**.

R Before attempting this activity, it would be a good idea to revise nationalities covered in the previous unit.

> Marco vive en Italia. Es italiano.
> Kate vive en Inglaterra. Es inglesa.

Then introduce *hablar* and the languages (see *el idioma* and *Gramática* boxes on page 29).

> Marco habla italiano.
> Kate habla inglés.

Teachers should check that pupils have understood by asking what languages celebrities speak: *¿Qué idioma habla Michael Schumacher?*

Answers

| 1 galés | 2 español | 3 alemán, francés | 4 catalán, español |

4b Escucha y comprueba tus respuestas. (AT1/2) [L3]

✉ *Listening for information and instructions – Level D*

Listening. Pupils listen to the dialogues and check their answers to activity **4a**.

Tapescript

1 – ¿Cómo te llamas?
– Me llamo Sara.
– ¿Dónde vives, Sara?
– Vivo en Swansea.
– ¿Qué idiomas hablas?
– Hablo inglés, galés … y español un poco.

2 – Hola, ¿cómo te llamas?
– Me llamo Elena.
– ¿De dónde eres?
– Soy de México pero vivo en Londres.
– ¿Qué idiomas hablas?
– Hablo español e inglés.

3 – ¿Cómo te llamas?
– Me llamo Dieter.
– ¿Dónde vives, Dieter?
– Vivo en París pero soy de Alemania.
– ¿Qué idiomas hablas?
– Hablo alemán, francés y un poco de español.

4 – Hola, me llamo Martí.
– Y yo me llamo Nuria.
– ¿Dónde vivís?
– Vivimos en Barcelona.
– ¿Qué idiomas habláis?
– Hablamos catalán, claro, y también hablamos castellano, es decir, español.
– ¿Catalán y español?
– Sí, eso es.

5a Haz un sondeo. ¿Cuántos idiomas habláis? Pregunta a tus compañeros/as de clase. (AT2/2) [W2,5; S4; L4]

✉ *Speaking and interacting with others – Level C/D*

Speaking. Pupils conduct a class survey of the languages spoken in the class. Before starting the survey, teachers may wish to check pupils know how to say the Spanish for all the languages spoken in the class. The easiest way to do this would be to brainstorm all the languages needed. Pupils could then prepare a grid for the survey, with the languages from the brainstorm as column headings.

módulo 2 Tú y yo

ICT activity

Pupils could create a spreadsheet based on the results of their survey and use the chart wizard function to produce a pie chart or bar graph of the languages spoken in the class.

5b Con tu compañero/a, haz entrevistas con Sara, Elena, Dieter, Martí y Nuria. (AT2/3) [W5; S4; L4]

Speaking and interacting with others – Level D

Speaking. Pupils prepare a role-play using the model, interviewing the people from activity **4a**.

5c Escribe dos de las entrevistas. (AT4/3) [W5; T6]

Writing to exchange information and ideas – Level D

Writing. Pupils write out two of the interviews from activity **5b** in full.

Plenary

In pairs, pupils choose a Spanish city from one of the five shown on the map of Spain on page 28 of the Pupil's Book. Ask pupils to invent as many sentences about themselves, imagining that they live there, e.g. *vivo en Madrid, me llamo Raúl, tengo diecisiete años, soy español, hablo español y inglés, no vivo en Londres*, etc.

R For lower-ability students, this could be done as a whole-class revision activity, or with some of the verbs required written on the board to start them off.

Cuaderno A, page 16

1 Escribe el idioma apropiado para cada país. (AT4/1) [W1]

Knowing about language

Writing. Pupils write the language spoken in each of the five countries listed.

Answers

| a alemán | b español | c francés | d inglés | e italiano |

2 Empareja las frases. (AT3/2) [W1,5]

Knowing about language

Reading. Pupils match up the sentences.

Answers

| 1 c | 2 b | 3 d | 4 a |

3a ¿Verdad (✓) o mentira (✓)? (AT3/2) [W1,5]

Reading for information and instructions – Level C

Reading. Pupils read the personal details forms and decide if the six sentences are true (*verdad*) or false (*mentira*).

Answers

| 1 ✓ | 2 ✓ | 3 ✗ | 4 ✗ | 5 ✗ | 6 ✓ |

3b Corrige las frases que son falsas. (AT4/2) [W1,5]

Writing to exchange information and ideas – Level C

Writing. Pupils correct the sentences in activity **3a** that are false.

Answers

3 Eduardo habla español.
4 Eleonora vive en Italia.
5 Callum vive en Escocia.

Cuaderno B, page 16

1a Busca cinco idiomas. (AT3/1) [W1,7]

Reading for enjoyment

Reading. Pupils find five languages in the wordsearch.

Answers

I	T	A	L	I	A	N	O
A	R	P	J	I	S	O	T
Q	F	E	M	N	N	A	P
B	R	F	L	G	Z	L	Q
I	A	I	Y	L	A	E	D
C	N	G	V	É	E	M	C
O	C	U	W	S	B	Á	F
D	É	H	T	S	R	N	G
E	S	P	A	Ñ	O	L	H

1b Escribe el idioma apropiado para cada país. (AT4/1) [W1]

Knowing about language

Writing. Pupils write the language spoken in each of the five countries listed.

Answers

| a alemán | b español | c francés | d inglés | e italiano |

Tú y yo — **módulo 2**

2 Empareja las frases. (AT3/2) [W1,5]

✠ *Knowing about language*

Reading. Pupils match up the sentences.

Answers

| 1 c | 2 b | 3 d | 4 a |

3a ¿Verdad (✓) o mentira (✗)? (AT3/2) [W1,5]

✠ *Reading for information and instructions – Level C*

Reading. Pupils read the personal details forms and decide if the six sentences are true (*verdad*) or false (*mentira*).

Answers

| 1 ✓ | 2 ✓ | 3 ✗ | 4 ✗ | 5 ✗ | 6 ✓ |

3b Corrige las frases que son falsas. (AT4/2) [W1,5]

✠ *Writing to exchange information and ideas – Level C*

Writing. Pupils correct the sentences in activity **3a** that are false.

Answers

3 Eduardo habla español.
4 Eleonora vive en Italia.
5 Callum vive en Escocia.

módulo 2

3 ¿Tienes hermanos?

(Pupil's Book pages 30–31)

Main topics

- Talking about your family

Key Framework Objectives

- Following speech 7L2 (Launch)
- Gist and detail 7L3 (Launch)
- Basic questions 7S4 (Reinforcement)
- Punctuation 7S8 (Reinforcement)

Grammar

- *llamarse: me llamo, te llamas, se llama, se llaman*
- *mi, tu, su; mis, tus, sus*

Key language

¿Tienes hermanos?
Sí, tengo un hermano y dos hermanas.
No, no tengo hermanos. Soy hija única/hijo único.
¿Cómo se llama/se llaman?
Mi madre se llama Clara.
Mi padre se llama Rafael.
Mi hermana tiene 5 años.
Somos gemelos/as.

Resources

Cassette A, Side 2
CD 1, track 13
Cuaderno A and B, page 17
Skills 1 and 2, Resource and Assessment File, pages 28 and 29
OHTs 7 and 8: Introducing the family

Starter 1: Number revision [W2; L2,3]

Aims: To revise numbers 1–10 and to encourage pupils to listen for specific details. (Timing: 5 minutes)

Activity: Read out the following text, which contains language that is unfamiliar to pupils, but numbers that are familiar: *Me llamo Carolina y vivo en Madrid. En mi piso hay tres dormitorios grandes y dos cuartos de baño. En mi familia hay ocho personas: tengo dos hermanos y tres hermanas. Mi amiga María Ángeles solo tiene cinco personas en su familia).* Pupils stand up when they hear a number in Spanish and then sit down when they hear the next one, etc. This may need to be repeated a number of times. Read the text again, stopping after each number, and ask pupils to tell you what that number is in English.

1 Escucha y lee. (AT1/2, AT3/2) [W1,2,4,5; S4,5; L1]

✶ *Knowing about language*

Listening/Reading. Pupils listen to the recording and read the text. See if they can deduce the meaning of *hermano* and *hermana* from the context, as well as the more difficult expressions *hijo único* and *hija única*.

Tapescript

1 – ¿Tienes hermanos?
  – Sí, tengo un hermano.
2 – ¿Tienes hermanos?
  – Tengo un hermano y una hermana.
3 – ¿Tienes hermanos?
  – No, no tengo hermanos. Soy hija única.
4 – ¿Tienes hermanos?
  – Sí, tengo una hermana.
5 – ¿Tienes hermanos?
  – Sí, tengo tres hermanas.
6 – ¿Tienes hermanos?
  – No, no tengo hermanos. Soy hijo único.

2 Escucha a los jóvenes. ¿Tienen hermanos? (1–6) (AT1/2) [W4; L3]

✶ *Listening for information and instructions – Level D*

Listening. Pupils listen to the six young people and draw stick figures to represent the answers. Agree in advance how to represent *hijo único* and *hija única*: it may be simplest just to write *no* since they don't have any brothers or sisters.

Answers

1 ♀♀ 2 no 3 ♀ 4 ♀♀♀♂ 5 ♂ 6 no

Tapescript

1 – ¿Tienes hermanos?
  – Sí, tengo un hermano y una hermana.
2 – ¿Tienes hermanos?
  – No, no tengo hermanos, soy hijo único.
3 – ¿Tienes hermanos?
  – Sí, tengo una hermana.
4 – ¿Tienes hermanos?
  – Sí.
  – ¿Cuántos tienes?
  – Tengo cuatro hermanos: dos hermanas y dos hermanos.
5 – ¿Tienes hermanos?
  – Sí, tengo un hermano.
6 – ¿Tienes hermanos?
  – No, soy hija única, no tengo hermanos. ¡Pero tengo muchos amigos!

Tú y yo — módulo 2

3 Lee y empareja las frases con las fotos. (AT3/2) [W4; S2]

✉ *Reading for information and instructions – Level D*

Reading. Pupils read the descriptions and match them up with the appropriate photo.

Answers

| 1 d | 2 a | 3 b | 4 c |

4 Con tu compañero/a, haz entrevistas con José, Claudia, Mateo y Gloria. (AT2/3) [W1,4,5; S4,5]

✉ *Speaking and interacting with others – Level D/E*

Speaking. Pupils work in pairs to make up interviews with the young people in activity 3.

Starter 2: Squashed sentences [S1,8; T2; L6]

Aims: To write simple sentences accurately and to reinforce knowledge of punctuation and spelling. (Timing: 10 minutes)

Pairwork activity: Write up the following sentences with no punctuation, accents or spacings, e.g. *mellamojoseytengodoshermanos: Me llamo José y tengo dos hermanos; Soy Carlos y soy hijo único; Me llamo Claudia y tengo tres hermanos; Hola, soy Gloria y no tengo hermanos.* Give pupils two minutes to say the sentences to each other. Ask different pupils to read out the sentences to the class. Pupils write down the sentences. Remind them that the sentences contain no punctuation so they must add capital letters, accents and full stops.

5 Escucha y lee. ¿Como se llaman las personas en el dibujo? (AT1/3, AT3/3) [W1,2,5; S2]

✉ *Listening for information and instructions – Level D*

Listening/Reading. Pupils read the text and listen to the recording to work out the names of the people a–e in the picture.

R Before starting this activity, teachers may wish to revise the structures *¿Cómo te llamas?* and *me llamo* learnt in the previous module. The *Gramática* box helps to introduce the structures *se llama* and *se llaman*.

Teachers may also wish to introduce the new vocabulary items *padre* and *madre*, or alternatively this may be left for pupils to deduce from the context.

Pupils should also be introduced to the structures *mi*, *tu* and *su*, in the second *Gramática* box. The quickest and easiest way to do this is by taking a pupil's pen and asking the class *¿Es mi bolígrafo?*. Hopefully the answer will be 'no'. Then ask a different student *¿Es tu bolígrafo?*, again hopefully prompting the answer 'no'. Finally return to the student whose pen it is and ask the class *¿Es su bolígrafo?*

If pupils are struggling with this activity, it may be simplest to establish which person in the picture is Adrián.

Answers

| a Rafael | b Clara | c Adrián | d Elisa | e Daniel |

Tapescript

– ¡Hola! ¿Cómo te llamas?
– ¡Hola! Me llamo Adrián.
– ¿Tienes hermanos, Adrián?
– Sí, tengo una hermana y un hermano.
– ¿Cómo se llaman tus hermanos?
– Mi hermana se llama Elisa.
– ¿Cuántos años tiene tu hermana?
– Tiene 5 años.
– Y tu hermano, ¿cómo se llama?
– Mi hermano se llama Daniel. Tiene 11 años.
– ¿Cómo se llaman tus padres?
– Mi madre se llama Clara y mi padre se llama Rafael.

6 Con tu compañero/a, haz una entrevista con Adrián. (AT2/3) [W1,2,4,5; S4; L4]

✉ *Speaking and interacting with others – Level D/E*

Speaking. In pairs, pupils take turns to interview Adrián about his family.

7a Con tu compañero/a, escribe una entrevista con Bart Simpson (o con otro personaje famoso). (AT4/3) [W1,2,4; S4]

✉ *Writing to exchange information and ideas – Level D/E*

Writing. In pairs, pupils make up and write out an interview with Bart Simpson. They should use the questions in the speech bubbles and the details on the personal details form as prompts.

7b Lee tu diálogo a la clase. (AT2/3) [T2; L1]

✉ *Speaking to convey information and ideas – Level D/E*

Speaking. In pairs, pupils read their dialogue out to the rest of the class.

💿 ICT activity

Pupils may use *PowerPoint* to write out the interview and then present it to the rest of the class using an interactive whiteboard. They could also record sound clips as part of the presentation instead of reading it back to the class.

módulo 2 Tú y yo

> **Plenary**
> Ask pupils in groups to prepare three questions on what they have learned in this module, to test other groups. Try to encourage a variety of questions that look at pronunciation, punctuation or spelling, as well as meaning. Pupils then take turns to ask different groups a question each. Reward interesting and inventive questions with points.

Cuaderno A, page 17

1 Elige una frase para cada dibujo. (AT3/2) [W1,4,5; S5]

✉ *Knowing about language*

Reading. Pupils match up each picture with the appropriate sentence.

Answers

| a 4 | b 1 | c 2 | d 3 |

2 Mira la foto y completa las frases. (AT4/1) [W1,2,4; S4]

✉ *Knowing about language*

Writing. Pupils look at the photo and use the words given to complete the answers to the questions.

Answers

| a llamo | b hermana | c hermano | d llama | e madre |

Cuaderno B, page 17

1 Elige una frase para cada dibujo. (AT3/2) [W1,4,5; S5]

✉ *Knowing about language*

Reading. Pupils match up each picture with the appropriate sentence.

Answers

| a 4 | b 1 | c 2 | d 3 |

2 Mira la foto y completa las frases. (AT4/1) [W1,2,4; S4,9]

✉ *Knowing about language*

Writing. Pupils look at the photo and use the words given to complete the answers to the questions.

Answers

| a llamo | b hermana | c hermano | d llama | e madre |

Skills 1 and 2, pages 28 and 29 [W4,6,7; S8; T7]

These activities provide pupils with opportunities to develop their language-learning skills, as detailed in paragraph 3 of the Programme of Study. Pupils work out the meanings of words and work out the grammatical rules.

módulo 2

4 ¿Tienes un animal en casa?

(Pupil's Book pages 32–33)

Main topics
- Talking about pets

Key Framework Objectives
- Stories and songs 7C4 (Launch)
- Gender/plural 7W4 (Reinforcement)
- Letters and sounds 7W6 (Reinforcement)
- Sound patterns 7L1 (Reinforcement)

Grammar
- Adjective agreement, singular and plural

Key language

¿Tienes un animal en casa?
Sí, tengo un perro/dos gatos.
Tengo seis peces dorados.
Se llama/Se llaman …
No, no tengo un animal.

un caballo	un gato
un pájaro	un pez
un perro	un ratón
un conejo	una tortuga
un cobayo	

Es grande/pequeño/a.
¿De qué color es/son?

blanco/a	rojo/a
negro/a	marrón
atigrado/a	azul
dorado/a	verde
amarillo/a	gris

Resources

Cassette A, Side 2
CD 1, track 14
Cuaderno A and B, page 18
Starter 1, Resource and Assessment File, page 31
Hojas de trabajo 1 and 2, Resource and Assessment File, pages 24 and 25
Grammar, Resource and Assessment File, page 27
OHTs 9 and 10: Pets and how to describe them (adjectives)

Starter 1: Sound spelling links [W6; L1]

Aims: To revise phonetic alphabet pronunciation by introducing the different pronunciations of *ja, jo, yo, llo* and *ño*. (Timing: 10 minutes)

Resources: Resource and Assessment File, page 31 (Starter 1)

Activity: Make an OHT using the sheet provided. Say the sounds displayed in the right-hand column on the OHT and show pupils how they are written in Spanish (left-hand column). Ask pupils to repeat them. Cover the sound column. Pupils look at the spelling and say the sound. Then cover the spelling. Pupils write the letter strings from the sounds. Explain to pupils that they will hear some new words which contain these sounds. Then read out the following, and ask pupils to fill in the missing letter strings : *un cobayo, un pájaro, un conejo, un caballo, pequeño*. Pupils can then look at the animals on page 32 in the Pupil's Book and have a go at pronouncing the words before listening to exercise 1a.

1a Escucha y repite. Pon atención a la pronunciación. (AT1/1) [W1; L1]

✠ *Knowing about language*

Listening. Pupils listen to the recording and repeat the names of the animals.

Tapescript

un pez, un conejo, un cobayo, un perro, un pájaro, un caballo, un gato, una tortuga, un ratón

---

As well as using flashcards, the OHP, photos of pets, or even real live animals to introduce vocabulary items, teachers may wish to play games to help pupils to recognise and use the names of animals.

1. Use mimes or animal noises to play a version of 'Simon Says'.

2. The teacher performs the mime and pupils have to shout out the name of the animal.

3. 'Soy un animal. ¿Qué animal soy?' Guessing game. Pupils have to guess what animal the teacher is thinking of.

4. Hangman is a useful way to revise the alphabet at this stage.

1b Escucha y escribe los nombres de los animales en el orden correcto. (1–9) (AT1/1, AT4/1) [W1; L1]

✠ *Listening for information and instructions – Level C*

Listening/Writing. Pupils listen to the recording and write down the names of the nine animals pictured in the order in which they hear them.

Answers

As tapescript

Tapescript

1 – un cobayo
2 – un caballo
3 – un conejo
4 – una tortuga

módulo 2 — Tú y yo

5 – un pájaro
6 – un gato
7 – un pez
8 – un ratón
9 – un perro

2 Escucha a los jóvenes. (1–6) ¿Tienen animales en casa? (AT1/2) [L3]

✗ *Listening for information and instructions – Level D*

Listening. Pupils listen to the six young people talking about their pets, and note down the animal(s) mentioned. Practise the plural form (use the grid next to activity **1b**) before attempting this activity: *un caballo, dos …; un perro, dos …; un pez, dos …*

Answers

1 un pájaro	2 un caballo
3 dos conejos y un gato	4 seis peces
5 un perro y una gata	6 no tengo animales

Tapescript

1 – *Carmen, ¿Tienes animales en casa?*
  – *Sí, tengo un pájaro. Es un canario.*
  – *¿Cómo se llama?*
  – *Se llama Kiki.*
2 – *¿Tienes un animal, Lola?*
  – *Sí, tengo un caballo.*
  – *¡Un caballo en casa!*
  – *Vivo en una granja.*
  – *¡Ah!*
3 – *¿Tienes animales en casa, Juan?*
  – *Tengo dos conejos.*
  – *¿Dos conejos?*
  – *Sí, también tengo un gato.*
4 – *Tienes animales en casa, ¿verdad, Pepe?*
  – *Sí, tengo peces.*
  – *¿Cuántos tienes?*
  – *Tengo seis.*
5 – *Merche, ¿Tienes animales en casa?*
  – *Sí, tengo un perro y una gata.*
  – *¿Cómo se llaman?*
  – *Se llaman Toto y Blanca.*
6 – *Javi, ¿Tienes animales en casa?*
  – *No, no tengo. Mis padres no los permiten.*

3 En grupos, pregunta y contesta. (AT2/2) [W4,5; S4,5; L4]

✗ *Speaking and interacting with others – Level D*

Speaking. Volunteers can be asked *¿Tienes un animal en casa?* to practise using the answer *tengo/no tengo*. Pupils then work in pairs using the example in activity **3** as a model.

✚ This could be extended to a class survey to reinforce the names of animals and parts of *tener* before introducing colours and adjectival agreements.

4 Escucha y repite. (AT1/1, AT2/1) [W4; L1]

✗ *Knowing about language*

Listening/Speaking. Pupils listen to the recording and repeat. Teachers may wish their pupils to hear the recording twice: during the first listening they point to the relevant captioned pictures in activity **4** in order to establish the relationship between sounds and writing. Then, after the second hearing, they repeat the phrases.

Teachers may wish to introduce the colours and adjectives used in this activity first.

R Before discussing adjectival agreements, the nationalities encountered on pages 26–27 can be revised in order to remind pupils that the adjective endings change. The teacher may then see if their pupils can work out the rule for the plural forms of adjectives before reading the **Gramática** box on page 32 of the Pupil's Book.

Tapescript

– *Un caballo blanco*
– *Una tortuga verde*
– *Un gato atigrado*
– *Un perro negro*
– *Un conejo gris*
– *Un pez dorado*
– *Un pájaro amarillo*
– *Un cobayo marrón*
– *Un pájaro azul*
– *Un ratón grande y un ratón pequeño*

5 Los jóvenes describen a sus animales. (1–4) Copia y rellena el cuadro. (AT1/3) [W1,2,4,5; L3]

✗ *Listening for information and instructions – Level D*

Listening/Writing. Pupils copy the grid and listen to the recording in order to fill in all the details.

✚ After completing this activity, teachers may wish to exploit the information in the grid to practise the structures in the vocabulary grid on page 33 of the Pupil's Book. *¿Cómo es?* could be added. Example:

  – *¿Tienes animales en casa, Rosa?*
  – *Tengo una gata.*
  – *¿De qué color es tu gata?*
  – *Es marrón y blanca.*
  – *¿Cómo es?*
  – *Es atigrada.*

Tú y yo — módulo 2

Answers

	Rosa	Manolito	Carmela	Oscar
Animal	gata	perro	caballo	pájaro
Años	9 años	1 año	12 años	5 meses
Color	marrón y blanca	negro	gris	azul
Descripción	atigrada	pequeño	muy grande	muy pequeño

Tapescript

1 – ¿Tienes animales en casa, Rosa?
 – Tengo una gata.
 – ¿De qué color es tu gata?
 – Es marrón y blanca. Es atigrada.
 – ¿Cuántos años tiene?
 – Tiene 9 años.
2 – ¿Tienes animales en casa, Manolito?
 – Sí, tengo un perro.
 – ¿De qué color es?
 – Es negro. Es pequeño.
 – ¿Cuántos años tiene?
 – Tiene un año.
3 – ¿De qué color es tu caballo, Carmela?
 – Es gris y muy grande.
 – ¿Cuántos años tiene?
 – Tiene 12 años.
4 – ¿De qué color es tu pájaro, Oscar?
 – Es azul. Es un periquito muy pequeño. Sólo tiene cinco meses.

Starter 2: Colour mixing [W1,2; L1] (any time after introducing colours)

Aims: To revise colours *(rojo, negro, blanco, azul, amarillo, verde, gris, marrón, naranja)* and build on thinking skills. (Timing: 5 minutes)

Pairwork activity: Pupils listen to the colours that will be mixed together in the following text, decide the colour that will be created and write it down in Spanish. Read out the following: *negro y blanco; azul y amarillo; rojo y amarillo; verde y rojo.* (Answers: *gris, verde, naranja, marrón*)

R Lower-ability pupils could hold up the correct piece of coloured paper or a colouring pencil, or write down the colour in English.

6a En grupos, pregunta y contesta. (AT2/3) [W1,2; S4,5; L4]

Speaking and interacting with others – Level D/E

Speaking. In small groups pupils ask and answer questions about their pets. Teachers may wish to add *¿Cómo es?*. In order to encourage pupils to talk about the full range of animals, the pairwork cards (*Hoja de trabajo 1*) could be used.

6b Escribe las informaciones de 6a. (AT4/3) [W5; S3]

Writing to exchange information and ideas – Level D/E

Writing. Teachers should check that pupils remember to use *tiene* for reporting back about someone else's pets. Pupils write short paragraphs about their classmates' pets.

7 Lee y escucha la canción. Contesta a las preguntas. (AT1/3, AT3/3) [W1,2,4; S4; C4]

Listening for enjoyment – Level D/E

Listening/Reading. Pupils read and listen to the song. It can be played more than once and pupils encouraged to sing along: the class could even have a talent show to see which group can sing with the best accent. Pupils then answer the questions to check they have understood the song.

Answers

a muy genial, pequeño	b un año
c negro y blanco	d pequeño
e tres peces	f en el corral

Tapescript

*En casa tengo un animal.
Es un perro muy genial.
Es pequeño, blanco y negro
Y de edad de sólo un año.*

*En mi casa tengo un gato,
Negro y blanco, atigrado.
Es un gato muy inteligente.
Y también es muy prudente.*

*En casa tengo un pájaro
Es pequeño y canario.
Y también tengo tres peces,
Un conejo y dos serpientes.*

*En casa tengo un animal
Que vive bien en el corral,
Mi mascota es un caballo
Es pequeño y castaño.*

*Para mí los animales
Son amigos especiales.
Tengo muchos en mi casa
Porque son buena compañía.*

8 ¿Tienes un animal en casa? Escribe una descripción de tu animal. (AT4/3) [T5,6]

Writing to establish and maintain personal contact – Level D/E

Writing. This is best set as a homework task, and pupils could be encouraged to use their descriptions

módulo 2 Tú y yo

as the basis of a presentation to the rest of the class. Teachers may want pupils to use presentation software such as *PowerPoint* to write and illustrate their descriptions.

Plenary
In groups, ask pupils to come up with a list of six invented animals. They take it in turns to read out their inventions and the rest of the class must correct any adjectival agreement mistakes (e.g. *un ratón azul y amarillo*).

Cuaderno A, page 18

1a Completa el crucigrama. (AT4/1) [W1,7]

✠ *Knowing about language*

Writing. Pupils do the crossword, inserting the names of the animals.

Answers

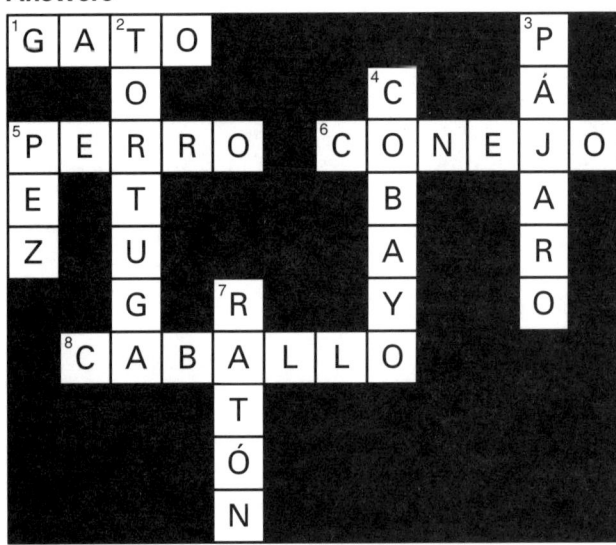

Crossword:
- 1 across: GATO
- 2 down: TORTUGA
- 3 down: PÁJARO
- 4 down: CONEJO (with C at top)
- 5 across: PERRO
- 5 down: PEZ
- 6 across: CONEJO
- 6 down: CABALLO (B column)
- 7 down: RATÓN
- 8 across: CABALLO

1b Lee las frases y colorea los animales en **1a**. (AT3/2) [W1,4,5]

✠ *Reading for information and instructions – Level C*

Reading/Writing. Pupils read the descriptions and colour in the animals in activity 1a appropriately.

2 Lee la ficha y rellena la descripción. (AT3/2) [T5]

✠ *Knowing about language*

Reading/Writing. Pupils read the details and complete the sentences.

Answers

En casa tengo un caballo. Se llama Zar. Es gris. Tiene siete años.

Cuaderno B, page 18

1 Empareja los animales con los adjetivos apropiados. (AT3/1, AT4/1)

✠ *Knowing about language*

Reading/Writing. Pupils match up the pictures of animals with the adjectives.

Answers

a grande	b atigrado	c blanco
d verde	e pequeño	f blanco y negro

2a Lee la descripción y rellena la ficha. (AT3/2) [W1,4,5]

✠ *Reading for information and instructions – Level C*

Reading/Writing. Pupils read the description and fill in the details.

Answers

| *Animal:* caballo | *Color:* gris |
| *Nombre:* Zar | *Edad:* 7 años |

2b Lee la ficha y rellena la descripción. (AT3/2) [W1,4,5]

✠ *Knowing about language*

Reading/Writing. Pupils read the details and complete the sentences.

Answers

En casa tengo un gato.
Se llama Leo.
Es negro.
Tiene dos años.

3 Completa las descripciones con las frases apropiadas. (AT3/2) [W1,2,4,5]

✠ *Knowing about language*

Reading. Pupils match up the sentences.

Answers

1 c 2 d 3 a 4 b

Hoja de trabajo 1, page 24

Cards for pairwork featuring pets: pupils match the pictures to the correct words.

Hoja de trabajo 2, page 25

Identity cards of eight people and three cards for pupils to fill in. These can be used to practise:

Tú y yo — módulo 2

¿Cómo te llamas?
¿Qué idiomas hablas?
¿Tienes un animal en casa?
¿Tienes hermanos?

They can be used as a class, group or pairwork activity. It is suggested that pupils ask three partners the questions and fill in the three blank cards with the information that they receive.

Grammar, Resource and Assessment File, page 27

Activities to practise adjective endings, followed by an activity to insert the correct verb. Teachers should train their pupils at this stage to use the clues in the question and answer to help decide which verb is most appropriate.

1a [W4]

Answers

a	un perro	*blanco*	blanca	blancos	blancas
b	un gato	*atigrado*	atigrada	atigrados	atigradas
c	una tortuga	negro	*negra*	negros	negras
d	tres peces	dorado	dorada	*dorados*	doradas
e	dos conejos	pequeño	pequeña	*pequeños*	pequeñas
f	dos pájaros	verde	verde	*verdes*	*verdes*

1b

Answers

Singular	Plural
un perro pequeñ*o*	dos perros pequeñ*os*
un gato negr*o*	dos gatos negr*os*
un conejo blanc*o*	dos conejos blanc*os*
un pez dorad*o*	dos peces dorad*os*
un caballo blanc*o*	dos caballos blanc*os*
una tortuga pequeñ*a*	dos tortugas pequeñ*as*

2 [W5]

Answers

a ¿De dónde ......*eres*......?

b ......*Hablo*...... inglés.

c ......*Vive*...... en México.

d ¿Cómo se ......*llama*...... tu madre?

e ¿......*Tienes*...... hermanos?

No ......*tengo*...... hermanos.

......*Soy*...... hija única.

módulo 2

5 Los ojos y el pelo

(Pupil's Book pages 34–35)

Main topics

- Describing your eyes and hair

Key Framework Objectives

- Gender/plural 7W4 (Reinforcement)
- Word order 7S1 (Reinforcement)
- Adapting sentences 7S3 (Reinforcement)

Key language

¿De qué color son tus ojos?
Tengo los ojos …
marrones   negros
azules   verdes
¡Tengo el ojo morado!
¿De qué color es tu pelo?
Tengo el pelo …
castaño   rubio
negro   pelirrojo
largo   rizado
liso   ondulado
corto   ni largo ni corto
Tengo pecas.
Llevo barba y bigote.
Llevo gafas.

Resources

Cassette A, Side 2
CD 1, track 15
Cuaderno A and B, page 19
Hoja de trabajo 3, Resource and Assessment File, page 26
OHTs 11 and 12: describing facial features

Starter 1: Spot the mistake [W4]

Aims: To develop reading skills by getting pupils to focus very closely on the text; to develop pupils' skills in using correct adjectival agreement and to introduce some vocabulary for descriptions. (Timing: 5–10 minutes)

Activity: Write the following incorrect sentences on the board or transparency: 1 *Un ratón blanco y negra*; 2 *Una tortuga verda*; 3 *Dos conejos gris*; 4 *Tres perro marrones*. Give pupils a couple of minutes to spot the mistake in each sentence. Pupils then feed back with correct versions, justifying their answers (Correct answers: *un ratón blanco y negro, una tortuga verde, dos conejos grises, tres perros marrones*).

1 Escucha y repite. Pon atención a la pronunciación. (AT1/1, AT2/1) [W1,4; S1; L1]

✴ *Knowing about language*

Listening/Speaking. Pupils listen to the recording and repeat the descriptions of hair and eyes. Teachers may wish pupils to hear the recording twice: during the first listening they point to the pictures in order to establish the relationship between sounds and writing, and then after a second hearing they repeat the phrases.

Before attempting this activity, teachers should introduce the key words *pelo* and *ojos* and remind students that the adjective follows the noun. To make this as realistic as possible, teachers may wish to use the OHP for an 'identikit' style activity, changing the colour of hair and eyes.

Tapescript

1 – *Tengo los ojos marrones y el pelo castaño.*
2 – *Tengo los ojos negros y el pelo negro.*
3 – *Tengo los ojos azules y el pelo rubio.*
4 – *Tengo los ojos verdes y el pelo pelirrojo.*
5 – *Tengo los ojos negros y el pelo castaño.*
6 – *¡Tengo el ojo morado!*

2a ¿De qué color son los ojos y el pelo de las personas? Copia y rellena el cuadro. (AT1/2) [W1,4; S1; L3]

✴ *Listening for information and instructions – Level D*

Listening. Pupils copy the grid and listen to the descriptions, filling in the eye and hair colour of the four people.

Answers

Marta: pelo negro, ojos marrones
José: pelo castaño, ojos marrones
Carmen: pelo rubio, ojos verdes
Oscar: pelo pelirrojo, ojos azules

Tapescript

– ¿De qué color es tu pelo, Marta?
– Tengo el pelo negro.
– ¿Y de qué color son tus ojos?
– Tengo los ojos marrones.

– ¿De qué color es tu pelo, José?
– Tengo el pelo castaño.
– ¿Y de qué color son tus ojos?
– Tengo los ojos marrones.

– ¿De qué color es tu pelo, Carmen?
– Tengo el pelo rubio.
– ¿Y de qué color son tus ojos?
– Tengo los ojos verdes.

– ¿De qué color es tu pelo, Oscar?
– Tengo el pelo pelirrojo.
– ¿Y de qué color son tus ojos?
– Tengo los ojos azules.

Tú y yo — módulo 2

2b Con tu compañero/a, pregunta y contesta. ¿Qué dicen las personas en **2a**? (AT2/2) [W2,5; S4; L4]

✉ *Speaking to convey information – Level D*

Speaking. Working in pairs, pupils ask and answer questions on what the people in activity **2a** say.

2c Haz un sondeo. Pregunta a tus compañeros/as de clase. Copia y rellena el cuadro. (AT2/3) [W1,2,4,5; S1,4; L4]

✉ *Speaking and interacting with others – Level D*

Speaking. Pupils copy the grid and conduct a survey of at least five of their classmates, asking for their name, eye and hair colour.

2d Describe a cinco de tus compañeros/as. (AT4/2–3) [W1,4,5; S3; T6]

✉ *Writing to establish and maintain personal contact – Level D/E*

Writing. Pupils write descriptions of five classmates, using the information from activity **2c**. Teachers may wish pupils to write two or more sentences for each person in order to achieve level 3. Pupils should be reminded to use *tiene* when describing other people.

> *Starter 2:* **Match up** [S1,3; T1,5]
>
> *Aims:* To reinforce the understanding of gender, adjectival agreement and sentence structure. (Timing: 5–10 minutes)
>
> *Activity:* Write the following phrases on the board or on a transparency in two rows and four columns: (Row 1) *Tengo el pelo; Daniel tiene los ojos; Tengo el pelo corto; Sofía tiene los;* (Row 2) *y liso; marrón y los ojos azules; azules y el pelo castaño; ojos verdes y el pelo rubio.* Pupils match up the correct sentence halves. Correct any sentences and ask for justification of their answers. (Correct sentences: *Tengo el pelo marrón y los ojos azules; Tengo el pelo corto y liso; Daniel tiene los ojos azules y el pelo castaño; Sofía tiene los ojos verdes y el pelo corto.*) Then pupils have three minutes to change one detail in every sentence. This could be a grammatical detail (i.e. from singular to plural) or a meaning. Pupils then read out sentences to the class.

3 Escucha y repite. (AT1/1, AT2/1) [W1,4,5; L1]

✉ *Knowing about language*

Listening/Speaking. Pupils listen to the recording and repeat.

Tapescript

– Tengo el pelo largo y liso.
– Tengo el pelo corto y rizado.
– Tengo el pelo ondulado. No es ni largo ni corto.
– Tengo pecas.
– Llevo barba.
– Llevo barba y bigote.
– Llevo gafas.

---

4 Empareja las descripciones con las personas. (AT3/2) [W1,4,5; S2]

✉ *Reading for information and instructions – Level D*

Reading. Pupils read the descriptions and match them with the people a–f.

Answers

| 1 b | 2 d | 3 c | 4 a | 5 f | 6 e |

5 Con tu compañero/a, adivina quién es en tu clase. (AT2/2) [W1,4,5; L4]

✉ *Speaking and interacting with others – Level D/E*

Speaking. Play this guessing game as a whole-class activity first. Someone describes a pupil's hair and eyes, and the rest of the class try to guess who it is. This can then be played as a pair or small-group activity.

6 Escribe una descripción de ti. (AT4/2–3) [W1,2,4,5; S3; T5]

✉ *Writing to establish and maintain personal contact – Level D/E*

Writing. Pupils write a description of their own hair and eyes, starting the description with *tengo*.

✚ As an extension activity they may wish to write a description of their partner, starting the description with *tiene*.

Plenary

Throw-and-catch game, using a soft ball or object. Throw it to a pupil and ask a question about them in Spanish from those introduced previously (*¿Cómo te llamas?*, etc.) and then questions from this unit (*¿De qué color son/es … ? ¿Tienes un animal en casa? ¿Tienes hermanos?*). Pupils answer and throw the ball back to you. When you have asked the questions a number of times a pupil can replace you and throw the ball and ask the questions. Eventually the ball can be thrown to a pupil who will answer a question and then pose another question, throwing the ball to another pupil.

módulo 2 Tú y yo

Cuaderno A, page 19

1 Lee las descripciones. Colorea los ojos y el pelo. (AT3/2) [W1,5; S2,6]

✠ *Reading for information and instructions – Level C*

Reading. Pupils read the descriptions in order to colour the eyes and draw and colour the hair.

Answers

a brown eyes, brown hair	**b** blue eyes, red hair
c brown eyes, fair hair	

2 Mira los dibujos y lee las descripciones. Escribe el nombre de cada persona. (AT3/2) [W1,5; S2,5]

✠ *Reading for information and instructions – Level C*

Reading. Pupils look at the pictures and read the descriptions, then write the names below the people that match the descriptions.

Answers

1 d Javier	**2** c Alba	**3** b Carina	**4** a David

3 Dibuja y colorea el pelo y los ojos. Escribe tres frases para describir a la persona. (AT4/3) [T6]

✠ *Writing to exchange information and ideas – Level C/D*

Writing. Pupils draw and colour in the eyes and hair on the picture, and then write a short paragraph to describe the person. Teachers may wish to provide a writing frame to help pupils. *Tiene los ojos ... Tiene el pelo ... Su pelo es ...*

Cuaderno B, page 19

1 Lee las descripciones. Colorea los ojos. Dibuja y colorea el pelo. (AT3/2) [W1,5; S2,5,6]

✠ *Reading for information and instructions – Level D*

Reading. Pupils read the descriptions in order to colour the eyes and draw in and colour the hair.

Answers

a brown eyes, long wavy brown hair
b brown eyes, medium-length curly fair hair
c blue eyes, short red hair

2 Empareja las descripciones con los dibujos apropiados. (AT3/2) [W1,5; S2,5]

✠ *Reading for information and instructions – Level D*

Reading. Pupils match up the descriptions with the pictures.

Answers

a 2	**b** 1	**c** 3	**d** 5	**e** 4

3 Describe a dos personas famosas. (AT4/3) [T6]

✠ *Writing to exchange information and ideas – Level D/E*

Writing. Pupils write short paragraphs to describe the hair and eyes of two famous people.

Hoja de trabajo 3, page 26 [W1,2,4,5; S4; L4]

Cards for pairwork, practising questions about eye and hair colour.

módulo 2

6 ¿Cómo eres?

(Pupil's Book pages 36–37)

Main topics

- Describing your size
- Describing your colouring

Key Framework Objectives

- Reading using cues 7T1 (Launch)
- Checking before reading 7T3 (Launch)
- Assembling text 7T5 (Launch)
- Gender/plural 7W4 (Reinforcement)

Key language

¿Cómo eres?
alto/a
Soy/Es …
bajo/a
de talla mediana
blanco/a
moreno/a
negro/a
Soy/Es …
pelirrojo/a
rubio/a

Resources

Cassette A, Side 2
CD 1, track 16
Cuaderno A and B, page 20
Starter 1, Resource and Assessment File, page 32

Starter 1: **Drawing from written text** [W1,4; S2; T1]

Aims: To develop reading skills by getting pupils to focus very closely on the text; to develop pupils' skills in scanning texts and to encourage pupils to commit language to memory (*Me llamo … Tengo … años … Tengo los ojos … y el pelo … , Mis ojos son … , Mi pelo es …*). (Timing: 10 minutes)

Resources: Resource and Assessment File, page 32 (Starter 1)

Pairwork activity: Make an OHT using the sheet provided. Reveal one of the texts on the OHT for up to one minute, then cover the text. Ask pupils to draw what they have read from memory. They can use colours or label the picture to note the details. Repeat the exercise with the other texts. Numbers 3 and 4 are more difficult as the structure of the key phrases is different.

1a ¿Quién habla? Escucha y escribe el orden en que se menciona cada persona. (1–6) (AT1/2) [W1,2,4,5; L1]

✉ *Listening for information and instructions – Level D*

Listening. Pupils listen to the recording and work out which of the family members is speaking, according to whether they are *alto/a, bajo/a* or *de talla mediana*.

For example, the first person says '*soy baja*' so pupils are looking for a short female, so the answer for 1 is Isabel.

Before attempting this activity, introduce *alto/a, bajo/a, de talla mediana* and remind your pupils of masculine and feminine endings (the *Gramática* box will help).

Answers

1 Isabel	2 Miguel	3 Luis
4 Esther	5 Beatriz	6 Francisco

Tapescript

1 – Me llamo Isabel. Soy baja.
2 – Me llamo Miguel. Soy alto.
3 – Soy Luis y soy bajo.
4 – Mi nombre es Esther. Soy alta.
5 – Soy Beatriz y soy de talla mediana.
6 – Me llamo Francisco. Soy de talla mediana también.

1b Con tu compañero/a, ¿qué dicen los jóvenes? (AT2/2) [W1,2,4,5; S4; L4]

✉ *Speaking and interacting with others – Level C/D*

Speaking. In pairs, pupils work out what each person from activity 1a would say to describe their size.

1c ¿Cómo son? (AT4/2) [W1,4,5; S3]

✉ *Writing to exchange information and ideas – Level C/D*

Writing. Pupils write a sentence to describe each of the six people in activity 1a. Teachers may wish to practise ¿*Cómo es …?* and *Es …* before pupils start this activity.

Answers

Miguel es alto.
Esther es alta.
Francisco es de talla mediana.
Beatriz es de talla mediana.
Luis es bajo.
Isabel es baja.

2a Escucha y repite. (AT1/1) [W4,5; L1]

✉ *Knowing about language*

Listening. Pupils listen to the descriptions and repeat. Teachers may wish to vary this activity by asking volunteers to predict how each phrase will be pronounced before playing the recording, and then comparing to see how well pupils can match sounds and writing.

módulo 2: Tú y yo

Teachers should ensure that pupils remember that the adjectival ending changes for males and females.

Tapescript
– Soy rubia.
– Soy moreno.
– Soy negra.
– Soy blanca.
– Soy pelirrojo.

2b ¿Verdad (✓) o mentira (✗)? (AT3/2) [W1,4; S2]

✉ *Reading for information – Level C*

Reading. Pupils decide whether the descriptions of the people in activity **2a** are true (*verdad*) or false (*mentira*).

Answers

| a ✗ | b ✗ | c ✓ | d ✗ | e ✗ |

Starter 2: Odd one out [W4,7]

Aims: To reinforce the understanding and knowledge of gender and meaning with descriptions, and to use thinking skills. (Timing: 5 minutes)

Pairwork activity: Copy the following onto a grid with three columns and three rows: (Row 1) 1 *pelo rubio* 2 *ojos verdes* 3 *pelo corto* (Row 2) 4 *soy alto* 5 *soy baja* 6 *soy moreno* (Row 3) 7 *es negro* 8 *es blanco* 9 *es de talla mediana*. Pupils must locate the odd one out in each row. Encourage use of the target language by giving an example and putting keywords on the board (*masculino, femenino, diferente, número tres es la excepción porque …*), but allow pupils to communicate in English for more complex ideas. Pairs feed back to the whole class and justify their decision (in English). Accept all valid suggestions. You can repeat the process using the columns instead of the rows, or ask pupils to construct sentences using the language in the grid, e.g. *tengo el pelo rubio y soy alto y moreno*.

3 Con tu compañero/a, describe a las personas. (AT2/3) [W4,5; S1,3]

✉ *Speaking and interacting with others – Level D/E*

Speaking. Depending on the ability of the pupils, teachers may wish to start with a guessing game. The teacher describes the physical characteristics of one of the people in activity **3** and the pupils guess who is being described. Volunteers can take the 'teacher' role. Pupils then work in pairs, taking turns to describe the people.

4 Empareja las descripciones con los dibujos de los criminales. (AT3/3) [T1,3]

✉ *Reading for information and instructions – Level D*

Reading. Pupils read the wanted posters and find the criminal's picture to match each description.

Answers

| a 3 | b 1 | c 4 |

National Literacy Strategy

This activity is an ideal opportunity for shared writing, which would provide a clear model for pupils to attempt activity **5** independently. There is no description for criminal number 2, and the teacher could elicit and edit suggestions for a wanted poster which pupils could then copy into their exercise books for future reference. Teachers with more confident learners may prefer their pupils to make up their own wanted poster, which would provide opportunities to write using different registers.

🖱 ICT activity

Pupils could use desk-top publishing software, such as *MS Publisher*, to produce a wanted poster.

5 Describe a una persona famosa. (AT4/3) [T5,6]

✉ *Writing to exchange information and ideas – Level D/E*

Writing. This is an ideal homework assignment. Pupils write a description of a famous person. They should include name, hair, eyes, colouring and build. They could also include age, birthday, nationality and country of origin. This could also be set as an ICT activity using desk-top publishing software, using a *newsletter* format, and could include an interview with the star, using the *yo* and *tú* forms, and an article about the star, using *él* or *ella* forms of the verbs learnt, as well as pictures of the star, the star's country of birth, etc.

Plenary

Ask pupils to use the **Resumen** section on page 38 of the Pupil's Book to test each other on the language that has been introduced during the module. Pupils can award each other a point for each correct answer. Pupils with the most points after three minutes can take up the challenge of the 'hot seat', where they have to accurately answer questions asked by the teacher and/or other students to stay in the seat.

Tú y yo — módulo 2

Cuaderno A, page 20

1 Escribe las palabras que faltan. (AT4/1) [W4]

✉ *Knowing about language*

Writing. Pupils fill in the missing words, giving the masculine or feminine form of the adjectives.

Answers

baja, blanco, moreno, negra, pelirroja, rubio

2 Escribe una frase para cada dibujo. (AT4/2) [W3,4; S6]

✉ *Knowing about language*

Writing. Pupils write a sentence for each of the four people illustrated.

Answers

a Soy alto y negro.	b Soy baja y rubia.
c Soy bajo y rubio.	d Soy alta y negra.

3 Escribe una frase para cada persona. (AT3/2) [W1,2,4,5]

✉ *Knowing about language*

Reading/Writing. Pupils complete the sentences, inserting the appropriate names.

Answers

a Gregorio	b Elvira
c Pepe	d Nuria

4 Describe a una persona famosa. (AT4/3) [T6]

✉ *Writing to exchange information and ideas – Level D*

Writing. Pupils write a short paragraph describing a famous person of their choice.

Cuaderno B, page 20

1 Escribe las palabras que faltan. (AT4/1) [W4]

✉ *Knowing about language*

Writing. Pupils fill in the missing words, giving the masculine or feminine form of the adjectives.

Answers

baja, blanco, moreno, negra, pelirroja, rubio

2 ¿Quién es? (AT3/2) [W1,2,4,5]

✉ *Knowing about language*

Reading. Pupils fill in the names to match the descriptions.

Answers

a Gregorio	b Pepe	c Nuria/Elvira
d Pepe	e Elvira	f Nuria

3 Escribe una frase para cada persona famosa. (AT4/2–3) [W3,4; S6; T6]

✉ *Writing to exchange information and ideas – Level D/E*

Writing. Pupils write a sentence or short paragraph to describe the four famous people.

Answers

Marilyn Monroe es baja. Tiene el pelo rubio, corto y rizado y los ojos azules.
Barney Rubble es bajo. Tiene el pelo rubio y corto y los ojos marrones.
Venus Williams es alta. Tiene el pelo negro y largo y los ojos marrones.
Will Smith es alto. Tiene el pelo negro y corto y los ojos marrones.

módulo 2

Resumen y Prepárate

(Pupil's Book pages 38–39)

Resumen

This is a checklist of language covered in Module 2. There is a comprehensive *Resumen* list for Module 2 in the Student's Book (page 38) and a *Resumen* test sheet in Cuaderno A and B (page 24).

Key Framework Objectives

- Basic questions 7S4 (Reinforcement)
- Reading using cues 7T1 (Reinforcement)
- Gist and detail 7L3 (Reinforcement)

Prepárate

A revision test to give practice for the test itself at the end of the module.

Resources

Cassette A, side 2
CD 1, track 17
Cuaderno A and B, Repaso (previously ¡Extra!), pages 21–22; Gramática, page 23

1 Escucha y empareja cada persona con el dibujo apropiado. (AT1/2) [L3]

✉ *Listening for information and instructions – Level D*

Listening. Pupils listen and match up the descriptions of the people 1–5 with the pictures a–e.

Answers

| 1 b | 2 d | 3 a | 4 c | 5 e |

Tapescript

1 – Tengo el pelo corto y rubio.
2 – Tengo el pelo negro.
3 – Tengo el pelo pelirrojo y rizado.
4 – Tengo el pelo castaño, largo y ondulado.
5 – Tengo el pelo castaño y llevo gafas.

2a Con tu compañero/a, empareja las preguntas con las respuestas. (AT2/2–3, AT3/2–3) [W1,5; S4,9]

✉ *Speaking and interacting with others – Level D*

Speaking/Reading. In pairs, pupils match up the six questions and answers and then practise asking and answering the questions.

Answers

| 1 c | 2 e | 3 b | 4 d | 5 a | 6 f |

2b Pregunta y contesta para ti. (AT2/3) [W1,5; S3,4,9]

✉ *Speaking to convey information – Level D/E*

Speaking. In pairs, pupils take turns to ask the questions from activity **2a** and answer for themselves.

3 Lee las entrevistas. Elige la persona apropiada. (AT3/3) [T1]

✉ *Reading for information and instructions – Level D*

Reading. Pupils read the interviews and choose the correct person from the choice of three for each one.

Answers

| a Michael Owen | b Jennifer López | c Penélope Cruz |

4 Copia y rellena la ficha sobre ti. (AT4/1–3) [T5]

✉ *Writing to establish and maintain personal contact – Level D*

Writing. Pupils copy the grid and fill it in for themselves, either using single words or one or more sentences.

Cuaderno A, pages 21–22

Repaso (previously ¡Extra!)

1 Descifra los anagramas de los países. (AT3/1, AT4/1) [W1,7]

✉ *Knowing about language*

Reading/Writing. Pupils solve the anagrams of countries.

Answers

| 1 Escocia | 2 Inglaterra | 3 Gales |
| 4 Irlanda | 5 España | 6 Paquistán |

2 Escribe una lista de los animales en el dibujo. (AT4/1) [W2,4]

✉ *Knowing about language*

Writing. Pupils write a list of the animals in the picture.

Answers

| un gato, una tortuga, un conejo, un cobayo, un ratón, un perro, dos peces, un caballo, un pájaro |

3 Completa las frases sobre las familias de las personas famosas. (AT3/2) [W1,2,4,]

✉ *Knowing about language*

Resumen y Prepárate módulo 2

Reading. Pupils complete the sentences about famous people and characters with the appropriate word.

Answers

| a hijo | b padre | c hermana | d hermano | e madre |

4 ¿Tienes hermanos? ¿Cómo se llaman? ¿Cómo se llaman tus padres? Escribe tres frases. (AT4/3) [S9; T5]

✉ *Writing to establish and maintain personal contact – Level D/E*

Writing. Pupils write a short paragraph of three sentences to answer the questions about their own family.

5a Empareja las respuestas con las preguntas apropiadas. (AT3/2–3) [W1,2,5; S4]

✉ *Knowing about language*

Reading. Pupils match up the questions and answers.

Answers

| 1 b | 2 a | 3 d | 4 f | 5 e | 6 g | 7 c |

5b Contesta a las preguntas sobre ti. (AT4/3) [S9]

✉ *Writing to establish and maintain personal contact – Level D/E*

Writing. Pupils write the answers to the questions from activity **5a** with information about themselves.

➕ Teachers may also like to use this activity for extended speaking practice, either for pairwork, or as a framework for pupils to prepare a short presentation about themselves.

Cuaderno B, pages 21–22

Repaso (previously ¡Extra!)

1 Descifra los anagramas de los países. (AT3/1, AT4/1) [W1,7]

✉ *Knowing about language*

Reading/Writing. Pupils solve the anagrams of countries.

Answers

| 1 Escocia | 2 Inglaterra | 3 Gales |
| 4 Irlanda | 5 España | 6 Paquistán |

2 Escribe una descripción para cada animal en el dibujo. (AT4/2) [W1,2,4]

✉ *Knowing about language*

Writing. Pupils write a description of each animal illustrated, including the colour with the correct adjectival agreement.

Answers

| un gato blanco/un conejo blanco |
| un cobayo negro/una tortuga negra |
| un pájaro gris/ un ratón gris |
| un perro grande/un pez grande |
| un pez pequeño/un caballo pequeño |

3 Completa las frases sobre las familias de las personas famosas. (AT3/2) [W1,2,4]

✉ *Knowing about language*

Reading. Pupils complete the sentences about famous people and characters with the appropriate word.

Answers

| a hijo | b padre | c hermana | d hermano | e madre |

4 ¿Tienes hermanos? ¿Cómo se llaman? ¿Cómo se llaman tus padres? Escribe tres frases. (AT4/3) [S9; T5]

✉ *Writing to establish and maintain personal contact – Level D/E*

Writing. Pupils write a short paragraph of three sentences to answer the questions about their own family.

5a Empareja las respuestas con las preguntas apropiadas. (AT3/2–3) [W1,2,5; S4]

✉ *Knowing about language*

Reading. Pupils match up the questions and answers.

Answers

| 1 b | 2 a | 3 f | 4 d | 5 g | 6 e | 7 h | 8 c |

5b Contesta a las preguntas sobre ti. (AT4/3) [S9]

✉ *Writing to establish and maintain personal contact – Level D/E*

Writing. Pupils write the answers to the questions from activity **5a** with information about themselves.

➕ Teachers may also like to use this activity for extended speaking practice, either for pairwork, or as a framework for pupils to prepare a short presentation about themselves.

módulo 2 — Tú y yo

Cuaderno A, page 23

Gramática

1 Completa las frases con las palabras apropiadas. (AT3/2) [W2,4]

✉ *Knowing about language*

Reading/Writing. Pupils choose the correct word to complete each sentence. They should read the box to revise possessive adjectives before attempting this activity.

Answers

a Mi	b Mis	c Mi	d Mi	e Mi	f Mis

2 Completa las frases con *es* o *son*. (AT3/2) [W5]

✉ *Knowing about language*

Reading/Writing. Pupils choose the correct word to complete each sentence. They should read the box to revise the verb *ser* before attempting this activity.

Answers

a es	b son	c son	d es	e es	f son

3 Completa las frases con la forma apropiada de los verbos. (AT3/2) [W5]

✉ *Knowing about language*

Reading/Writing. Pupils choose the correct word to complete each question and answer. They should read the box to revise the verbs *llamarse, hablar, vivir* and *tener* before attempting this activity.

Answers

1 llamo	2 vives	3 Tengo
4 hablas	5 llaman	6 tiene, tiene

Cuaderno B, page 23

Gramática

1 Completa las frases con las palabras apropiadas. (AT3/2) [W2,4]

✉ *Knowing about language*

Reading/Writing. Pupils choose the correct word to complete each sentence. They should read the box to revise possessive adjectives before attempting this activity.

Answers

a Mi	b tu	c Mis	d tus	e Mi	f Mi

2 Completa las frases con *es* o *son*. (AT3/2) [W5]

✉ *Knowing about language*

Reading/Writing. Pupils choose the correct word to complete each sentence. They should read the box to revise the verb *ser* before attempting this activity.

Answers

a es	b son	c son	d es	e es	f es	g son	h es

3 Completa las frases con la forma apropiada de los verbos. (AT3/2) [W5]

✉ *Knowing about language*

Reading/Writing. Pupils choose the correct word to complete each question and answer. They should read the box to revise the verbs *llamarse, hablar, vivir* and *tener* before attempting this activity.

Answers

1 llamas, llamo	2 vives, Vivo	3 tienes, Tengo
4 hablas, Hablo	5 llaman, llaman	6 tienen, tiene, tiene

módulo 2

¡Extra! 7 Se habla español
(Pupil's Book pages 40–41)

Main topics
This is an optional unit which reviews some of the key language of the module: it consists of activities based on a map showing where Spanish is spoken throughout the world.

Key Framework Objectives
- Geographical facts 7C1 (Launch)

Resources
Cassette A, Side 2
CD 1, track 18

Suggestion
The TLF inititative (Teaching and Learning Foundation subjects) will have a significant impact on the relationship between MFL and humanities subjects. This topic is an ideal opportunity to reinforce links between Spanish and Geography in your school. Teachers should not overestimate their pupils' ability to name countries, much less say where they are on a map. Also, they should not be surprised if their pupils think that Spanish is spoken in the strangest places! It may even be possible to work together on delivering a cultural awareness unit: a number of case studies will be available. CILT and Canning House, as well as the embassies of Hispanic countries, are able to provide a wide variety of information. Better still, the Internet can be used.

The real point to emphasise here is the importance of Spanish as a world language.

This is also a good starting point for comparing cultures, which will enhance both the Citizenship and Spriritual Moral Social and Cultural (SMSC) delivery of Schemes of Work. There are a number of charities who work with Spanish-speaking countries and produce some excellent resources.

Starter 1: Find the missing country [L2; C1]
Aims: To build on existing knowledge of countries in Spanish; to encourage pupils to listen carefully for detail and to develop memory skills. (Timing: 5–10 minutes)

Activity: Pupils can either work individually or with partners/groups. Read out five countries from the following Spanish-speaking countries/islands: *España, Menorca, Mallorca, Ibiza, Las Islas Baleares, Tenerife, Gran Canaria, Lanzarote, Las Islas Canarias, Argentina, Uruguay, Paraguay, Perú, Ecuador, Colombia, Venezuela, Panamá, El Salvador, Costa Rica, Honduras, Nicaragua, Belice, Guatemala, México, Cuba, La República Dominicana, Puerto Rico, Los Estados Unidos.* Repeat the list in a different order but leave out one country, e.g. (first time) *España, Tenerife, Ibiza, Costa Rica, Cuba;* (second time) *Tenerife, Cuba, España, Costa Rica.* Pupils write down the missing country, using page 40 in the Pupil's Book as a reference to check spellings if necessary. Repeat this a number of times with different countries.

R For lower-ability pupils, start with a list of three and work up to five.

+ For those pupils who are coping well, increase the number of countries from five to six, and more.

1 Mira la información en el mapa y contesta a las preguntas. (AT3/1) [C1]

Knowing about language

Reading. This activity should go beyond simple recognition of the names of countries: both questions are good starting points for exploring the history of Spanish influence in the Americas, spanning six centuries.

Answers

1	21
2	more than 20 million Americans are of Hispanic origin

2 ¿De dónde son? Busca en el mapa el país de cada persona famosa. (AT3/2) [C1,2]

Reading for information and instructions – Level D

Reading. Pupils read the descriptions of famous Spanish speakers and find the country they come from based on their nationality.

Answers

a Cuba	b Argentina	c America
d Mexico	e Chile	f Spain

3 Escucha y anota los países. (AT1/2) [C1]

Listening for information and instructions – Level D

Listening. Pupils listen and note the countries mentioned.

Answers

Mexico, Cuba, Spain, Argentina, Chile, Colombia, Puerto Rico, Venezuela

Tapescript
– Se habla español en México.
– Se habla español en México y Cuba.

módulo 2 Tú y yo

– Se habla español en México, Cuba y España.
– Se habla español en México, Cuba, España y Argentina.
– Se habla español en México, Cuba, España, Argentina y Chile.
– Se habla español en México, Cuba, España, Argentina, Chile y Colombia.
– Se habla español en México, Cuba, España, Argentina, Chile, Colombia y Puerto Rico.
– Se habla español en México, Cuba, España, Argentina, Chile, Colombia, Puerto Rico y Venezuela.

4 ¿Dónde se habla español? Juega al juego de la memoria. (AT2/2) [C1]

✕ *Speaking to convey information – Level D*

Speaking. Pupils play this memory game that they have just heard on the recording in activity 3. If you have more than 21 pupils in your class you will need to allow the Canary and Balearic Islands.

5a Lee las palabras. ¿Qué significan? (AT3/1) [C2]

✕ *Knowing about language*

Reading. Pupils read the words on the wall and see how many they already understand. This is also a language awareness activity.

Answers

¡vamos! – let's go!, patio, guacamole, ¡ándale! – let's go!, pronto – ready, paella, plaza, ¡hasta la vista! – goodbye!, gracias – thank you, tortilla

5b ¿Qué otras palabras sabes en español? (AT4) [W1]

✕ *Knowing about language*

Speaking. This language awareness activity follows on from activity 5a. Students may need some 'prodding' to get their brains working. Cartoon characters are a good starting point! Most pupils will know ¡Ay caramba!

Plenary

In groups, ask pupils to invent four sentences in Spanish, either true or false, concerning Spanish and the countries and places that speak it. Each group presents the sentences to the class and other students must decide if the statements are true or false, and justify their answers. You could draw students' attention to the sentence structures of exercises 2 and 4 on page 41 of the Pupil's Book to help them.

R For lower-ability classes, ask students to invent the four true or false sentences in English.

Optional Thinking Skills lesson

Aims

To develop reading and thinking skills; to help pupils think laterally; to revise pets, brothers and sisters and description language. (Timing: 40 minutes)

Resources

Resource and Assessment File, page 33 (Thinking Skills)

Logic problem [S2; T1,2]

Pairwork activity: Make worksheets and an OHT using the master provided. Give each pair of pupils a copy of the blank grid and answer options and explain that they must read the ten clues you are about to show them and work out the information to complete the grid for each person. Explain that each person on the grid needs one piece of information for each category: *Aspecto Físico, Familia, Animales*, and that the options listed below the grid can only be used once. Check that pupils can identify which are boys and which are girls from the names in the grid. Reveal the first clue on the OHT and give pupils two minutes to fill in the grid. Pupils must also decide what other incomplete information they have received. One by one reveal the ten sentences. Pupils must not ask you for the answer. If pupils run into difficulties, stop, go back to the first two or three sentences and go through them with the class.

Answers

Pilar: ojos marrones, 1 hermano, perro;
Pablo: alto, 2 hermanos, conejo;
Mercedes: pelo rubio, 0 hermanos y 0 hermanas, gato;
Felipe: pelo corto, 1 hermana, pez;
Yolanda: ojos azules, 1 hermano y 1 hermana, pájaro).

Pairs then feed back their answers. Select the least able pupils to feed back first, as they will give the most straightforward answers. Then discuss with pupils how this technique helped them to work out the language and how it made them think. Try to ask open questions, such as: 'What did you learn? What did you find easy/difficult? How did you tackle the task? How might you approach it differently next time? How does a task like this help you with learning Spanish? What skills have you developed/used? Where else might you use these skills?'.

módulo 2 *Te toca a ti*

(Pupil's Book pages 118–119)

- Self-access reading and writing at two levels.

A Reinforcement

1 Elige dos frases apropiadas para cada dibujo. (AT3/2) [W1,4; S2]

✉ *Reading for information and instructions – Level C*

Reading. Pupils choose two speech bubbles to go with each picture.

Answers

1 f, l	2 e, g	3 b, h	4 c, k	5 a, j	6 d, i

2a Copia y completa las frases con las palabras apropiadas. (AT4/2) [W1,4; T1]

✉ *Knowing about language*

Writing. Pupils copy out and complete the sentences using the information for Penélope Cruz contained in the ID tag.

Answers

1 Penélope Cruz	2 veintiocho
3 española	4 hermana, un
5 hermana, Mónica, Eduardo	6 Aitana
7 ojos	8 castaño

2b Escribe seis frases sobre ti. (AT4/3) [S3,9]

✉ *Writing to establish and maintain personal contact – Level D/E*

Writing. Pupils write six sentences about themselves using activity **2a** as a model.

B Extension

1 Empareja los anuncios y elige el anuncio apropiado para cada dibujo. (AT3/2) [W1,4; T1]

✉ *Reading for information and instructions – Level D*

Reading. Pupils match up the two parts of each advert and then work out which animal goes with which advert.

Answers

1 d, B	2 c, A	3 a, D	4 b, C

2a Empareja cada descripción con el dibujo apropiado. (AT3/2) [W4; T1]

✉ *Reading for information and instructions – Level D*

Reading. Pupils match up the descriptions with the correct pictures.

Answers

1 b	2 a	3 c	4 d	5 e

2b Describe a una persona de tu familia, un amigo o una amiga. (AT4/3) [S9; T6]

✉ *Writing to exchange information and ideas – Level D/E*

Writing. Pupils write a short paragraph to describe a friend or family member, using activity **2a** as a model.

módulo 3 ¡Vamos al instituto!

(Pupil's Book pages 44–61)

Unit/topics	Key Framework Objectives	PoS	Key language and Grammar
1 Me encanta la informática (pp. 44–45) Talking about school subjects Expressing likes and dislikes	7S6 Compound sentences (L) 7W1 Everyday words (R) 7W4 Gender/plural (R) 7L3 Gist and detail (R)	1a sounds and writing 2c ask/answer questions 5c express opinions	School subjects ¿Te gusta la geografía? ¿Te gustan las ciencias? Me gusta (mucho) la historia. Me gustan las matemáticas. Me gusta(n) bastante. Me encanta(n). Odio/Detesto.
2 La historia es interesante (pp. 46–47) Giving opinions about school and school subjects	7T7 Improving written work (L) 7W4 Gender/plural (R) 7W5 Verbs present (R) 7T2 Reading aloud (R)	1b grammar and how to apply it 2c ask/answer questions 5c express opinions	Adjective agreement, singular and plural ¿Te gusta el instituto? aburrido/a divertido/a pensar preferir
3 ¿Qué hora es? (pp. 48–49) Asking the time Saying the time Talking about your school timetable	7T4 Using resources (L) 7T6 Texts as prompts (L) 7C3 Contact with native speakers (L)	1c how to express themselves 2a listen for gist/detail 2c ask/answer questions 3c use knowledge of English 4c compare cultures 4d consider experiences in other countries	Clock times Days of the week (Monday–Friday) ¿Qué hora es? Son las tres y cinco. ¿A qué hora empieza(n)/termina(n) …? Las clases empiezan a las ocho y media. No hay recreo. Tenemos media hora de recreo. Termina a las once. El viernes tenemos ciencias a las nueve.
4 La hora de comer (pp. 50–51) Talking about meal times Saying what you have to eat and drink	7S7 Time and tenses (Part-L) 7W5 Verbs present (R) 7S3 Adapting sentences (R) 7T6 Texts as prompts (R)	2a listen for gist/detail 2f adapt language for different contexts 5i working in a variety of contexts	Food and drink Expressions of frequency ¿Qué comes/bebes/tomas? Siempre como un bocadillo. Generalmente bebo una naranjada. Nunca tomo fruta. el desayuno la comida meriendo ceno
5 Mi instituto (pp. 52–53) Describing your school	7W6 Letters and sounds (R) 7S5 Basic negatives (R) 7T5 Assembling texts (R)	2f adapt language for different contexts 2h scan texts 4c compare cultures 4d consider experiences in other countries	Rooms and facilities in a school Estudio en un instituto mixto. ¿Qué tiene tu instituto? Mi instituto tiene dieciséis aulas. Tiene tres laboratorios de idiomas. Tiene un comedor. (No) Hay uniforme.
6 ¡Ya llegamos! (pp. 54–55) Saying how you get to school	7L5 Spontaneous talk (L) 7W6 Letters and sounds (R) 7L1 Sound patterns (R)	1a sounds and writing 2c ask/answer questions 2f adapt language for different contexts	Means of transport ¿A qué hora llegas al instituto? Llego a las ocho y media. ¿Cómo llegas? Llego en autobús/a pie. Llego pronto/tarde.

¡Vamos al instituto! módulo 3

Unit/topics	Key Framework Objectives	PoS	Key language and Grammar
Resumen y Prepárate (pp. 56–57) Pupils' checklist and practice test	7S4 Basic questions (R) 7S9 Simple sentences (R) 7L3 Gist and detail (R)	**3a** memorising **3d** use reference materials **3e** develop their independence	
¡Extra! 7 Un instituto en España (pp. 58–59) Optional unit: Being at school in Spain	7C2 Everyday culture (L) 7S6 Compound sentences (R) 7S7 Time and tenses (R) 7T1 Reading using cues (R)	**2f** adapt language for different contexts **2g** deal with the unpredictable **2h** scan texts	
Te toca a ti (pp. 120–121) Self-access reading and writing at two levels		**2f** adapt language for different contexts	

módulo 3

1 Me encanta la informática

(Pupil's Book pages 44–45)

Main topics
- Talking about school subjects
- Expressing likes and dislikes

Key Framework Objectives
- Compound sentences 7S6 (Launch)
- Everyday words 7W1 (Reinforcement)
- Gender/plural 7W4 (Reinforcement)
- Gist and detail 7L3 (Reinforcement)

Key language
las asignaturas
¿Te gusta la geografía?
¿Te gustan las ciencias?
Me gusta la historia.
Me gusta mucho la música.
Me gustan las matemáticas.
Me encantan el español y el francés.
Me gusta bastante el inglés.
No me gusta la tecnología.
No me gusta nada la educación física.
Odio la informática.
Detesto la religión.
pero
también
y

Resources
Cassette B, side 1
CD 2, track 2
Cuaderno A and B, page 25
Starter 1, Resource and Assessment File, page 54
Hojas de trabajo 1 and 2, Resource and Assessment File, pages 45 and 46
OHTs 13 and 14: school subjects, likes and dislikes

Starter 1: **Sound spelling links** [W1,6; L1]

Aims: To revise phonetic alphabet pronunciation by introducing the different pronunciation of *fía, gía, geo, ción* and *gión* and to introduce some school subjects. (Timing: 5 minutes)

Resources: Resource and Assessment File, page 54 (Starter 1)

Activity: Make an OHT using the master provided. Using the OHT, say the sounds in the right-hand column and show pupils how they are written in Spanish (left-hand column). Pupils repeat them. Cover the right-hand column. Pupils look at the spelling in the left-hand column and say the sound. Then cover the left-hand column and ask pupils to write the letter strings from the sounds. Read out the following: *la geografía, la religión, la educación física, la geografía, la biología.* Pupils fill in the missing letter strings on the OHT. Then ask pupils to look at page 44 of the Pupil's Book and try to pronounce the school subjects before listening to exercise 1a.

1a Escucha y empareja cada asignatura con el dibujo apropiado. (AT1/1) [W3,4]

✉ *Listening for information and instructions – Level C*

Listening. Pupils listen to the recording and match each school subject to the correct picture.

Suggestion
Before attempting this activity, teachers could introduce the school subjects using a timetable, starting with the subjects that sound similar to English. Alternatively, teachers may prefer to use the symbols from page 44 and do a matching game using an OHT in order to prepare pupils for activity 1a.

Answers
As tapescript

Tapescript
a – las matemáticas
b – la geografía
c – la historia
d – las ciencias
e – el inglés
f – la educación física
g – la música
h – la informática
i – la tecnología
j – el español
k – la religión
l – el francés

1b Escucha otra vez y comprueba tus respuestas. (AT1/1) [W3,4]

✉ *Knowing about language*

Listening. Pupils listen to the recording again to check their answers to activity 1a.

2 Con tu compañero/a, practica las asignaturas. (AT2/1) [W3,4; L1]

✉ *Speaking to convey information – Level C*

Speaking. In pairs, pupils practise saying the subjects.

3 ¿Les gustan o no les gustan las asignaturas? Escucha y dibuja ☺ o ☹. (1–8) (AT1/2) [W3,4,5; L3]

✉ *Listening for information and instructions – Level C/D*

¡Vamos al instituto! módulo 3

Listening. Pupils listen to the recording and note whether the people like the subjects or not. Teachers should make sure that pupils have been introduced to the expressions *me gusta* and *no me gusta* before attempting this activity.

➕ Teachers may wish to extend their pupils by asking them to write down the name of the subject mentioned as well as whether or not the people like the subjects.

Answers

1 ☺ 2 ☹ 3 ☺ 4 ☹ 5 ☺ 6 ☹
7 ☺ 8 ☺

Tapescript

1 – Me gusta la historia.
2 – No me gusta la geografía.
3 – Me gusta la informática.
4 – No me gustan las matemáticas.
5 – Me gustan las ciencias.
6 – No me gusta el francés.
7 – Me gusta la educación física.
8 – Me gusta la música.

Starter 2: Opposites [W1,2; S3,5,9; T2,7] (any time after introducing *(no) me gusta*)

Aims: To revise school subjects and the verb *gustar*; to introduce more opinions (*me encanta(n), detesto, odio*) and to reinforce knowledge of forming negative sentences. (Timing: 5–10 minutes)

Pairwork activity: Using the text on Raúl on page 45 of the Pupil's Book, pupils read out each opinion that he gives about his school subjects. Pupils then write down the opposite opinions to Raúl, e.g. *Me gusta la geografía* becomes *No me gusta la geografía*. Pupils then read out their sentences and the class indicates if the word order in the sentences is correct.

➕ For higher-ability groups, or students who complete this quickly, do the same with the other texts on page 45 (*Alba, Pedro and Elisabet*).

4 Con tu compañero/a, pregunta y contesta. (AT2/2) [W3,4,5; S4,5]

✎ *Speaking and interacting with others – Level D*

Speaking. In pairs, pupils take it in turns to ask whether or not their partner likes the subjects on page 44.

Note Before attempting this activity, teachers should read through the **Gramática** with the class and make sure that all pupils are clear about *(no) me gusta/gustan* as well as the need to retain the definite article *el, la, los, las* before the school subject.

5a Escucha y lee. Escribe los nombres en el orden correcto. (1–4) (AT1/3, AT3/3) [S6; T1; L3]

✎ *Listening for information and instructions – Level D*

Listening/Reading. Pupils listen to the recording and match up the correct text with the person who is speaking. Teachers may wish to introduce the new expressions of opinion before attempting this activity, or pupils could be encouraged to work out the meanings from the context.

Answers

| 1 Pedro | 2 Elisabet | 3 Alba | 4 Raúl |

Tapescript

– Me gusta mucho la educación física y me encanta el francés. No me gusta la tecnología y odio las matemáticas.
– No me gustan nada las ciencias y detesto las matemáticas. Me gusta bastante el inglés y también me encantan la música y la religión.
– Me gusta mucho la informática. Es mi asignatura favorita. Me gustan también las ciencias y las matemáticas. No me gusta la historia.
– Me gusta la geografía y me gusta el español. Me gusta bastante la religión. Me gusta el francés. No me gusta la música.

5b Copia y rellena el cuadro. (AT3/3) [W2; S6; T1]

✎ *Reading for information and instructions – Level D*

Reading. Pupils copy the grid and fill in the appropriate ticks and crosses below the subjects that are mentioned by the four young people in activity 5a.

Answers

	📖	♻	✏	🌍	👕	🎵	📐	💻	🗣
Alba	✓	✓		✗					✓✓
Pedro	✗✗✗				✓✓✓		✗		✓✓
Raúl				✓	✓	✓	✗	✓/✗	
Elisabet	✗✗✗	✗✗	✓/✗			✓✓✓	✓✓✓		

6 Escribe sobre las asignaturas que te gustan y no te gustan. (AT4/2–3) [W5; S5,6; T6]

✎ *Writing to establish and maintain personal contact – Level D/E*

Writing. Pupils write sentences, or a short paragraph similar to those written by the young people in activity 5a, about the school subjects they like and dislike.

Literacy activity

Teachers may wish to give their students some guidance in the structure of paragraphs and use of the connectives *pero, también* and *y*. It may be worthwhile consulting the school's literacy policy or literacy co-ordinator on the use of connectives, as these are an important tool for pupils to vary and add sophistication to their writing. Teachers may wish to start by brainstorming phrases as a shared writing activity, and asking pupils to choose connectives to link or contrast phrases. Another useful strategy is to insist that pupils find a way of including all three connectives at least once in their paragraph, and then feed back to the rest of the class.

Plenary

Ask pupils, in groups, to prepare three questions on what they have learned to test other groups. Try to encourage a variety of questions that look at pronunciation, punctuation or spelling, as well as meaning. Pupils then take turns to ask different groups a question each. Reward interesting and inventive questions with points.

Cuaderno A, page 25

1a Busca diez asignaturas. (AT3/1)

Knowing about language

Reading. Pupils find the names of ten school subjects in the wordsearch.

Answers

z	i	b	e	d	o	i	n	f	o	r	m	á	t	i	c	a	m
m	a	t	e	m	á	t	i	c	a	s	q	n	a	z	a	s	ú
s	i	n	e	c	a	i	c	r	e	l	i	g	i	ó	n	u	s
s	é	l	g	n	i	f	r	a	n	c	é	s	p	r	b	o	i
j	s	h	a	ñ	t	n	t	e	c	n	o	l	o	g	í	a	c
b	n	a	c	i	s	í	f	n	ó	i	c	a	c	u	d	e	a
h	i	s	t	o	r	i	a	a	í	f	a	r	g	o	e	g	h

1b Escribe *el, los, la* o *las.* (AT4/1) [W1,2]

Knowing about language

Writing. Pupils write out the subjects from the wordsearch grid, adding *el, los, la* or *las.*

Answers

1 las matemáticas **2** la informática **3** la religión
4 el inglés **5** el francés **6** la tecnología
7 la educación física **8** la historia **9** la geografía
10 la música

2a Rellena el cuadro con los símbolos apropiados para Marcos. (AT3/3) [W1,5; S2,5]

Reading for information and instructions – Level C/D

Reading. Pupils read the paragraph about Marcos' likes and dislikes, and fill in the grid with the appropriate symbols.

Answers

Science: 🙂 Maths: 😃 PE: ☹ English: 😧

2b Escribe una carta similar para Silvia. (AT4/2–3) [W2,5; S5; T6]

Writing to exchange information and ideas – Level C

Writing. Pupils copy and complete the letter about Silvia's likes and dislikes. Teachers should remind pupils to use the connectives from Pupil's Book page 45.

Answers

¿Qué tal? Me llamo Silvia. Me encantan el inglés y las ciencias. Odio las matemáticas. Me gusta la educación física. No me gustan la tecnología ni el español.

Cuaderno B, page 25

1a Busca diez asignaturas. (AT3/1) [W1,7]

Knowing about language

Reading. Pupils find the names of ten school subjects in the wordsearch.

Answers

z	i	b	e	d	o	i	n	f	o	r	m	á	t	i	c	a	m
m	a	t	e	m	á	t	i	c	a	s	q	n	a	z	a	s	ú
s	i	n	e	c	a	i	c	r	e	l	i	g	i	ó	n	u	s
s	é	l	g	n	i	f	r	a	n	c	é	s	p	r	b	o	i
j	s	h	a	ñ	t	n	t	e	c	n	o	l	o	g	í	a	c
b	n	a	c	i	s	í	f	n	ó	i	c	a	c	u	d	e	a
h	i	s	t	o	r	i	a	a	í	f	a	r	g	o	e	g	h

1b Escribe *el, los, la* o *las.* (AT4/1) [W1,2,4]

Knowing about language

Writing. Pupils write out the subjects from the wordsearch grid, adding *el, los, la* or *las.*

Answers

1 las matemáticas **2** la informática **3** la religión
4 el inglés **5** el francés **6** la tecnología
7 la educación física **8** la historia **9** la geografía
10 la música

2a Rellena el cuadro con los símbolos apropiados para Marcos. (AT3/3) [W1,5; S2,5]

Reading for information and instructions – Level D

¡Vamos al instituto!

módulo 3

Reading. Pupils read the paragraph about Marcos' likes and dislikes, and fill in the grid with the appropriate symbols.

Answers

Science: ☺	Maths: 😐	IT: ☺	PE: ☹
English: ☹	Spanish: 😀		

2b Escribe una carta similar para Silvia.
(AT4/2–3) [W2,5; S5; T6]

✉ *Writing to exchange information and ideas – Level D/E*

Writing. Pupils copy and complete the letter about Silvia's likes and dislikes using the symbols in the grid in activity 2a. Teachers should remind pupils to use the connectives from page 45 in the Pupil's Book.

Answers

¿Qué tal? Me llamo Silvia. Me encantan las ciencias y odio las matemáticas. No me gusta la informática. Me gusta la educación física. Me encanta el inglés pero no me gusta el español.

Hojas de trabajo 1–2, pages 45–46 [W3]

12 picture cards and 12 cards with corresponding labels, which can be used for matching activities.

módulo 3

2 La historia es interesante

(Pupil's Book pages 46–47)

Main topics
- Giving opinions about school and school subjects

Key Framework Objectives
- Improving written work 7T7 (Launch)
- Gender/plural 7W4 (Reinforcement)
- Verbs present 7W5 (Reinforcement)
- Reading aloud 7T2 (Reinforcement)

Grammar
- Adjective agreement, singular and plural
- Plural forms with *las ciencias*, etc.
- Present tense of radical changing verbs *pensar* and *preferir*

Key language

¿Te gusta el instituto?
¿Te gustan las matemáticas?
Las matemáticas son aburridas.
Los profesores son simpáticos.
Pienso que el francés es difícil.
Prefiero las ciencias.
Es/Son …

aburrido/a	aburridos/as
bueno/a	buenos/as
difícil	difíciles
divertido/a	divertidos/as
fácil	fáciles
inteligente	inteligentes
interesante	interesantes
relajante	relajantes
simpático/a	simpáticos/as
útil	útiles

Resources

Cassette B, side 1
CD 2, track 3
Cuaderno A and B, page 26
Grammar, Resource and Assessment File, page 52

Starter 1: **Cognates** [W1,2,8; S9; T1]

Aims: To show pupils that there are many words in Spanish that are very similar to English and build confidence in their learning. (Timing: 5 minutes)

Activity: Write out the following opinions on a transparency: *es … aburrido, divertido, fácil, interesante, bueno, relajante, inteligente, útil; son … difíciles, simpáticos*. Ask pupils to identify what type of language this is or the topic it is from. The discussion should lead pupils to the conclusion that this language can be used for many topics and concerns opinions. In groups, pupils then work out what the equivalents are for these opinions in English. Point out that many are cognates, but the last one, *simpáticos*, is a 'false friend', as it does not mean 'sympathetic', but 'nice', or 'pleasant'. Groups feed back and justify their answers.

Suggestion

Pupils have already encountered adjectives and adjectival endings twice in Module 2, first describing nationalities and then the colour of their pets. In order to reinforce this grammar point as well as encourage pupils to make the connection and start to transfer their language knowledge, it would be a good idea to revise pets and descriptions at this point, before introducing some cognates for giving opinions about school subjects: *interesante* and *difícil* are both easily recognisable. Teachers could then introduce the meaning of the six new adjectives before attempting activity 1a, or, if preferred, this vocabulary could be introduced within the context of the activity.

1a Escucha y mira los dibujos. (1–8) (AT1/2) [W3,4,5]

✄ *Knowing about language*

Listening. Pupils listen to the recording and look at the pictures to work out the meaning of the adjectives, giving opinions about school and school subjects.

Tapescript

1 – El inglés es fácil.
2 – El español es interesante.
3 – El instituto es bueno.
4 – La música es relajante.
5 – La educación física es divertida.
6 – La informática es aburrida.
7 – Los profesores son simpáticos.
8 – Las matemáticas son difíciles.

1b Empareja las asignaturas con las opiniones y escribe una frase para cada dibujo. (AT3/2, AT4/2) [W3,4,5]

✄ *Reading for information and instructions – Level D*

Reading/Writing. Pupils use the pictures from activity 1a to help them match the sentence halves to give the appropriate opinion for each subject. They should then listen to the recording of activity 1a again to check their answers.

Answers

As tapescript to activity **1a**.

¡Vamos al instituto! módulo 3

2 Escribe frases con tus opiniones sobre las asignaturas. (AT4/2) [W3,4,5; S3]

✉ *Writing to establish and maintain personal contact – Level D/E*

Writing. Pupils use the sentences they have written for activity 1b to help them write their own opinions about their school subjects. Teachers should encourage pupils to use the *¡OJO!* and *Gramática* boxes to help them with their sentences.

✚ More-able pupils can be extended by the introduction of the connective *porque* to enable them to write a paragraph about their likes and dislikes (using the structures from pages 44–45), giving reasons.

Starter 2: **Spot the mistake** [W4; S9; T7]

Aims: To develop reading skills by requiring pupils to focus very closely on the text, and to develop pupils' skills in using correct adjectival agreement. (Timing: 5–10 minutes)

Pairwork activity: Write the following sentences (containing errors) on the board or a transparency: 1 *Los profesores no son bueno*; 2 *Me gusta las ciencias porque son fáciles*; 3 *Odio el religión – es aburrida*; 4 *La música son relajante e interesante*. Ask pupils to identify and note down the mistake in each sentence. Pupils feed back to class, justifying their answers, and together write the correct version. (Correct sentences: 1 *Los profesores no son buenos*; 2 *Me gustan las ciencias porque son fáciles*; 3 *Odio la religión – es aburrida*; 4 *La música es relajante e interesante*.)

✚ For higher-ability pupils who finish early, ask them to write the opposite of each sentence (see also 'Optional Thinking Skills lesson' on page 85.)

3a Escucha y lee. (AT1/3, AT3/3) [W4,5; S4; T2; L3]

✉ *Knowing about language*

Listening/Reading. Pupils listen to the dialogue between Neus and Eduard, and follow the script in their books. Teachers may wish to ask pupils to read the dialogue in pairs after hearing the recording. Alternatively, the class could be split into two, and one half assigned the part of Neus, the other half Eduard's part, and they could chorus the dialogue after they hear each phrase on the recording. This is a fun and inclusive way to practise pronunciation.

Tapescript

– ¡Hola, Neus! ¿Qué tal?
– Bien, ¿y tú?
– Muy bien, fenomenal. ¿Te gusta el instituto?
– Sí, sí, me gusta. Los profesores son buenos y los alumnos … son simpáticos. ¿Qué asignaturas prefieres?
– Me gustan las ciencias pero prefiero las matemáticas. La informática es interesante … pero pienso que el francés es difícil.
– ¿Te gusta el inglés?
– ¡Qué va! ¡Odio el inglés! ¿Y tú?
– Me gusta el inglés. Mi madre es inglesa y hablamos inglés en casa. ¡A ver si hablamos inglés un día!
– Vale. ¡Ahora me gusta el inglés!

3b ¿Verdad (✓) o mentira (✗)? (AT3/3) [W5; T1,4]

✉ *Reading for information and instructions – Level D*

Reading. Pupils read the text of the dialogue between Neus and Eduard and decide whether the phrases are true (*verdad*) or false (*mentira*). Before attempting this activity pupils should read the *Gramática* box in order to understand the meaning of *piensa* and *prefiere*. Pupils could also be asked to correct the phrases that are false.

Answers

| a ✓ | b ✓ | c ✗ | d ✓ | e ✗ | f ✓ |

---

4 Con tu compañero/a, haz frases con tus opiniones. (AT2/2) [W4,5; L1]

✉ *Speaking about experiences, feelings and opinions – Level D/E*

Speaking. In pairs, pupils practise giving opinions using the structure *pienso que*.

5a Con tu compañero/a, mira el diálogo de Neus y Eduard y escribe otro similar. (AT4/3) [W4,5; S4; T6]

✉ *Writing to exchange information and ideas – Level D/E*

Writing. In pairs, pupils reread the conversation between Neus and Eduard and then make up their own dialogue about school subjects. Pupils need to be encouraged to use the dialogue on page 47 as a model, to ensure that they use the key language for this unit. Teachers may wish to give pupils a checklist of structures to incorporate, for example at least one *prefiero, pienso que …*

5b Lee el diálogo a la clase. (AT2/3) [T2]

✉ *Speaking and interacting with others – Level D*

Speaking. Pupils read out their dialogues to the rest of the class. If possible, pupils could be videoed or tape recorded. They should be encouraged to make their pronunciation as natural and authentic as possible. Time should be made to play back the recording, as this is both motivating and instructional.

módulo 3 — ¡Vamos al instituto!

Plenary

Working in groups of four, ask pupils to recap orally on the language covered on pages 46–47 of the Pupil's Book. In each group, pupil 1 talks for as long as they can, with a limit of 15 seconds, about their opinions of school subjects. The other pupils listen for mistakes in pronunciation. Pupil 2 does the same, but this time the others listen for grammatical errors. This is repeated until all the students have spoken twice on their school subjects and the rest of the group has corrected both their pronunciation and their grammar. This can lead to a homework where pupils prepare for a 45-second oral presentation on school subjects.

R For low-ability classes, pupils can give one opinion at a time and give each other marks for pronunciation and accuracy.

Cuaderno A, page 26

1 Empareja las frases con los dibujos. (AT3/2) [W1,5]

Reading for information and instructions – Level C

Reading. Pupils match up the phrases with the pictures.

Answers

1 a Es difícil.	2 c Es aburrido.	3 d Es divertida.
4 e Son fáciles.	5 b Es interesante.	6 g Es bueno.
7 f Es relajante.	8 h Es simpático.	

2 Elige la palabra apropiada. (AT3/2) [W4]

Knowing about language

Reading. Pupils choose the correct word to complete the sentences.

Answers

1 interesantes	2 fácil	3 aburridas	4 divertido
5 divertido	6 relajante	7 buenos	

Cuaderno B, page 26

1 Empareja las frases con los dibujos. (AT3/2) [W1,5]

Reading for information and instructions – Level C

Reading. Pupils match up the phrases with the pictures.

Answers

1 a Es difícil.	2 c Es aburrido.	3 d Es divertida.
4 e Son fáciles.	5 b Es interesante.	6 g Es bueno.
7 f Es relajante.	8 h Es simpático.	

2a Escribe *es* o *son*. (AT3/2, AT4/1) [W5]

Knowing about language

Reading/Writing. Pupils complete the sentences by inserting *es* or *son*.

Answers

1 son	2 es	3 son	4 es	5 es	6 es	7 son

2b Elige la palabra apropiada. (AT3/2) [W4]

Knowing about language

Reading. Pupils choose the correct word to complete the sentences.

Answers

1 interesantes	2 fácil	3 aburridas	4 divertido
5 divertido	6 relajante		

2c Completa las frases con tu opinión. (AT4/2) [W4,5; S3]

Writing to establish and maintain personal contact – Level D

Writing. Pupils complete the sentences using *es* or *son* and an opinion.

Grammar, Resource and Assessment File, page 52

Activities to practise the verbs *gustar*, *pensar* and *preferir*.

1 [W3,5]

Answers

- b No me gusta la historia.
- c No me gusta el inglés.
- d No me gustan las matemáticas.
- e Me gustan la música y el francés.
- f Me gustan las ciencias.
- g No me gusta la educación física.
- h Me gustan el español y la geografía.

2 [W5]

Answers

a Prefiero	e Piensas
b Prefiere	f Piensa
c Piensas	g Pienso
d Prefiero	

¡Vamos al instituto!

módulo 3

Optional Thinking Skills lesson

Aims
To develop thinking skills, consolidate language of opinions and develop basic sentence construction, comparing Spanish and English sentence structure. (Timing: 40 minutes)

Resources
Resource and Assessment File, page 54 (Thinking Skills)

Categories [W2,3,5; S1,2,3,5]

Activity: Ask each group of three or four pupils to cut out the game cards on the sheet provided and place them on the table, face up. Explain to pupils that they can lay out their cards and group them into categories of their own choosing. Then play the game as follows: The groups share with the others how they have categorised their cards and why. Discuss and ask pupils to categorise the cards in terms of verbs, nouns, connectives and time indicators. Go through each category and check that pupils have identified the correct words. Ask pupils to use a card from each category to construct a sentence. Discuss with the group the usual word order and write up a model on the board, e.g. *verbo + sustantivo + conectador + verbo + sustantivo; indicativo del tiempo + verbo + sustantivo*. Pupils then have to make a sentence which follows the model from the board, e.g. *Odio el inglés y detesto la geografía; A veces me encanta el español*. Pupils then have time in groups to make the longest sentence possible, the shortest sentence, the one with the most verbs and the one with the most nouns. After the exercise, discuss the difficulties with it and the importance of categorising words in order to express yourself in a foreign language.

módulo 3

3 ¿Qué hora es?

(Pupil's Book pages 48–49)

Main topics
- Asking the time
- Saying the time
- Talking about your school timetable

Key Framework Objectives
- Using resources 7T4 (Launch)
- Texts as prompts 7T6 (Launch)
- Contact with native speakers 7C3 (Launch)

Key language

¿Qué hora es? Es la una.
Son las dos y cinco. Son las tres y cuarto.
Son las cuatro y media.
Son las cinco menos veinte.
Son las seis menos cuarto.
¿A qué hora empieza(n)/termina(n) …
Las clases empiezan a las ocho y media y terminan a las dos.
No hay recreo.
Tenemos media hora de recreo.
Empieza a las diez y media y termina a las once.
No tenemos clases por la tarde.
Después tenemos inglés.
El viernes tenemos ciencias a las nueve.
lunes   martes   viernes
miércoles   jueves

Resources

Cassette B, side 1
CD 2, track 4
Cuaderno A and B, page 27
Starters 1 and 2, Resource and Assessment File, page 55
Hojas de trabajo 3, 4 and 5, Resource and Assessment File, pages 47, 48 and 49

Suggestion

Teachers should not underestimate how long it will take to teach pupils the time. It is worth investing some effort in making sure they can all say the hours first; once they are confident with the hours, introduce and practise *y, menos, cuarto* and *media*. Pupils may have difficulty in remembering that the minutes always come after the hours: teachers should establish and continue to reinforce this point clearly at this early stage.

Starter 1: Noughts and Crosses [W1,2; L1,4,6]

Aims: To revise numbers 1–30. (Timing: 5 minutes)

Resources: Resource and Assessment File, page 55 (Starter 1).

Activity: Make an OHT using the master provided. Use the first and second grids as a whole-class game, with the class divided into two teams. The last grid is left blank for you to fill with numbers that the class find difficult to remember or pronounce. Give pupils a copy of the OHT and they can play the games with a partner. Pupils can make up more games using numbers 1–30 if there is time.

1 Escucha y lee. (AT1/2) [W1,5; T2; L1]

✄ *Knowing about language*

Listening/Reading. Pupils listen to the recording and follow the dialogues on page 48. Pupils could act out the dialogues in pairs, or the group could be split into two to repeat the dialogue.

Tapescript

1 – ¿Qué hora es?
– Son las nueve.
2 – ¿Qué hora es?
– Son las doce y cuarto.
3 – ¿Qué hora es?
– Son las siete y veinte.
4 – ¿Son las doce?
– No, es la una.
5 – ¿Qué hora es?
– Son las cinco menos cuarto. ¡Oh no!

2 Con tu compañero/a, elige un dibujo en **1** y pregunta a qué hora es. (AT2/2) [W1,5; T2; L1,4]

✄ *Speaking and interacting with others – Level C*

Speaking. In pairs, pupils ask and say the time using the pictures in activity 1.

3a Empareja las horas con los relojes apropiados. (AT3/2) [W1,5; S9]

✄ *Reading for information and instructions – Level D*

Reading. Pupils match up the times with the correct clocks. Before attempting this activity, teachers should make sure that pupils understand how to read the time using a digital clock, and that they know that XX.30 is half past and XX.15 is quarter past.

Answers

| 1 c | 2 a | 3 b | 4 f | 5 j | 6 d | 7 i |
| 8 g | 9 e | 10 h | | | | |

3b Escucha y comprueba tus respuestas. (AT1/2) [W1; L1]

✄ *Listening for information and instructions – Level D*

¡Vamos al instituto! — módulo 3

Listening. Pupils listen to the recording to check their answers to activity 3a. Pupils could read out how they think the times should be said before hearing them on the recording, in order to compare pronunciation.

Tapescript

1 – Es la una.
2 – Son las diez.
3 – Son las nueve y cuarto.
4 – Son las doce y media.
5 – Son las cuatro menos cuarto.
6 – Son las dos y diez.
7 – Son las once y veinte.
8 – Son las nueve menos cinco.
9 – Es la una y veinte.
10 – Son las ocho menos veinticinco.

Starter 2: Time sequencing [W1; S2,9] (any time after introducing quarter- and half-past)

Aims: To reinforce knowledge of times (*es la … / son las …* (numbers 1–12), *y media, y cuarto*) and to develop memory skills and thinking skills. (Timing: 10 minutes)

Resources: Resource and Assessment File, page 55 (Starter 2)

Activity: Make an OHT using the master provided. Ask pupils to work in pairs or groups of three. Reveal the first set of four options on the OHT. Ask pupils to play the 'fastest finger first' game and to write down the letters in ascending numerical order. One member of each pair/group brings their answer to the front when finished and pupils stand in finishing order. When all groups are represented at the front, they reveal their answers and the correct solution is ascertained. Repeat with the other options.

➕ Higher-ability students could do two or more options at a time.
🅁 Lower-ability classes can work on one option at a time.

4 Con tu compañero/a, escribe o dibuja la hora. Pregunta y contesta. (AT2/2) [W1,5; L1,4]

✖ *Speaking and interacting with others – Level D*

Speaking. Pupils draw a clock face with the time, or simply write down the time, and practise asking and answering the question *¿Qué hora es?*

5 Escucha los diálogos y mira el horario. ¿De qué días hablan Neus y Eduard? (1–3) (AT1/3, AT3/3) [W1,3; L3]

✖ *Listening for information and instructions – Level D*

Listening/Reading. Pupils listen to the conversations 1–3 and look at the timetable to work out which days Neus and Eduard are talking about. Before attempting this activity, teachers should make sure that their pupils understand the layout of the timetable, revising the days of the week, as well as introducing the new words *recreo, empieza, termina* and *tenemos*.

Answers

| 1 viernes | 2 martes | 3 miércoles |

Tapescript

1 – ¿Qué asignaturas tenemos hoy?
 – Tenemos matemáticas a las ocho y media.
 – Y después, ¿qué tenemos?
 – Después, tenemos ciencias … A las diez y media empieza el recreo.
 – ¡Y a las once termina!
 – ¡Claro! Luego tenemos música.
2 – ¿Tenemos inglés hoy?
 – Sí, y también tenemos español.
 – ¿A qué hora tenemos matemáticas?
 – A la una.
3 – Hoy tenemos matemáticas y después hay inglés. Tenemos diseño y tecnología a las doce …
 – Y a la una tenemos educación física, ¡qué bien!

6 Con tu compañero/a, habla del horario. Tu compañero/a tiene que adivinar el día. (AT2/2–3) [W3,5; S4; L1,4]

✖ *Speaking and interacting with others – Level D*

Speaking. In pairs, pupils take turns to talk about the timetable using the structure *tenemos … a las …* Their partner has to guess the day.

7a Lee el correo electrónico. ¿Verdad (✓) o mentira (✗)? (AT3/3–4) [W3,8; S9; T4]

✖ *Reading for information and instructions – Level D/E*

Reading. Pupils read the e-mail message and decide if the statements are true (*verdad*) or false (*mentira*). There is some unfamiliar language in the message which would make this a level 4 activity if pupils work out the meaning using a glossary or dictionary.

Answers

| a ✗ | b ✓ | c ✗ | d ✗ | e ✓ |

7b Escribe una respuesta al correo electrónico. Cambia las palabras subrayadas y describe tu horario. (AT4/3–4) [W3; S3; T6]

✖ *Writing to establish and maintain personal contact – Level D/E*

Writing. Pupils write a reply to the e-mail, changing the underlined words. They may wish to change more details and add opinions, which would enable them to meet the criteria for level 4.

módulo 3 ¡Vamos al instituto!

ICT activities [C3]

Pupils could send their e-mail message to their partner in a Spanish-speaking country. For help in setting up an e-mail link, go to www.heinemann.co.uk/hotlinks, or read the useful book produced by CILT on using e-mail.

Pupils could also produce their own computer-generated timetable, using the *insert, table* function on word-processing software such as *Microsoft Word*.

Plenary

If pupils have the same timetable then you can play a 'true or false?' game. Read out sentences about their timetable and pupils must identify if they are true or false, using a thumbs up or thumbs down, e.g. *Tenemos historia a las nueve.*

Alternatively, if pupils have different timetables, use a soft ball or object for a throwing game. Ask pupils to translate sentences from and into Spanish when the object is thrown to them, e.g. *¿Cómo se dice: 'Las clases empiezan a las nueve' en inglés?; ¿Cómo se dice 'I have English at ten' en español?*, etc.

Cuaderno A, page 27

1 Empareja la hora con el reloj apropiado. (AT3/2) [W1; S9]

✉ *Reading for information and instructions – Level C*

Reading. Pupils match up the times with the correct clocks.

Answers

| 1 b | 2 c | 3 a | 4 f | 5 d | 6 e |

2a Mira el horario y contesta a las preguntas. (AT3/2, AT4/2) [W1,2,3,5; S4,9]

✉ *Reading for information and instructions – Level C*

Reading/Writing. Pupils use the timetable to answer the questions.

Answers

| 1 a las dos | 2 a las nueve y cinco | 3 a las dos |
| 4 a las nueve y cinco | 5 a las doce menos diez |
| 6 a las once menos veinte |

2b Completa las frases con la(s) palabra(s) que falta(n). (AT3/2, AT4/1) [W1,2,3,5; S9]

✉ *Knowing about language*

Reading/Writing. Pupils insert the missing word or words to complete the sentences about the timetable in activity 2a.

Answers

| 1 martes | 2 las nueve y cinco | 3 ciencias | 4 viernes |
| 5 historia | 6 tenemos, las dos |

Cuaderno B, page 27

1 Dibuja la hora apropiada en cada reloj. (AT3/2) [W1; S9]

✉ *Reading for information and instructions – Level D*

Reading. Pupils draw the correct times on the clock faces.

Answers

| 1 6.30 | 2 11.45 | 3 3.15 | 4 1.10 | 5 4.40 | 6 12.55 |

2a Lee las frases y rellena el horario. (AT3/2) [W1,3,5; S2]

✉ *Reading for information and instructions – Level D*

Reading. Pupils read the sentences and use the information to complete the gaps in the timetable.

Answers

	lunes	martes	miércoles	jueves	viernes
9.05 – 10.20	español	inglés	matemáticas	ciencias	educación física
10.20 – 10.40	R E C R E O				
10.40 – 11.50	geografía	francés	música	tecnología	informática
11.50 – 1.00	informática	ciencias	ciencias	religión	matemáticas
1.00 – 2.00	H O R A D E C O M E R				
2.00 – 3.10	matemáticas	español	inglés	francés	religión

2b Completa las frases con la(s) palabra(s) que falta(n). (AT3/2, AT4/1) [W1,2,3,5; S9]

✉ *Knowing about language*

Reading/Writing. Pupils insert the missing word or words to complete the sentences about the timetable in activity 2a.

Answers

| 1 martes | 2 las nueve y cinco | 3 ciencias | 4 viernes |
| 5 tecnología | 6 tenemos, las dos |

Hojas de trabajo 3–4, pages 47–48 [W1,3]

12 picture cards and 12 corresponding label cards which can be used for matching games.

Hoja de trabajo 5, page 49

Pupils interview their partners to find out the times and days of the subjects missing from their sheets. Pupils can either ask *¿A qué hora tienes …?* to guess the subjects that are missing and find out the days and time, or alternatively they could fill in the blanks by asking *¿Qué asignatura tienes el (lunes) a las (10.10)?*

módulo 3

4 La hora de comer

(Pupil's Book pages 50–51)

Main topics

- Talking about meal times
- Saying what you have to eat and drink

Key Framework Objectives

- Time and tenses 7S7 (Part-launch. See also 5.6 and 6.5)
- Verbs present 7W5 (Reinforcement)
- Adapting sentences 7S3 (Reinforcement)
- Texts as prompts 7T6 (Reinforcement)

Grammar

- Expressions of frequency

Key language

¿Qué comes/bebes/tomas?
Normalmente como un bocadillo.
Siempre bebo una naranjada.
Nunca tomo fruta.
Desayuno tostadas y café con leche.
Como a las dos.
Generalmente meriendo a las seis.
A veces ceno espaguetis.

el desayuno	*la comida*
la merienda	*la cena*
un bocadillo	*un agua mineral*
una ensalada	*un café con leche*
unos espaguetis	*una Coca Cola*
fruta	*una limonada*
una hamburguesa	*una naranjada*
unas patatas fritas	*un zumo de naranja*
una pizza	*una tostada*

Resources

Cassette B, side 1
CD 2, track 5
Cuaderno A and B, page 28
Hoja de trabajo 6, Resource and Assessment File, page 50

Starter 1: Guess the gender [W1,4,8]

Aims: To introduce food vocabulary and develop knowledge of gender patterns; to develop thinking skills. (Timing: 10 minutes)

Activity: Write the following words on a transparency: *bocadillo, hamburguesa, pizza, ensalada, patatas fritas, espaguetis, fruta, naranjada, limonada, Coca Cola, agua mineral, zumo de naranja*. Pupils must identify if the words are masculine or feminine. For some classes, it may be appropriate to give a couple of examples of gender. Responses can be written on a whiteboard (under headings M or F) or pupils can give a physical response, such as staying seated for masculine and standing up for feminine. Reveal one word at a time and await the response. Discuss with the class which words are feminine or masculine and why. Explain why *agua mineral* takes *un/el*. Ask pupils to write down the rule for determining gender in their own words.

1a Escucha y empareja los jóvenes con las horas de comer. (AT1/2) [W1,2; L3]

✉ *Listening for information and instructions – Level C*

Listening. Pupils listen to the recording and match up the young people with their meal times. Before attempting this activity, pupils should be introduced to the 24-hour clock, which may be a new concept for some of them, and practise saying the times in activity 1a using both the 24- and 12-hour clocks.

Answers

Lourdes b, **Marcos** d, **Bárbara** e, **Aurora** c, **Francisco** a

Tapescript

– ¿Cuándo es la hora de comer en tu instituto, Lourdes?
– Es a las 2.00.

– Marcos, ¿cuándo es la hora de comer?
– Es de 1.00 a 4.00.

– ¿Cuándo es la hora de comer en tu instituto, Bárbara?
– Es a la 1.00.

– Aurora, ¿cuándo es la hora de comer?
– Es a las 12.30.

– ¿Cuándo es la hora de comer en tu instituto, Francisco?
– Es de 12.00 a 3.00

1b Con tu compañero/a, pregunta y contesta. (AT2/2) [W1,2,4,5; L4]

✉ *Speaking and interacting with others – Level D*

Speaking. In pairs, pupils ask and answer when the meal times are for the five young people in activity 1a.

2a Escucha y lee el menú. ¿Qué comen y beben los jóvenes? (1–5) (AT1/3) [W1,5; L3]

✉ *Listening for information – Level D*

Listening. Pupils listen to the recording and read the menu, noting down what the five young people from activity 1a eat and drink. Before attempting this activity, teachers should make sure that their pupils understand the items of food and drink, the verb

módulo 3 — ¡Vamos al instituto!

forms *como*, *bebo* and *tomo*, and the expressions of frequency. This is quite a complex listening activity and could be broken down, listening first for the food and drink items, leaving the expressions of frequency until activity 2b. It may be easiest to use a grid with the headings *nombre*, *come* and *bebe*.

Answers

Lourdes – bocadillo, fruta, agua
Marcos – pizza/espaguetis, agua/zumo
Bárbara – hamburguesa con patatas fritas
Aurora – ensalada
Francisco – nunca come en el comedor

Tapescript

1 – Lourdes, ¿qué comes normalmente en el instituto?
 – Normalmente como un bocadillo y fruta.
 – ¿Y para beber?
 – Bebo agua.
2 – Marcos, ¿qué comes en el instituto?
 – Generalmente como pizza o espaguetis en el comedor del instituto y bebo agua o un zumo.
3 – Bárbara, ¿qué comes generalmente?
 – Normalmente como una hamburguesa con patatas fritas, pero a veces voy a casa a comer.
4 – Aurora, ¿qué comes en el comedor del instituto?
 – Siempre tomo ensalada.
5 – Y tú, Francisco, ¿qué comes en el comedor?
 – Nunca como en el comedor. La comida es muy mala. Siempre voy a casa a comer.

2b Escucha otra vez. ¿Con qué frecuencia comen y beben las cosas? (AT1/3) [W1,2; L3]

✉ *Listening for information and instructions – Level D*

Listening. Pupils listen to this recording again, this time picking the correct expression of frequency for each speaker.

Answers

Lourdes – normalmente, **Marcos** – generalmente, **Bárbara** – normalmente, a veces **Aurora** – siempre, **Francisco** – nunca, siempre

Tapescript

As for activity 2a

2c ¿Qué comen los cinco jóvenes? (AT4/2–3) [W1,2; L1]

✉ *Writing to exchange information and ideas – Level D*

Writing. Pupils write a sentence or short paragraph for each person, giving details of what they eat and drink, as well as the frequency.

Answers

Generalmente Lourdes come un bocadillo y fruta y bebe agua.
Generalmente Marcos come pizza o espaguetis y bebe agua o un zumo.
Normalmente Bárbara come una hamburguesa con patatas fritas.
Aurora siempre come ensalada.
Francisco no come nunca en el comedor.

Starter 2: Squashed sentences [S1,2,9; T2; L6]

Aims: To write simple sentences accurately and to reinforce knowledge of punctuation and spelling. (Timing: 5–10 minutes)

Pairwork activity: Write up sentences using the language grid from page 50 of the Pupil's Book on the board or projector with no punctuation or spacing, e.g. *normalmentecomounapizza* (normalmente/generalmente/siempre/a veces/nunca … como/bebo/tomo … un bocadillo, una pizza). Give pupils two minutes with their partner to say the sentences to each other. Ask different pupils to read aloud the sentences to the class. Pupils write down the sentences with the correct word-spacing and punctuation. Pupils then compare their versions with the language grid on page 50.

3a En España las horas de comer son diferentes. Copia y rellena el cuadro. (AT1/3) [W1,2; S7; C2]

✉ *Listening for information and instructions – Level D*

Listening. Pupils listen to Carlos (who is Spanish) and Charlie (who is British) talking about their meal times. Before attempting this activity, teachers should make sure that all pupils know and understand the names of the meals listed in the box.

Answers

	España	Reino Unido
Desayuno	7.00	–
Comida	2.30	12.30
Merienda	6.00	4.00
Cena	9.30	7.00

Tapescript

– ¿A qué hora desayunas, Carlos?
– Desayuno a las 7.00. ¿Y tú, Charlie?
– No desayuno.
– ¿Nunca?
– Bueno, a veces los sábados o domingos. ¿A qué hora comes?
– Normalmente comemos a las 2.30. ¿Y tú?
– Generalmente como a las 12.30. ¿A qué hora meriendas?

¡Vamos al instituto! módulo 3

– Meriendo a las 6.00. ¿Y tú?
– Meriendo a las 4.00. Y, ¿a qué hora cenas?
– Generalmente cenamos a las 9.30.
– Y nosotros a las 7.00.

3b Con tu compañero/a, pregunta y contesta. (AT2/2–3) [W1; S4; L4]

⚑ *Speaking and interacting with others – Level D*

Speaking. In pairs, pupils ask and answer questions about their own meal times.

4a Lee el texto. ¿Qué come Eduard y a qué hora? (AT3/3) [W1; S7; T1]

⚑ *Reading for information and instructions – Level D*

Reading. Pupils copy the grid and fill in the details for what Eduard eats for each meal and at what time.

Answers

	Desayuno	Comida	Merienda	Cena
Hora	7.00	2.00	6.00	9.00
Qué toma	tostadas y café con leche	bocadillo	fruta/ chocolate	espaguetis y ensalada

4b Escribe un texto similar. Cambia las palabras subrayadas. (AT4/3–4) [W1; S3; T6]

⚑ *Writing to establish and maintain personal contact – Level D/E*

Writing. Pupils write a similar text about their own meals, changing the underlined words in the text for activity 4a.

➕ More-able pupils may wish to extend the description, adding more detail, connectives and opinions. [S6]

Plenary

Ask pupils to find the Spanish for phrases you give them which cover vocabulary and instruction language from pages 50–51 of the Pupil's Book, e.g. *I have breakfast at seven during the week.* Then ask pupils to do the same in pairs for two minutes. Pupils can give their partner a three-second time limit to find the Spanish in the book (if necessary).

Cuaderno A, page 28

1 Completa el crucigrama. (AT4/1) [W1,7]

⚑ *Knowing about language*

Writing. Pupils complete the crossword with the names of the food and drink items illustrated.

Answers

(Crossword solution with entries including: ESPAGUETIS, PATATAS FRITAS, PIZZA, LIMONADA, BOCADILLO, ZUMO DE NARANJA, ENSALADA, FRUTA, NARANJADA)

2 Empareja los dibujos con las comidas. (AT3/1) [W1]

⚑ *Knowing about language*

Reading. Pupils match up the names of the meals with the illustrations.

Answers

a el desayuno	b la comida	c la merienda	d la cena

3a Rellena el cuadro con las horas de comer de Matilde. (AT3/3) [S6,7; T3]

⚑ *Reading for information and instructions – Level D*

Reading. Pupils read the description of Matilde's meal times and use the information to fill in the times on the grid.

Answers

	breakfast	lunch	snack	dinner
Juan	7.00	1.30	5.00	9.00
Matilde	6.30	1.00	4.30	9.30

3b Escribe un texto similar para Juan. (AT4/3) [T6]

⚑ *Writing to exchange information and ideas – Level C*

Writing. Pupils use Juan's details in the grid for activity 3a to write a short text about his meal times.

módulo 3 ¡Vamos al instituto!

Answers

| ¿Qué tal? Me llamo Juan. Desayuno a las siete. |
| Como a la una y media. |
| Meriendo a las cinco. |
| Ceno a las nueve. |

Cuaderno B, page 28

1 Completa el crucigrama. (AT4/1) [W1,7]

✠ *Knowing about language*

Writing. Pupils complete the crossword with the names of the food and drink items illustrated.

Answers

	¹E			²P
	S		³P		A
	P	⁴L		I	⁵B		T
	A	I		Z	O		A
	G	M		Z	C		T
⁸Z	U	M	O	D	⁶E	N	A	R	A	N	J	A
	E	N		N		D		S
	T	A		S		I		F
	I	D		A		L		R
	S	A		L		L		I
⁷F			A		O		T
⁹N	A	R	A	N	J	A	D	A			A
	U			A			S
	T
	A

2 Empareja los dibujos con las comidas. (AT3/1) [W1]

✠ *Knowing about language*

Reading. Pupils match up the names of the meals with the illustrations.

Answers

| **a** el desayuno | **b** la comida | **c** la merienda | **d** la cena |

3a Rellena el cuadro con las horas de comer de Matilde. (AT3/3) [S6,7; T3]

✠ *Reading for information and instructions – Level D*

Reading. Pupils read the description of Matilde's meal times and use the information to fill in the times on the grid.

Answers

	breakfast	lunch	snack	dinner
Juan	7.00	1.30	5.00	9.00
Matilde	6.30	1.00	4.30	9.30

3b Escribe un texto similar para Juan. (AT4/3) [T6]

✠ *Writing to exchange information and ideas – Level C*

Writing. Pupils use Juan's details in the grid for activity 3a to write a short text about his meal times.

Answers

| ¿Qué tal? Me llamo Juan. Desayuno a las siete. Como en casa a la una y media. Por la tarde meriendo a las cinco. Siempre cenamos a las nueve. |

Hoja de trabajo 6, page 50 [L4]

1 Pupils find out what their partners have to eat and drink using the picture cues on the pairwork card.

2 Pupils find out what time their partners have their meals.

módulo 3

5 Mi instituto
(Pupil's Book pages 52–53)

Main topics
- Describing your school

Key Framework Objectives
- Letters and sounds 7W6 (Reinforcement)
- Basic negatives 7S5 (Reinforcement)
- Assembling text 7T5 (Reinforcement)

Grammar
- hay/no hay

Key language

¿Dónde estudias?
Estudio en un instituto mixto/masculino/femenino.
(No) Es un instituto moderno.
(No) Hay uniforme.

¿Qué tiene tu instituto?
Mi instituto tiene …
Hay/No hay …
un aula (de inglés)
una biblioteca
una cafetería
un comedor
un gimnasio
el despacho de la directora
un laboratorio (de idiomas/ciencias)
un patio
una pista polideportiva
una sala de profesores
un salón de actos
unos servicios

los alumnos
los profesores

Resources
Cassette B, side 1
CD 2, track 6
Cuaderno A and B, page 29

Starter 1: Sound spelling links [W6; T2; L1]

Aims: To revise the pronunciation of the letter string *ay* and the silent property of the letter 'h' at the start of a word. (Timing: 5 minutes)

Activity: Write the following words on a transparency: *mayo, raya, ¡vaya!, historia, hola, Héctor*. Explain that some words will be familiar to pupils and others won't. Ask pupils to find links between the words. Accept all valid suggestions. Ask different pupils to read the words aloud and remind pupils of the pronunciation of the sound *ay* with a familiar word such as *mayo* and of the silent property of 'h' with a familiar word such as *historia*. Then ask pupils to learn the correct pronunciation of each word by repeating it in unison. Pupils now work in pairs to decide on the correct pronunciation of the word *hay* and feed back to the class. Write up the following tongue-twister for pupils to practise in pairs: *¡Vaya! En mayo hay historia con Héctor.*

1a ¿Dónde estudias? Escucha y empareja las frases con las fotos. (AT1/2–3, AT3/2–3) [W1,2,3,5; S4]

✉ *Knowing about language*

Listening/Reading. Pupils listen to the recording and read the texts to match up the descriptions with the pictures. The level will vary according to the level of support given. Teachers may wish to introduce the key words *instituto, colegio* and *uniforme* first, and then do the listening without reading the text: pupils could cover the texts and identify the picture for each person they hear.

R If pupils need more support, they could read the text at the same time as hearing the recording, matching the sounds with the words.

Answers

1 c	2 a	3 b

Tapescript

1 – ¿Dónde estudias?
  – Estudio en un instituto masculino.
  – ¿Hay uniforme?
  – Sí, hay uniforme.
2 – ¿Dónde estudias?
  – Estudio en un instituto mixto.
  – ¿Hay uniforme?
  – No hay uniforme.
3 – ¿Dónde estudias?
  – Estudio en un colegio femenino.
  – ¿Hay uniforme?
  – Sí, hay uniforme.

1b Con tu compañero/a, pregunta y contesta. (AT2/3) [W1,2,3,5; S4; L4]

✉ *Speaking and interacting with others – Level D*

Speaking. Pupils work in pairs to ask and answer questions based on the model given about their own school and uniform.

2a Escucha y repite. (AT1/2, AT2/2) [W1,3; T2; L1]

✉ *Knowing about language*

Listening/Speaking. Pupils listen to the recording and repeat the names of the school facilities. They should follow the words in the box to match the sounds with the words.

R After listening to the recording, pupils could practise the names of school facilities more before the next activity. They could work in pairs, taking turns to name something in the school while their

módulo 3 ¡Vamos al instituto!

partner finds it on the school plan. Alternatively, they could take it in turns to ask *¿Qué es (a)?*

Tapescript

– ¿Qué tiene tu instituto?
– Tiene ...
a – unas aulas
b – unos laboratorios
c – unos despachos de la directora y las secretarias
d – un salón de actos
e – una sala de profesores
f – una biblioteca
g – un comedor
h – un patio
i – un gimnasio
j – unas pistas polideportivas
k – unos servicios

2b Mira el plano. ¿Qué instalaciones mencionan los jóvenes? (1–4) (AT1/3) [W1,3; L3]

✉ *Listening for information and instructions – Level D*

Listening. Pupils look at the school plan and listen to the four young people describing their schools and write down the letters of the facilities mentioned.

Answers

Raúl: a, b, f	
Yolanda: a, b, g	
Héctor: i, j	
Bea: d, f, h	

Tapescript

1 – ¿Qué tiene tu instituto, Raúl?
   – Pues, tiene 24 aulas y cuatro laboratorios.
   – ¡24 aulas y cuatro laboratorios!
   – Sí, y tiene una biblioteca ...
   – Biblioteca ...
2 – ¿Qué tiene tu instituto, Yolanda?
   – Tiene tres aulas de tecnología.
   – ¡Tres aulas de tecnología ...!
   – Y tiene dos laboratorios de idiomas.
   – ¡Dos laboratorios de idiomas! ¿Tiene comedor?
   – Sí, un comedor muy grande.
3 – ¿Qué instalaciones deportivas tiene tu instituto, Héctor?
   – Tiene gimnasios.
   – ¿Cuántos?
   – Dos gimnasios, y tiene tres pistas polideportivas.
4 – Bea, ¿qué tiene tu instituto de interés?
   – Pues, tiene un salón de actos muy bonito y tres bibliotecas.
   – Un salón de actos y tres bibliotecas.
   – Y tiene un patio muy grande.
   – Un patio grande.

2c Escucha otra vez. ¿Cuántos de cada hay? (AT1/3) [W1,3; L3]

✉ *Listening for information and instructions – Level D*

Listening. Pupils listen to the four young people again, and this time note down how many of each facility each person mentions.

Answers

Raúl: a – 24, b – 4, f – 1
Yolanda: a – 3, b – 2, g – 1
Héctor: i – 2, j – 3
Bea: d – 1, f – 3, h – 1

Tapescript

As for activity 2b

2d Con tu compañero/a, pregunta y contesta. ¿Qué tienen los institutos de Raúl, Yolanda, Héctor y Bea. (AT2/2–3) [W1,3,5; S4,9; L4]

✉ *Speaking to convey information – Level D*

Speaking. In pairs, pupils take turns to ask and answer questions about the four schools described in activities 2b and 2c.

> **Starter 2: Match up** [W4; S2,3,5,9; T1,5]
>
> *Aims:* To reinforce the understanding of gender and sentence structure. (Timing: 5 minutes)
>
> *Activity:* Write up the following sentence halves in two columns. Column 1: *Mi colegio es; En mi instituto hay; Mi colegio; El uniforme.* Column 2: *un gimnasio y unas pistas deportivas; no es obligatorio; que es bueno; mixto y muy grande; tiene muchas instalaciones.* Pupils must match them correctly. Pupils feed back their answers, justifying their choices. (Answers: *Mi colegio es mixto y muy grande; En mi instituto hay un gimnasio y unas pistas deportivas; Mi colegio tiene muchas instalaciones; El uniforme no es obligatorio que es bueno.*) Give pupils three minutes to change one detail in every sentence. This could be a grammatical detail (i.e. from singular to plural) or a meaning. Pupils then read out the sentences to the class.

3a El instituto de Neus está en obras. ¿Dónde estudia sus asignaturas? (AT1/3) [W1,2,3; L3]

✉ *Listening for information and instructions – Level D/E*

Listening. Pupils listen to Neus describing where she has her lessons now that her school is having building work done. Pupils could arrange their answers in two columns headed *asignatura* and *aula*.

¡Vamos al instituto! módulo 3

R If pupils are struggling with this activity, teachers could fill in the information in the *asignatura* column so that pupils can focus on the names of the rooms.

Answers

matemáticas – aula de inglés, inglés – laboratorio, ciencias – aula de tecnología, tecnologia – gimnasio, educación física – salón de actos

Tapescript

– ¿Dónde estudias matemáticas?
– De momento estudio matemáticas en el aula de inglés.
– ¿Y dónde estudias inglés?
– Estudio inglés en el laboratorio.
– ¿Pues, dónde estudias ciencias?
– Por ahora estudio ciencias en el aula de tecnología.
– ¿Y dónde estudias tecnología?
– Estudio tecnología en el gimnasio.
– ¿Pues dónde estudias educación física?
– Estudio educación física en el salón de actos.
– ¡Qué desastre!

3b Con tu compañero/a, pregunta y contesta. (AT2/2–3) [W2,3; S4,9; L4]

✳ *Speaking and interacting with others – Level D*

Speaking. Pupils work in pairs and take turns to ask and answer questions about where their partner has lessons. Teachers may wish to suggest that pupils note down their partner's responses to further consolidate this structure: pupils could use their partner's responses to write phrases about what lessons they have and where.

4a Lee la descripción del instituto de Eva. ¿Verdad (✓) o mentira (✗)? (AT3/3–4) [W8; T1,4]

✳ *Reading for information and instructions – Level D/E*

Reading. Pupils read the description of Eva's school and decide whether the sentences are true (*verdad*) or false (*mentira*). There are a number of new words in the text which teachers may wish pupils to look up for themselves in a dictionary or glossary. This would provide evidence of a higher level of reading comprehension.

Answers

1 ✗	2 ✗	3 ✗	4 ✓	5 ✗	6 ✓

4b Corrige las frases en **4a** que son falsas. (AT3/3–4, AT4/2) [S3]

✳ *Knowing about language*

Reading/Writing. Pupils correct the sentences from activity 4a that are incorrect.

Answers

1 Es un instituto mixto.
2 No hay uniforme.
3 Tiene dieciséis aulas y varias aulas especiales; también tiene cuatro laboratorios.
5 No tiene comedor pero tiene una cafetería.

4c Escribe una descripción de tu instituto. (AT4/2–4) [S9; T5,6]

✳ *Writing to establish and maintain personal contact – Level D/E*

Writing. Pupils write a description of their own school. There are a number of ways in which teachers may wish to differentiate this activity. Some pupils could label a picture of their school as a first step, which would provide a stimulus for writing sentences using the structures encountered in this unit. Pupils could, alternatively, adapt the description of Eva's school. Some teachers may prefer to brainstorm words and phrases that could be used, before sequencing these into a more structured description as part of a shared writing activity.

Plenary

Ask pupils, in groups of three, to look at the sentences for exercise 4a on page 53 of the Pupil's Book. They must change one part of the sentence to give it a different meaning. Brainstorm with pupils what they could change (verb, person, negative, individual words, numbers, endings of phrases, etc.). Go through an example and encourage the class to invent as many different phrases as possible to cover all the different ideas they have just collected. Then give pupils one word from the spread (e.g. *biblioteca* or *mixto*) and ask the groups to invent a sentence using that word.

Cuaderno A, page 29

1 Rellena los espacios en blanco con las palabras apropiadas. (AT3/3) [W1; S2]

✳ *Knowing about language*

Reading. Pupils choose the appropriate words to fill in the blanks, using the picture cues.

Answers

femenino, uniforme, aulas, informática, laboratorios, gimnasio, biblioteca, salón de actos, pistas polideportivas, despachos, sala de profesores, cafetería

2 Empareja las preguntas con las respuestas. (AT3/2) [W1,2; S4,5,7]

✳ *Knowing about language*

módulo 3 ¡Vamos al instituto!

Reading. Pupils match up the questions with the appropriate answers.

Answers

| 1 f | 2 e | 3 c | 4 g | 5 a | 6 d | 7 b |

Cuaderno B, page 29

1 Rellena los espacios en blanco con las palabras apropiadas. (AT3/3) [W1, S2]

✉ *Knowing about language*

Reading. Pupils choose the appropriate words to fill in the blanks, using the picture cues.

Answers

femenino, uniforme, aulas, informática, laboratorios, gimnasio, biblioteca, salón de actos, pistas polideportivas, despachos, sala de profesores

2a Empareja las preguntas con las respuestas. (AT3/2) [W1,2; S4,5,7]

✉ *Knowing about language*

Reading. Pupils match up the questions with the appropriate answers.

Answers

| 1 f | 2 e | 3 c | 4 g | 5 a | 6 d | 7 b |

2b Contesta a las preguntas sobre tu instituto. (AT4/2–3) [W1,2; S3,4,5,7]

✉ *Writing to establish and maintain personal contact – Level D*

Writing. Pupils answer the questions from activity 2a for their own school.

módulo 3

6 ¡Ya llegamos!

(Pupil's Book pages 54–55)

Main topics
- Saying how you get to school

Key Framework Objectives
- Spontaneous talk 7L5 (Launch)
- Letters and sounds 7W6 (Reinforcement)
- Sound patterns 7L1 (Reinforcement)

Grammar
- Present tense of *llegar*

Key language
¿A qué hora llegas/llega al instituto?
Llego/llega a las ocho y media.
Llego/llega pronto/a tiempo/tarde.
¿Cómo llegas?
Llego a pie.
Llego en …
autobús   metro
bici   moto
coche   tren

Resources
Cassette B, side 1
CD 2, track 7
Cuaderno A and B, page 30
Starters 1 and 2, Resource and Assessment File, page 56
Hoja de trabajo 7, Resource and Assessment File, page 51
Skills, Resource and Assessment File, page 53
OHTs 15 and 16: forms of transport to school

Starter 1: Letter strings [W6; L1]

Aims: To introduce transport vocabulary and to make links between the spelling and pronunciation of words. (Timing: 5 minutes)

Resources: Resource and Assessment File, page 56 (Starter 1)

Activity: Make an OHT using the master provided. Read out the following list of transport words: *autobús, bicicleta, coche, metro, moto, pie*. Explain to pupils that some of them are cognates and therefore easily recognisable. Pupils must write down the transport word using the letter strings on the OHT. Pupils then look at the language grid on page 54 of the Pupil's Book and find the missing mode of transport (answer: *tren*).

R For lower-ability pupils, correct the transport words one by one.

1a ¿Cómo llegan al instituto? Escucha y escribe las letras de las fotos en el orden correcto. (AT1/2) [W5; S9; L3]

✉ *Listening for information and instructions – Level C*

Listening. Pupils listen to the recording and look at the photos. They write the letters of the photos in the order they hear the modes of transport mentioned. Teachers should point out to pupils that the order does not follow the times on the clocks. Before attempting this activity, teachers should use flashcards or OHT to introduce the forms of transport, as well as revising the times learnt earlier in this module.

Answers

| 1 d | 2 g | 3 f | 4 a | 5 c | 6 b | 7 e |

Tapescript
1 – Llego a las 8.30. A pie.
2 – Llego a las 8.25. En metro.
3 – Llego a las 8.35. En tren. Llego a tiempo.
4 – Llego a las 9.10. En autobús. ¡Llego tarde!
5 – Llego a las 8.15. En bici. ¡Llego pronto!
6 – Llego a las 8.20. En moto. ¡Llego pronto!
7 – Llego a las 9.00. En coche. ¡Llego tarde!

1b Completa las frases. (AT4/3) [W2,5; S3,9]

✉ *Writing to establish and maintain personal contact – Level D*

Writing. Pupils write a short paragraph about what time they themselves arrive at school, the form of transport used, and whether they arrive at school on time, late or early. Teachers should practise these structures with pupils orally first. Pupils should use the writing frame at the bottom of the page to help them: this activity will help pupils have their answers ready for the survey in the following activity.

1c Haz un sondeo. Pregunta a tus compañeros/as de clase. (AT2/3) [W2,5; S4,9; L4]

✉ *Speaking and interacting with others – Level D*

Speaking. Pupils should read through *Gramática* to ensure that they are confident with the verb *llegar*, with the question form ¿*llegas*? and the answer *llego* … They should then copy the survey grid and ask at least 10 classmates what time they arrive at school and how they travel.

🖱 ICT activity

Pupils could enter their results onto a spreadsheet such as *Microsoft Excel*, and produce pie charts or bar graphs to show the proportion of the class who arrive

módulo 3 — ¡Vamos al instituto!

on time, take the bus, etc. This software will also generate percentages which can be added to the charts, and used by pupils to write up a summary of the results, which will provide extra practice of the verb *llegar*. For example: *60% de los alumnos en mi clase llegan a las 8.30 …*

Starter 2: Battleships [W5; S9; L1,5] (any time after introducing verb *llegar*)

Aims: To revise transport language and the verb *llegar* in the present tense. To develop pupils' memory skills. (Timing: 10 minutes)

Resources: Resource and Assessment File, page 56 (Starter 2)

Pairwork activity: Make game-sheets using the master provided. Give a copy to each pupil to play battleships. One pupil has the ship (Pupil A) and the other is trying to destroy it (Pupil B). Pupil A secretly marks out five squares to represent the position of the battleship. These can be horizontal, vertical or diagonal. Pupil B then reads out sentences in Spanish using part of the verb *llegar*, followed by a mode of transport. Pupil A says *golpe* (hit) or *nada* (miss). This continues until the ship is found.

➕ Pupils who finish quickly can be given more copies of the worksheet and swap roles.

🅁 For lower-ability students, create a transparency with the key language in Spanish to display on the projector.

2a ¿Quién habla? Empareja las frases con los dibujos. (AT3/2) [W1,5; S7,9]

✖ *Knowing about language*

Reading. Pupils match up the phrases with the pictures. They check their answers in the following activity.

Answers

| a 6 | b 5 | c 1 | d 2 | e 3 | f 4 |

2b Escucha y comprueba tus respuestas. (AT1/2) [W1,5; S7,9]

✖ *Knowing about language*

Listening. Pupils check their answers to activity 2a.

🅁 Teachers may want pupils to practise these useful phrases which give more exposure to the verb *llegar* by setting them a short speaking activity in pairs, or as a whole-class quickfire game.

Tapescript

a – Llegan a tiempo.
b – Llega el tren.
c – ¡Ya llegamos!

d – ¡Llego tarde!
e – ¡Llegas pronto!
f – ¿A qué hora llegáis?

3a Rellena los espacios en blanco con la forma correcta del verbo *llegar*. (AT3/3) [W1,5; S2]

✖ *Knowing about language*

Reading. Pupils have the opportunity to practise the verb *llegar* by filling in the correct form of the verb in the gaps in the text.

Answers

| 1 llegamos | 2 llega | 3 llegan | 4 llego | 5 llega | 6 llegáis |

3b Escribe a qué hora y cómo llegan los miembros de tu familia a casa. (AT4/2) [W5; S9; T5]

✖ *Writing to exchange information and ideas – Level D/E*

Writing. Pupils write sentences about how and at what times the members of their family arrive home. Teachers may wish to prescribe the forms of *llegar* for the pupils to use, for example, *yo llego, mi … llega, mis … llegan …*

Plenary

Read out five different times of day during the school day and, for each time, pupils must create a sentence in Spanish. Pupils may work in pairs or groups. For example, (Teacher): *A las nueve;* (Students) *Tengo las matemáticas a las nueve; Llego al instituto a las nueve,* etc. Pupils then choose one of the times given and invent as many sentences about this time as they can (orally or, if preferred, written down).

Cuaderno A, page 30

1 Completa el crucigrama. (AT4/1) [W1,7]

✖ *Knowing about language*

Writing. Pupils fill in the correct forms of transport to complete the crossword.

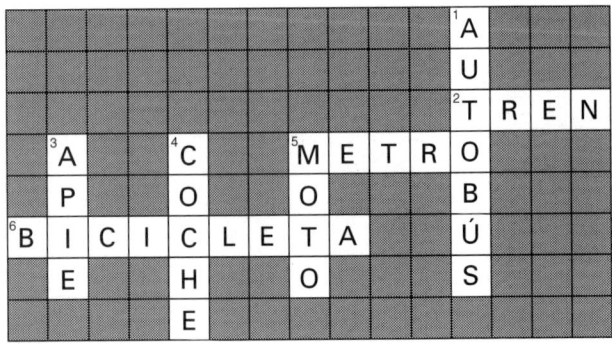

Answers

Across: 2 TREN, 5 METRO, 6 BICICLETA
Down: 1 AUTOBÚS, 3 APIE, 4 COCHE

¡Vamos al instituto!

módulo 3

2a Mira el sondeo. Completa los globos para Gregorio, Javier, Elvira y Lola. (AT4/2) [W1; S2,7]

✉ *Writing to exchange information and ideas – Level C/D*

Writing. Pupils complete the speech bubbles for the four young people using the information in the survey and the text given for Nicolás.

Answers

Gregorio: en bici, nueve menos diez
Javier: autobús, nueve menos veinte
Elvira: moto, ocho y media
Lola: coche, nueve menos cuarto

2b Completa las frases sobre ti. (AT4/2–3) [W1; S3,9]

✉ *Writing to establish and maintain personal contact – Level C*

Writing. Pupils write similar sentences about how they themselves get to school, and at what time.

Cuaderno B, page 30

1a Mira el sondeo. Escribe unas frases para Javier y Lola. (AT4/3) [W1; S2,3,9]

✉ *Writing to exchange information and ideas – Level D*

Writing. Pupils use the information in the survey grid to write sentences about Javier and Lola, adapting the information about Nicolás.

Answers

Lola:	Llego al instituto en coche. Llego a tiempo. No llego tarde.
Javier:	Llego al instituto a pie. Llego pronto.

1b Mira la lista. Las clases empiezan a las nueve menos cuarto. Contesta a las preguntas. (AT3/2–3) [W1,2; S4,7]

✉ *Reading for information and instructions – Level D/E*

Reading/Writing. Pupils use the details in the survey to answer the questions. They should be reminded that school starts at 8.45, which will help them to answer the first two questions.

Answers

1 tres	**2** 0	**3** a las nueve menos veinticinco	**4** dos
5 dos	**6** una		

1c Contesta a las preguntas sobre ti. (AT4/2–3) [W1,2; S4,7,9]

✉ *Writing to establish and maintain personal contact – Level D/E*

Writing. Pupils answer the questions for themselves.

Hoja de trabajo 7, page 51

Cards for teachers to cut out for pupils to play 'dominoes'. Tip: photocopy this sheet onto card.

Pupils put the 'dominoes' face down. They pick four each and start playing as in a normal dominoes game. If they can't put anything down they should pick another domino or miss their turn. The first one who manages to put all their dominoes down is the winner.

During the game pupils could read the words aloud (good for pronunciation), translate the words orally, and try to work out in advance what the words for the symbols they have will be in Spanish.

Skills Resource and Assessment File, page 53 [W2,6; S1]

These activities provide pupils with the opportunity to practise asking and answering questions, including the meanings of question words.

módulo 3

Resumen y Prepárate

(Pupil's Book pages 56–57)

Resumen

This is a checklist of language covered in Module 3. There is a comprehensive **Resumen** list for Module 3 in the Student's Book (page 56) and a **Resumen** test sheet in Cuaderno A and B (page 34).

Key Framework Objectives

- Basic questions 7S4 (Reinforcement)
- Simple sentences 7S9 (Reinforcement)
- Gist and detail 7L3 (Reinforcement)

Prepárate

A revision test to give practice for the test itself at the end of the module.

Resources

Cassette B, side 1
CD 2, track 8
Cuaderno A and B, Repaso (previously ¡Extra!), pages 31–32; Gramática, page 33

---

1 ¿Qué hora es? Escribe el orden en que se mencionan las horas. (AT1/2) [W1; L1]

✉ *Listening for information and instructions – Level C*

Listening. Pupils write down the times in the order in which they are mentioned.

Answers

c, d, e, a, b

Tapescript

1 – Las nueve y veinte.
2 – Las tres y cuarto.
3 – Las seis y cinco.
4 – La una y media.
5 – Las dos menos diez.

2 Escucha. ¿Qué asignaturas les gustan a estos jóvenes? Copia y rellena el cuadro. (AT1/3) [W3,5; L3]

✉ *Listening for information and instructions – Level D*

Listening. Pupils listen to the young people's opinions about their school subjects and mark on the grid the subjects that they like. Teachers may wish pupils to put a tick by the subjects the people like, and a cross by the subjects they do not like. In number 3 the expression *me da igual* may need some explanation before pupils listen.

Tapescript

1 – Hola. Me llamo Miguel. Me gustan mucho las matemáticas y las ciencias. Odio la historia y el inglés.
2 – ¿Qué tal? Me llamo Nicolás. Me gusta la informática. Detesto la geografía.
3 – Me llamo Esperanza. Me gustan la geografía y la historia. No me gustan nada las ciencias.
4 – Me llamo Montse. El francés me da igual. Me encanta la educación física.
5 – ¿Qué tal? Me llamo Andrés. No me gusta nada la tecnología pero me gustan las ciencias. ¡Ah! Y la música, me gusta mucho la música.

3a Con tu compañero/a, empareja las preguntas con las respuestas. (AT2/2–3) [W3; S4,9]

✉ *Speaking to convey information – Level D*

Speaking. In pairs, pupils match up the questions with the answers, and then take turns to ask and answer the questions.

Answers

1 e	2 b	3 d	4 a	5 c

3b Pregunta y contesta para ti. (AT2/3) [W3; S4,9; L4]

✉ *Speaking and interacting with others – Level D/E*

Speaking. Pupils take turns to ask and answer the questions from activity 3a for themselves.

Answers

	la historia	la tecnología	la geografía	el francés	las matemáticas	la educación física	el inglés	la música	la informática	las ciencias
Miguel	✗				✓		✗			✓
Nicolás		✗							✓	
Esperanza	✓		✓						✗	
Montse				=		✓				
Andrés		✗						✓		✓

¡Vamos al instituto! módulo 3

4a Mira el horario. ¿Verdad (✓) o mentira (✗)? (AT3/2–3) [W1,3; S7]

✉ *Reading for information and instructions – Level D*

Reading. Pupils use the timetable to decide whether the sentences are true (*verdad*) or false (*mentira*).

Answers

| 1 ✗ | 2 ✓ | 3 ✗ | 4 ✓ | 5 ✓ | 6 ✗ |

4b Corrige las frases en **4a** que son falsas. (AT3/3, AT4/2) [W3; S3]

✉ *Reading for information and instructions – Level D*

Reading/Writing. Pupils correct the sentences in activity 4a that are false.

Answers

1 Las clases empiezan a las ocho y media.
3 El recreo es a las diez y media.
6 Hay inglés el lunes a las once.

5 Escribe cinco frases para describir tu instituto. (AT4/3) [W3; S9; T5]

✉ *Writing to establish and maintain personal contact – Level D/E*

Writing. Pupils use the writing frame to write five sentences describing their school.

Cuaderno A, pages 31–32

Repaso (previously ¡Extra!)

1 Descifra los anagramas de las asignaturas. (AT3/1) [W1,7]

✉ *Reading for enjoyment*

Reading. Pupils work out the anagrams of the school subjects.

Answers

1 ciencias	2 religión	3 educación física	4 francés
5 geografía	6 historia	7 informática	8 inglés
9 música	10 matemáticas		

2 Completa las frases. (AT3/2) [W1; S1,2]

✉ *Knowing about language*

Reading. Pupils match up the sentence halves.

Answers

| 1 b | 2 d | 3 e | 4 a | 5 c | 6 g | 7 f |

3 Empareja las preguntas con las respuestas. (AT3/2–3) [W1,2,5; S4,7]

✉ *Knowing about language*

Reading. Pupils match up the questions and answers.

Answers

| 1 h | 2 c | 3 b | 4 f | 5 e | 6 a | 7 d |
| 8 g | | | | | | |

4 Completa la carta con las palabras apropiadas. (AT3/3) [W1; S2,9]

✉ *Knowing about language*

Reading. Pupils complete the letter, replacing the pictures with words from the box.

Answers

siete y media, café con leche, tostadas, una, bocadillo, cafetería, casa, fruta, nueve y media, espaguetis, agua mineral

5 Mira el plano. ¿Verdad (✓) o mentira (✗)? (AT3/2) [W1,5]

✉ *Knowing about language*

Reading. Pupils use the plan to decide whether the sentences are true (*verdad*) or false (*mentira*).

Answers

| 1 ✗ | 2 ✗ | 3 ✓ | 4 ✗ | 5 ✓ | 6 ✗ |

6 Escribe el número apropiado para cada dibujo. (AT3/2) [W1,5]

✉ *Knowing about language*

Reading. Pupils match up the sentences with the pictures.

Answers

| 1 c | 2 d | 3 a | 4 b |

Cuaderno B, pages 31–32

Repaso (previously ¡Extra!)

1 Completa las frases. (AT3/2) [W1; S1,2]

✉ *Knowing about language*

Reading. Pupils match up the sentence halves.

Answers

| 1 b | 2 d | 3 e | 4 a | 5 c | 6 g | 7 f |

módulo 3 ¡Vamos al instituto!

2a Empareja las respuestas con las preguntas. (AT3/2–3) [W1,2,5; S4,7]

✳ *Knowing about language*

Reading. Pupils match up the questions and answers.

Answers

1 h	2 c	3 b	4 f	5 e	6 a	7 d
8 g						

2b Contesta a las preguntas sobre ti. (AT4/2–3) [W1,2,5; S4,7,9]

✳ *Writing to establish and maintain personal contact – Level D*

Writing. Pupils answer the questions for themselves.

3 Lee la carta y contesta a las preguntas. (AT3/3, AT4/2–3) [W2,5; S4,9; T3]

✳ *Reading for information and instructions – Level D*

Reading/Writing. Pupils read the letter and answer the questions on it.

Answers

1 Elías desayuna a las siete y media.
2 La hora de comer es a la una.
3 Come en la cafetería.
4 Generalmente come un bocadillo.
5 Merienda fruta y un yogur.
6 A veces cenan espaguetis.

4 Mira el plano. ¿Verdad o mentira? Corrige las frases que son falsas. (AT3/2) [W1,5; S3]

✳ *Knowing about language*

Reading. Pupils use the plan to decide whether the sentences are true (*verdad*) or false (*mentira*). They then correct the sentences that are false.

Answers

1 ✗ Tiene dos laboratorios.
2 ✗ Tiene una biblioteca.
3 ✓
4 ✗ Tiene cuatro aulas.
5 ✓
6 ✗ Tiene un despacho.

5 Empareja los dibujos con las frases. (AT3/2) [W1,5]

✳ *Knowing about language*

Reading. Pupils match up the sentences with the pictures.

Answers

1 b	2 c	3 d	4 a

Cuaderno A, page 33

Gramática

1 Escribe la forma correcta de *gustar* en cada frase. (AT3/2) [W4,5]

✳ *Knowing about language*

Reading. Pupils complete the sentences with the correct form of *gustar*.

Answers

1 gusta	2 gusta	3 gustan	4 gustan	5 gusta	6 gustan

2 Escribe la forma correcta del adjetivo en cada caso. (AT3/2) [W1,4]

✳ *Knowing about language*

Reading. Pupils complete the sentences with the correct form of the adjective in brackets.

Answers

1 divertida	2 fácil	3 difíciles	4 interesante
5 útil	6 aburridas	7 buenos	8 morenas
9 dorados	10 inteligente		

3 Escribe la forma correcta del verbo en cada caso. (AT3/2) [W1,5]

✳ *Knowing about language*

Reading. Pupils complete the sentences with the correct form of the verb in brackets.

Answers

1 llega	2 estudias	3 cenamos	4 toman
5 desayunáis	6 cena	7 odio	8 merendan

Cuaderno B, page 33

Gramática

1 Completa las frases con *gusta* o *gustan*. (AT3/2) [W4,5]

✳ *Knowing about language*

Reading. Pupils complete the sentences with the correct form of *gustar*: *gusta* or *gustan*.

Answers

1 gusta	2 gusta	3 gustan	4 gustan	5 gusta
6 gusta	7 gustan	8 gusta	9 gusta	

¡Vamos al instituto!

módulo 3

2 Completa las frases con la forma apropiada del adjetivo. (AT3/2) [W1,4]

✉ *Knowing about language*

Reading. Pupils complete the sentences with the correct form of the adjective given in brackets.

Answers

1 divertida	**2** fácil	**3** difíciles	**4** interesante	**5** útil
6 aburridas	**7** simpáticos	**8** bueno		

3 Completa las frases con la forma apropiada del verbo. (AT3/2) [W1,5]

✉ *Knowing about language*

Reading. Pupils complete the sentences with the correct form of the verb in brackets.

Answers

1 llega	**2** estudias	**3** cenamos	**4** toman
5 desayunáis	**6** cena	**7** odio	**8** merendan
9 llamas	**10** llamo		

módulo 3

¡Extra! 7 Un instituto en España

(Pupil's Book pages 58–59)

Main topics

This is an optional unit which reviews some of the key language of the module: it consists of an activity based on a Spanish schoolboy's description of his school and timetable.

Key Framework Objectives

- Everyday culture 7C2 (Launch)
- Compound sentences 7S6 (Reinforcement)
- Time and tenses 7S7 (Reinforcement)
- Reading using cues 7T1 (Reinforcement)

Resources

Cassette B, side 1
CD 2, track 9

Suggestion

This is another excellent opportunity to get pupils to compare their experiences with those of young people in Spanish-speaking countries. If the school has a partner school, pupils could use Juan Ignacio's description as a model to write about their own school, either as a letter or e-mail to a penpal, or as a class project. Pupils could also create a web-based guide to their school, with descriptions and a plan (it is possible to highlight areas of the plan and link them to pictures, descriptions, video clips, audio clips, making it a truly interactive tour of the school). Pupils could also be encouraged to script, film and then edit a video diary or video tour of the school, and send the finished film to their Spanish-speaking partners.

Starter 1: **Verb search** [W2,5,8; S2,7; T1,3]

Aims: To develop reading skills by getting pupils to focus very closely on the text; to develop pupils' skills in text scanning; to develop pupils' appreciation of the different functions of language. (Timing: 5 minutes)

Activity: Ask pupils to work in pairs or in groups of three. Ask them to look at the first five lines of the text on page 58 of the Pupil's Book and to identify verbs in the present tense and time indicators. Go through a couple of examples from another part of the text. Tell pupils that they have to work fast as there is a time limit of two minutes to find the verbs. Pairs/groups then feed back and give the number of verbs and the time indicators they have found. Answers: verbs 8 (including *hay*), time indicators (2).

1a ¿Qué día de la semana prefiere Juan Ignacio? Escribe el horario de su día favorito. (AT3/4) [W8; T1,4; C2]

✉ *Reading for information and instructions – Level E*

Reading. This is a very detailed text which will require revision of all the points in this module, as well as looking up some new words. The comprehension activities break the text down into more manageable chunks. In the first activity, pupils need to correctly identify Juan Ignacio's favourite day, and use the text to complete the timetable for that day.

Answers

Viernes	
8.00	las matemáticas
9.00	la informática
10.30	EL RECREO
11.00	el español
12.00	las ciencias
1.00	la educación física

1b Elige los dibujos apropiados. (AT3/4) [W1,3,5; T1]

✉ *Reading for information and instructions – Level D*

Reading. Pupils use the information in the text to choose the correct picture.

Answers

1 c	2 c	3 b	4 b/c	5 b	6 b	7 b
8 a/b						

2 Elige las instalaciones que menciona Juan Ignacio. (AT3/4) [W3; T1]

✉ *Reading for information and instructions – Level D*

Reading. Pupils note down which school facilities Juan Ignacio mentions in the text.

Answers

e, c, a, b, d, h

Starter 2: **Odd one out** [W1,4]

Aims: To reinforce the understanding and knowledge of gender and to use thinking skills. (Timing: 5 minutes)

Pairwork activity: Copy the following words onto a grid with three columns and three rows: (Row 1) 1 *matemáticas* 2 *ciencias* 3 *informática*; (Row 2) 4 *aulas* 5 *laboratorios* 6 *gimnasio*; (Row 3) 7 *salón de actos* 8 *sala de profesores* 9 *biblioteca*. Pupils must locate the odd one out in each row. Encourage use of the target language by giving an example and putting keywords on the board:

¡Vamos al instituto! módulo 3

(*masculino, femenino, diferente, número tres es la excepción porque* …), but allow pupils to communicate in English for more complex ideas. Pairs feed back to the whole class and justify their decision (in English). Accept all valid suggestions. You can then repeat the process using the columns if there is time.

3 Escucha y elige las asignaturas que le gustan a Juan Ignacio. (AT1/3) [W3,5; L3]

Listening for information and instructions – Level D

Listening. Pupils listen to Juan Ignacio and note down the subjects that he likes.

Answers

j, a, f, i, k

Tapescript

Me gusta mucho la informática. Es mi asignatura preferida.
También me gustan las matemáticas y las ciencias.
Pienso que el inglés es importante pero no me gusta mucho. Es muy difícil.
Detesto el francés y pienso que la historia es aburrida.
Me gusta mucho el español y la educación física.
El día de la semana que prefiero es el viernes porque tenemos todas mis asignaturas preferidas.

4 Escribe una carta a Juan Ignacio. Describe tu instituto y tu horario. (AT4/3–4) [W3,5; S6,9; T5,6]

Writing to establish and maintain personal contact – Level D/E/F

Writing. Pupils write a letter to Juan Ignacio about their school and timetable. They may wish to use the text on page 58 as a model.

Plenary

Ask pupils to use the letters they have written for exercise 4 on page 59 of the Pupil's Book to summarise the language they have learned during the module. Pupils choose a sentence from their letters that they think is accurate and interesting and read it aloud. The rest of the class must translate what they have said into English (or summarise the main gist if the sentence is very long). Then ask the class to comment on the content, accuracy and any other points of interest.

módulo 3 — Te toca a ti

(Pupil's Book pages 120–121)

- Self-access reading and writing at two levels.

A Reinforcement

1 Empareja las asignaturas. (AT3/1) [W3,6]

✉ *Reading for enjoyment*

Reading. Pupils match up the word halves to find the names of subjects.

Answers

1 j (la historia)	**2** i (el inglés)	**3** g (el español)
4 h (las matemáticas)	**5** d (la educación física)	
6 f (la informática)	**7** b (la geografía)	
8 a (la tecnología)	**9** e (la música)	**10** c (las ciencias)

2 Empareja los relojes con las horas correctas. (AT3/2) [W1,5; S4]

✉ *Reading for information and instructions – Level D*

Reading. Pupils match up the clocks with the written times.

Answers

1 d	**2** i	**3** f	**4** h	**5** e	**6** a	**7** c
8 g	**9** b					

3a Copia y completa. (AT4/2) [W3; S2,3]

✉ *Writing to exchange information and ideas – Level D*

Writing. Pupils copy and complete the paragraph, replacing the pictures with words.

Answers

1 matemáticas	**2** inglés	**3** recreo	**4** música
5 español	**6** comida	**7** historia	**8** ciencias

3b Copia y completa las frases para ti. (AT4/3) [W3,5; S3,9]

✉ *Writing to establish and maintain personal contact – Level D*

Writing. Pupils adapt the paragraph in activity 3a to write about their own Monday at school.

B Extension

1 Copia y completa las frases con las palabras apropiadas. (AT3/3) [W3; T1]

✉ *Knowing about language*

Reading. Pupils copy the paragraph and use the words to fill in the gaps.

Answers

1 instituto	**2** mixto	**3** uniforme	**4** a pie	**5** llega
6 a tiempo	**7** empiezan	**8** terminan	**9** casa	
10 bocadillo	**11** cantina	**12** informática	**13** aula	
14 matemáticas	**15** aburridas	**16** inglés	**17** profesores	

2 ¿Qué hace Sebastián? Escribe una frase para cada dibujo. (AT4/2–3) [W3,5; S9]

✉ *Writing to exchange information and ideas – Level D*

Writing. Pupils write one or more sentence(s) to describe what Sebastián is doing in each picture.

Answers

- **a** Sebastián llega al instituto a las 8.15.
- **b** Las clases empiezan a las ocho y media.
- **c** Come en la cantina.
- **d** Después juega al fútbol.
- **e** No le gusta la música.
- **f** Las clases terminan a las cuatro.

módulo 4 — *En casa*

(Pupil's Book pages 62–79)

Unit/topics	Key Framework Objectives	PoS	Key language and Grammar
1 ¿Dónde vives? (pp. 62–63) Talking about your home Saying where it is	7W1 Everyday words (R) 7W5 Verbs present (R) 7W8 Finding meanings (R)	1b grammar and how to apply it 1c how to express themselves 2c ask/answer questions 5a communicating in the target language	Types of home Locations *¿Dónde vives? Vivo en una casa. Vivimos en un piso en el centro de la ciudad. Está en un pueblo en la costa. Está en el barrio en el sur de la ciudad.*
2 ¿Cómo es tu casa? (pp. 64–65) Describing your house	7S6 Compound sentences (R) 7S8 Punctuation (R) 7S9 Simple sentences (R) 7T2 Reading aloud (R)	1b grammar and how to apply it 1c how to express themselves 2c ask/answer questions 5c express opinions	*Mi casa es muy/bastante grande. Mi casa es adosada. Mi piso es antiguo. Mi chalet es de tres plantas. ¿Cuántas plantas/ habitaciones tiene? Tiene cinco habitaciones. (No) Me gusta porque es moderna.*
3 El plano de mi casa (pp. 66–67) Describing the rooms in your house	7W5 Verbs present (Part-L) 7W7 Learning about words (L) 7T6 Texts as prompts (R) 7L5 Spontaneous talk (R)	2a listen for gist/detail 3a memorising 4c compare cultures	Names of rooms *La cocina El salón En mi casa/piso hay una cocina. En la primera planta hay cuatro dormitorios.*
4 Mi dormitorio (pp. 68–69) Describing your bedroom	7W1 Everyday words (R) 7W6 Letters and sounds (R) 7C4 Stories and songs (R)	1b grammar and how to apply it 1c how to express themselves 5f using the TL creatively and imaginatively	Furniture, etc., in a bedroom Prepositions *En mi dormitorio hay un armario. Encima de la estantería hay pósters. La cama está al lado de la mesa.*
5 Por la mañana (pp. 70–71) Talking about your daily routine	7W2 High-frequency words (R) 7S1 Word order (R) 7T2 Reading aloud (R) 7L1 Sound patterns (R)	1b grammar and how to apply it 1c how to express themselves 2c ask/answer questions 2d initiate/develop conversations	Reflexive verbs *Me despierto a las siete. Me levanto tarde. Primero me ducho y me visto. ¿A qué hora desayunas? Desayuno a las siete.*
6 Por la tarde (pp. 72–73) Talking about what you do after school	7T3 Checking before reading (R) 7T4 Using resources (R) 7L6 Improving speech (R)	1b grammar and how to apply it 1c how to express themselves 2c ask/answer questions 2f adapt language for different contexts	Reflexive verbs *¿A qué hora te acuestas? Me acuesto a las once. ¡Me divierto con mis amigos! ¿A qué hora meriendas? Como en casa a la una. Después de cenar, hago los deberes.*
Resumen y Prepárate (pp. 74–75) Pupils' checklist and practice test	7S3 Adapting sentences (R) 7S4 Basic questions (R) 7T1 Reading using cues (R) 7T5 Assembling text (R)	3a memorising 3e develop their independence	
¡Extra! 7 Mi casa (pp. 76–77) Optional unit: Talking about houses	7T3 Checking before reading (R) 7T4 Using resources (R)	2h scan texts 4a working with authentic materials	
Te toca a ti (pp. 122–123) Self-access reading and writing at two levels		1b grammar and how to apply it 2f adapt language for different contexts	

módulo 4

1 ¿Dónde vives?

(Pupil's Book pages 62–63)

Main topics
- Talking about your home
- Saying where it is

Key Framework Objectives
- Everyday words 7W1 (Reinforcement)
- Verbs present 7W5 (Reinforcement)
- Finding meanings 7W8 (Reinforcement)

Grammar
- Present tense of *vivir*

Key language

¿Dónde vives?
Vivo en …
una casa
un piso (en un bloque moderno/antiguo)
un chalet
una granja
Vivimos en un piso en el centro de la ciudad.
Está en …
las afueras
el/un barrio
el campo
el centro
la/una ciudad
la costa
la montaña
el/un pueblo
el este
el norte
el oeste
el sur

Resources

Cassette B, side 2
CD 2, track 10
Cuaderno A and B, page 35
Starter 2, Resource and Assessment File, page 73
Skills, Resource and Assessment File, page 72

Starter 1: **Alphabetic order race** [W1,6,8; T4]

Aims: To expose pupils to new vocabulary and to build on their dictionary skills. (Timing: 5–10 minutes)

Activity: Ask pupils to look at the third column of the language grid on page 63 of the Pupil's Book (*una casa, un piso, un chalet, una granja, una ciudad, un pueblo, un barrio, las afueras, el campo, la costa, el norte, el sur, el oeste, el este*). Pupils must race to put the vocabulary in alphabetical order. You can divide up the vocabulary into three separate races using the three rows of the grid. Remind students that to look up or list words alphabetically in Spanish they should ignore the definite or indefinite articles.

R For less-able students, copy some of the words onto a card that can be cut out, so that it becomes more of a kinaesthetic activity.

+ Build on this activity by ending with a discussion on the possible topic the vocabulary is describing and look at any words which are similar in English.

1a Escucha y lee. Empareja las casas con las personas. (1–5) (AT1/2) [W1,2,5,6; S9; L1]

✉ *Knowing about language*

Listening. Pupils listen to the conversations with five young people saying where they live and match up the pictures of the homes with the people.

R Teachers may wish to introduce and practise the types of homes before attempting this activity, using the pictures on page 62. Pupils could say the number of the type of home mentioned by the teacher, to check the relationship between sound and writing. This could then be reversed, with the teacher saying the number and the pupils saying the type of home.

Answers

| José 5, David 1, Sandra 4, Asun 2, Barto 3 |

Tapescript

1 – ¿Dónde vives, José?
  – Vivo en una granja.
2 – ¿Dónde vives, David?
  – Vivo en un piso, en un bloque moderno.
3 – ¿Dónde vives, Sandra?
  – Vivo en un chalet.
4 – ¿Dónde vives, Asun?
  – Vivo en un piso, en un bloque antiguo.
5 – ¿Dónde vives, Barto?
  – Vivo en una casa.

1b Haz un sondeo. Pregunta a tus compañeros/as de clase. (AT2/2) [W1,2,5; S4,9; L4]

✉ *Speaking and interacting with others – Level D*

Speaking. Pupils copy out the grid and conduct a survey to find out where their classmates live.

R Before attempting this activity teachers may wish to practise the question and answer *¿Dónde vives, …? Vivo en …* either as a whole-class or pairwork activity.

💬 **ICT activity**

Pupils could enter the results of their survey on a spreadsheet, such as *Microsoft Excel*, and produce a

En casa · módulo 4

pie chart or bar graph to find out which type of home is most or least common. This could be used as a stimulus for activity 1c (see below).

1c Con tu compañero/a, pregunta y contesta. (AT2/2) [W1,2,5; S4,9; L4]

✖ *Speaking and interacting with others – Level D*

Speaking. In pairs, pupils ask and answer questions about the information in the survey.

Before attempting this activity, pupils need to know how to use the third person singular form of the verb *vivir.* Pupils should be allowed time to read through the *Gramática* box on page 63. Other parts of the verb could be practised, by asking *¿Cuántos alumnos viven en (una casa)?* If pupils have produced a pie chart or bar graph of their survey results the data should be easier to interpret.

2a Escucha y repite. Escribe los lugares en el plano en el orden correcto. (1–11) (AT1/1) [W1; L1]

✖ *Knowing about language*

Listening. Pupils listen to the names of places and find the words on the map. They should listen to the recording twice: the first time they repeat the words as they point to them on the map, reinforcing the relationship between sound and writing; they then write the names of the places in the correct order (1–11).

Answers

As tapescript.

Tapescript
1 – la ciudad
2 – el pueblo
3 – el centro
4 – las afueras
5 – el barrio
6 – el campo
7 – la costa
8 – el norte
9 – el sur
10 – el oeste
11 – el este

2b Indica dónde viven las personas en el plano (página 62). (AT3/2) [W1,5; S9; T1]

✖ *Reading for information and instructions – Level D*

Reading. Pupils read the descriptions in pairs and show their partner where on the map the young people live.

R Before attempting this activity, teachers may wish to practise the new words from the map, including the points of the compass. This would also be a good opportunity to introduce pupils to *está* and see if they can work out why it is used instead of *es* (for saying where places are).

Answers

Students should be indicating the following types of home/areas on the map.
1 Hugo: flat in a neighbourhood in the south of the city
2 Marina: a detached house on the outskirts, in a neighbourhood in the north of the city
3 Diego and Virginia: house in a town on the coast
4 Elisa: flat in an old block in the centre of the city
5 Montse: farm in the country

Starter 2: **Verb revision [W5; S3,5,9] (any time after introducing the verb *vivir*)**

Aims: To revise the present tense of the verb *vivir.* (Timing: 5 minutes)

Resources: Resource and Assessment File, page 73 (Starter 2)

Pairwork activity: Make an OHT using the master provided. Give pupils three minutes to write down the Spanish version that corresponds to the English written on the OHT, using the correct person of the verb. When correcting the exercise, ask pupils to justify their answers.

2c Con tu compañero/a, pregunta y contesta. ¿Dónde viven las personas? (AT2/3) [W1,5; S4,9; L4]

✖ *Speaking to convey information – Level D*

Speaking. In pairs, pupils ask and answer questions about the sort of home the people in activity 2b live in, and where their home is.

2d ¿Verdad (✓) o mentira (✗)? (AT3/2) [W1,5; S9]

✖ *Reading for information and instructions – Level D*

Reading. Pupils decide whether the statements about the people in activity 2b are true (*verdad*) or false (*mentira*).

✚ Teachers may wish to ask pupils to correct the sentences that are false, as an extension activity.

Answers

1 ✗	2 ✓	3 ✗	4 ✗	5 ✗

3a Haz un sondeo. Pregunta a tus compañeros/as de clase. (AT2/3) [W1,2,5; S4,9; L4]

✖ *Speaking and interacting with others – Level D/E*

módulo 4 En casa

Speaking. Pupils conduct a survey to find out where their classmates live.

Before attempting this activity, teachers may wish to make up a grid so that pupils can record their answers.

ICT activity

Pupils could enter the results of their survey on a spreadsheet such as *Microsoft Excel*, and produce a pie chart or bar graph to find out which type of home and location is the most or least common.

3b Escribe dónde vives tú y dónde viven tres o cuatro compañeros/as de clase. (AT4/2–3) [W1,2,5; S9]

✉ *Writing to establish and maintain personal contact – Level D/E*

Writing. Pupils use the data from the survey to write sentences or short paragraphs about where they and three or four classmates live. Teachers may wish to remind pupils to use the correct form of *vivir* and to restrict themselves to the vocabulary in the box, in order to practise these new words and structures as fully as possible.

Plenary

Classifying vocabulary. Ask pupils to use their memory or books to say words in Spanish that fall into the following categories: *sustantivos masculinos, sustantivos femeninos, preguntas, vocabulario sobre el tipo de casa, vocabulario sobre el lugar donde vives*. Check for understanding of the categories in English or give pupils examples to help. Pupils then repeat the exercise in pairs.

Cuaderno A, page 35

1 Empareja los dibujos con las frases. (AT3/2) [W1,5]

✉ *Knowing about language*

Reading. Pupils match up the sentences with the pictures.

Answers

| 1 b | 2 d | 3 c | 4 a |

2 Escribe una frase para cada dibujo. (AT4/2) [W1,2,5; S9]

✉ *Writing to exchange information and ideas – Level C*

Writing. Pupils use the writing frame to help them write a sentence about each picture.

Answers

1 Vivo en la costa.
2 Vivo en una ciudad.
3 Vivo en el campo.
4 Vivo en el sur de España.
5 Vivo en un pueblo.

Cuaderno B, page 35

1 Empareja los dibujos con las frases. (AT3/2) [W1,5]

✉ *Knowing about language*

Reading. Pupils match up the sentences with the pictures.

Answers

| 1 b | 2 c | 3 d | 4 a |

2a Rellena el cuadro para Ernesto. (AT3/3) [W1; S2]

✉ *Reading for information and instructions – Level C*

Reading. Pupils fill in the grid with the details about Ernesto from the speech bubble.

Answers

	Ernesto
ciudad	
pueblo	
barrio	✓
centro	
afueras	✓
campo	
norte/sur/oeste/este	norte
país	España

2b Escribe un texto similar para Carmela y Vicente. (AT4/2–3) [W1,2,5; S9]

✉ *Writing to exchange information and ideas – Level C*

Writing. Pupils write a sentence or short paragraph about Carmela and one about Vicente, using the details in the grid.

Answers

Me llamo Carmela. Vivo en un pueblo en el campo en el sur de México.
Me llamo Vicente. Vivo en un barrio en el centro de una ciudad en el oeste de Australia.

En casa — módulo 4

Skills, Resource and Assessment File, page 72 [W8; T4]

These activities provide pupils with opportunities to develop their use of word lists, and develop techniques for working out the meaning of words, as detailed in paragraph 3 of the Programme of Study.

módulo 4

2 ¿Cómo es tu casa?

(Pupil's Book pages 64–65)

Main topics

- Describing your house

Key Framework Objectives

- Compound sentences 7S6 (Reinforcement)
- Punctuation 7S8 (Reinforcement)
- Simple sentences 7S9 (Reinforcement)
- Reading aloud 7T2 (Reinforcement)

Key language

¿Cómo es tu casa/piso?
Mi casa es muy/bastante grande.
Mi piso es antiguo.
Mi chalet es de tres plantas.
Mi casa es adosada.

acogedor(a)	grande
adosado/a	moderno/a
antiguo/a	nuevo/a
bonito/a	pequeño/a
cómodo/a	reformado/a

¿Cuántas plantas/habitaciones tiene?
Tiene cinco habitaciones.
(No) Me gusta porque es moderno/a.

Resources

Cassette B, side 2
CD 2, track 11
Cuaderno A and B, page 36

Starter 1: Squashed sentences [W4; S1,8; T2; L6]

Aims: To write simple sentences accurately and to reinforce knowledge of punctuation and spelling. To introduce new adjectives (*grande, pequeño, nuevo, antiguo*). (Timing: 5–10 minutes)

Pairwork activity: Write up sentences using the language grid from page 63 of the Pupil's Book, but adding the adjectives listed above, with no punctuation or spacing, e.g. *vivoenunacasagrande*. Give pupils two minutes each to say the sentences to their partner. Ask different pupils to read out the sentences to the class. Pupils write down the sentences. Remind them about adding the correct punctuation. Pupils repeat this with three other sentences. Ask pupils to identify the new words and to categorise them.

1a Empareja las casas con las frases. (AT3/2) [W1,4,5,8; S9; T4]

✄ *Knowing about language*

Reading. Pupils match up the sentences in the speech bubbles with the pictures of different types of houses.

R Before attempting this activity, teachers may wish to revise the structure *es* + adjective that pupils have already encountered in describing people. The adjectives encountered in this activity could also be introduced and practised, or pupils could work out the meanings for themselves or look up new words in a dictionary or glossary.

Answers

| 1 b | 2 c | 3 f | 4 a | 5 e | 6 d |

1b Escucha y comprueba tus respuestas. (AT1/2) [W1,5; L3]

✄ *Knowing about language*

Listening. Pupils listen to the recording and check their answers to activity 1a.

Tapescript

a – Mi piso es antiguo.
b – Mi casa es grande. Tiene ocho habitaciones.
c – Mi piso es pequeño.
d – Mi chalet es de tres plantas.
e – Mi casa es adosada.
f – Mi casa es nueva.

1c Escucha otra vez y repite. Pon atención a la pronunciación. (AT1/2, AT2/2) [W1,6; T2; L1]

✄ *Knowing about language*

Listening/Speaking. Pupils listen to the recording again and repeat the phrases, paying attention to the relationship between sound and writing.

Tapescript

As for activity 1b

2a Identifica las casas. (AT1/3) [W4; S9; L3]

✄ *Listening for information and instructions – Level D*

Listening. Pupils listen to the recording and identify the houses described.

Before attempting this activity, teachers may wish to read through the vocabulary box and ensure that pupils understand all the words.

Answers

| 1 d | 2 c | 3 a | 4 b |

Tapescript

1 – ¿Cómo es tu casa?
– Es grande.
– ¿Cuántas plantas tiene?
– Es de tres plantas.
– ¿Cuántas habitaciones tiene?

En casa — módulo 4

– Tiene siete habitaciones.
–¿Te gusta?
– Sí, me gusta porque es moderna.

2 – ¿Cómo es tu piso?
– Mi piso es pequeño y antiguo.
–¿Cuántas habitaciones tiene?
– Tiene tres.
–¿Te gusta tu piso?
– Sí, me gusta porque es bonito.

3 – ¿Cómo es tu casa?
– Es adosada.
–¿De cuántas plantas es?
– Es de dos plantas y cinco habitaciones.
–¿Te gusta?
– Sí, porque es grande.

4 – ¿Cómo es tu piso?
– Es bastante grande.
–¿Cuántas habitaciones tiene?
– Tiene cinco.
–¿Te gusta tu piso?
– Sí, me gusta porque es antiguo.

2b Con tu compañero/a, pregunta y contesta. (AT2/3–4) [W1,4,5; S4,5,9; L4]

Speaking and interacting with others – Level D/E

Speaking. Pupils work in pairs to ask and answer questions about the houses in activity 2a, asking what the house is like, how many floors it has, how many rooms it has, and whether or not they like it.

Starter 2: **Shrink-me sentences** [S2,3,9]

Aims: To look at sentence construction and the essential part of a sentence. (Timing: 5 minutes)

Activity: Copy the following sentences onto the board or a transparency: *Manuel y su hermano viven en un piso pequeño en una ciudad; Natalia vive en una casa antigua de dos plantas en el campo.* Reveal the first sentence and ask pupils to take away words that would not render the sentence nonsense. For example, pupils may point out that you cannot take away the people as the verb would be incorrect, or that the sentence would still make sense if *pequeño* were removed. Then reveal the second sentence and give pupils one minute to 'shrink' it, in pairs.

3a Lee las descripciones de las casas de Neus y Eduard. Busca las palabras que no conoces en el diccionario. (AT3/4) [W1; T1,4]

Knowing about language

Reading. Pupils read the descriptions of Neus and Eduard's houses and look up any new words in a glossary or dictionary.

Teachers may wish to play a game to check that pupils have picked out and understood all of the key words. This could be hangman, *¿Cómo se dice (renovated)?*, word bingo, etc.

3b ¿Verdad (✓) o mentira (✗)? (AT3/4) [W1; S9; T1]

Reading for information and instructions – Level D

Reading. Pupils reread the descriptions of the houses in activity 3a and decide whether the sentences are true (*verdad*) or false (*mentira*).

Answers

1 ✗	2 ✗	3 ✗	4 ✓	5 ✓	6 ✗	7 ✗
8 ✗						

3c Con tu compañero/a, pregunta y contesta. (AT2/4) [W1,4,5; S4,6,9; L4]

Speaking to convey information – Level D

Speaking. Pupils work in pairs to ask and answer questions similar to those in activity 2b about Neus and Eduard's houses.

Before attempting this activity, teachers may wish to revise the parts of the verb *vivir* on page 63.

Answers

Neus:	**Eduard:**
Vive en las afueras.	Vive en el centro de la ciudad.
Es una casa adosada.	Es un piso en un bloque antiguo.
Es de tres plantas.	Es de cinco plantas.
Tiene ocho habitaciones.	Tiene cuatro habitaciones.
Le gusta porque es muy bonita.	Le gusta porque es antiguo.

3d Escribe una descripción de tu casa. (AT4/3–4) [W1; S6,9; T6]

Writing to establish and maintain personal contact – Level D

Writing. Pupils use the writing frame to help them write a description of their own home.

Plenary

Grow-me sentences. Remind pupils about basic sentence construction. Then ask pupils to embellish a basic sentence by adding adjectives, connectives, etc., e.g. *Vivo en una casa* or *Vicente y su hermana viven en una granja*. This is an opportunity to revisit adjectival agreements, verb endings and word order. Once the whole class has looked at a sentence, ask pupils to work in teams to make the longest possible sentence that makes sense, based on one very basic sentence.

módulo 4 — En casa

Cuaderno A, page 36

1 Busca y escribe las palabras. (AT3/1, AT4/1) [W1,7]

✉ *Reading for enjoyment*

Reading/Writing. Pupils write down the 10 words contained in the word snake.

Answers

1 jardín	2 garaje	3 habitaciones	4 plantas
5 grande	6 pequeño	7 antiguo	8 adosado
9 nuevo	10 moderno		

2a Empareja las descripciones con los dibujos apropiados. (AT3/3) [W1,5; S9; T3]

✉ *Reading for information and instructions – Level D*

Reading. Pupils read the descriptions and match them up with the appropriate picture.

Answers

1 b   2 a

2b Completa la descripción de la casa que falta con las palabras apropiadas. (AT3/3) [W1,4; S1,6]

✉ *Knowing about language*

Reading. Pupils use the words in the box to complete the paragraph.

Answers

Es una casa adosada. Es de tres plantas. Tiene ocho habitaciones. Tiene jardín pero no tiene garaje. Es nueva y bastante grande.

Cuaderno B, page 36

1a Empareja las descripciones con los dibujos apropiados. (AT3/3) [W1,7]

✉ *Reading for information and instructions – Level D*

Reading. Pupils read the descriptions and match them up with the appropriate picture.

Answers

1 b   2 a

1b Contesta a las preguntas. (AT3/3) [W1,2,5; S4,9]

✉ *Reading for information and instructions – Level D*

Reading. Pupils answer the questions about the homes in activity 1a.

Answers

1 El chalet de Esteban es de dos plantas.
2 Tiene cinco habitaciones.
3 Le gusta porque es moderno.
4 El piso de Juana es muy pequeño.
5 No tiene jardín.

1c Completa la descripción de la casa 'c' con las palabras apropiadas. (AT3/3) [W1,4; S1,6]

✉ *Knowing about language*

Reading. Pupils use the words in the box to complete the paragraph.

Answers

Es una casa adosada. Es de tres plantas. Tiene ocho habitaciones. Tiene jardín pero no tiene garaje. Es nueva y bastante grande.

2 Mira el dibujo y escribe una descripción. (AT4/3) [S9; T5,6]

✉ *Writing to exchange information and ideas – Level D*

Writing. Pupils write a description of the house pictured.

módulo 4

3 El plano de mi casa

(Pupil's Book pages 66–67)

Main topics
- Describing the rooms in your house

Key Framework Objectives
- Verbs present 7W5 (Part-launch. See also 1.3)
- Learning about words 7W7 (Launch)
- Texts as prompts 7T6 (Reinforcement)
- Spontaneous talk 7L5 (Reinforcement)

Key language
En mi casa/piso hay una cocina.
En la planta baja hay un salón.
El la primera planta hay tres dormitorios.
Hay un jardín.
Tiene un ático/un ascensor/un sótano.

aseo(s)
cocina(s)
comedor(es)
(cuarto(s) de) baño
despacho(s)
dormitorio(s)
escalera(s)
pasillo(s)
salón/salones
salón-comedor(es)
garaje(s)
jardín/jardines
terraza(s)

Resources
Cassette B, side 2
CD 2, track 12
Cuaderno A and B, page 37
Starter 1, Resource and Assessment File, page 73
Hoja de trabajo 1, Resource and Assessment File, page 67
OHTs 17 and 18: rooms in a house

Starter 1: Missing vowels [W1,7]

Aims: To introduce rooms of the house (*la cocina, el salón, el comedor, el (cuarto de) baño, el dormitorio, el despacho, el aseo, el pasillo, la escalera, la terraza, el garaje, el jardín*) and to focus on the accurate spelling and gender of the new vocabulary. (Timing: 10 minutes)

Resources: Resource and Assessment File, page 73 (Starter 1)

Activity: Make an OHT (or worksheet) using the master provided. Put up the OHT with the first word revealed, and ask pupils to complete the word using the *Las habitaciones* box on page 66 of the Pupil's Book.

R Lower-ability pupils could be shown the words one at a time.

+ Higher-ability pupils could be given one minute to study the words and then 30 seconds to complete as much of the worksheet as possible. Repeat three or four times until the vocabulary list is complete.

1a Escucha y escribe las habitaciones en el orden correcto. (AT1/1, AT3/1) [W1,4]

✂ *Knowing about language*

Listening/Reading. Pupils listen to the recording and write down the numbers of the rooms in the order they hear the rooms mentioned, showing that they recognise the link between sounds and writing.

R Teachers may wish to introduce the names of the rooms in the house first, using flashcards or OHT, or the picture and words on page 66. The question *¿Qué número es (la cocina)?* could be asked to get pupils to recognise the names of the rooms, followed by questions such as *¿Qué habitación es el número (3)?*

Answers
5, 1, 12, 2, 3, 4, 7, 8, 9, 6, 10, 11

Tapescript
– el dormitorio
– la cocina
– el jardín
– el salón
– el comedor
– el cuarto de baño
– el aseo
– el pasillo
– la escalera
– el despacho
– la terraza
– el garaje

1b Escucha y repite. Pon atención a la pronunciación. (AT1/1, AT2/1) [W1,4; T2; L1]

✂ *Knowing about language*

Listening/Speaking. Pupils listen to the recording and repeat the names of the rooms. They should follow the names of the rooms in the box, in order to reinforce the relationship between sound and writing.

Tapescript
– la cocina
– el salón
– el comedor
– el cuarto de baño
– el dormitorio
– el despacho
– el aseo
– el pasillo
– la escalera
– la terraza
– el garaje
– el jardín

módulo 4 En casa

1c Con tu compañero/a, pregunta y contesta. (AT2/2) [W1,5; S4,9; L4]

✖ *Speaking and interacting with others – Level D*

Speaking. Pupils work in pairs to ask and say the names of the rooms on the plan.

2a Escucha y empareja las casas de las personas con los planos. (1–3) (AT1/3) [W1,2,5; S9; L3]

✖ *Listening for information and instructions – Level D*

Listening. Pupils listen to the descriptions of the three homes and match up each description with the appropriate plan.

R Teachers may wish to brainstorm descriptions of the plans with pupils before attempting this activity, and compare this with the descriptions on the recording. The language support box and *¡OJO!* box supply the relevant vocabulary and structures.

Answers

| 1 c | 2 a | 3 b |

Tapescript

1 En mi piso hay dos dormitorios, una cocina, un salón-comedor y un cuarto de baño.
2 Mi casa es de dos plantas. En la planta baja hay una cocina, un salón, un comedor, un cuarto de baño y un dormitorio. En la primera planta hay otro dormitorio, un aseo y un salón pequeño.
3 Mi casa es también de dos plantas. En la planta baja hay una cocina, un salón grande, un cuarto de baño y una terraza. En la primera planta hay dos dormitorios.

2b Con tu compañero/a, describe las casas de las personas en **2a**. (AT2/2–3) [W1,2,5; S4,9; L4]

✖ *Speaking and interacting with others – Level D/E*

Speaking. Pupils take turns to ask and answer questions about the plans in activity 2a.

➕ Teachers may wish to extend pupils by allowing them to ask more open-ended questions, such as *¿Qué hay en la casa c? ¿Qué hay en la primera planta?*

> **Starter 2:** La casa de Jennifer López [W1,4,5; S1,3,7,9; L5]
>
> *Aims:* To revise rooms of the house and how to formulate plurals for nouns and adjectives; to expose students to the preterite tense (*Fui a la casa de J-Lo y vi ... un(a), dos, tres, cuatro, etc ...*); to build on memory skills. (Timing: 5–10 minutes)
>
> *Activity:* Start with a quick revision of plural forms, asking questions such as *¿Cómo se dice* 'two bedrooms' *en español?*. Then explain to pupils that they are going to play a memory game similar to 'I went to market and I bought ... '. However, you have been to Jennifer López's house and you are telling your friends what you saw. The use of the preterite tense here is to expose pupils (in the form of set phrases) to the past tense as required by Words 5 of the Modern Languages Framework. Play an example game as a whole class: *Fui a la casa de J-Lo y vi ocho dormitorios; Fui a la casa de J-Lo y vi ocho dormitorios y dos cocinas; Fui a la casa de J-Lo y vi ocho dormitorios, dos cocinas y un jardín,* etc. Then pupils divide into groups of four and play the game themselves.

3a Escucha y repite. Pon atención a la pronunciación. (AT1/1, AT2/1) [W1,4; T2; L1]

✖ *Knowing about language*

Listening/Speaking. Pupils listen to the recording and repeat the names of the floors. They should follow the names of the floors in the boxes, in order to reinforce the relationship between sound and writing.

Pupils should already be familiar with the terms *planta baja* and *primera planta*.

Tapescript

– el sótano
– la planta baja
– la primera planta
– la segunda planta
– la tercera planta
– la cuarta planta
– la quinta planta
– el ático
– el ascensor

3b ¿Qué personas se mencionan y dónde viven? (1–8) (AT1/2) [W1,2,5; S9; L3]

✖ *Listening for information – Level D*

Listening. Pupils write down the names of the people or families mentioned on the recording as well as the floor they live on. They could write their answers in two columns headed *nombre* and *planta* if preferred.

Answers

1 Juan Oeste Zárate – la tercera planta
2 Don Ajamil Ferreiro – el ático
3 Concha Matamala – la quinta planta
4 la familia Martín Martín – la segunda planta
5 la familia Pardo González – la planta baja
6 Doña Pérez de Santos – la primera planta
7 la señorita Urdangarín – la cuarta planta
8 Señor Aguirre Castro – la cuarta planta

En casa — módulo 4

Tapescript

1 – ¿Dónde vive Juan Oeste Zárate?
– Vive en la tercera planta.
2 – ¿Dónde vive don Ajamil Ferreiro?
– Vive en el ático.
3 – ¿Dónde vive Concha Matamala?
– Vive en la quinta planta.
4 – ¿Dónde vive la familia Martín Martín?
– Vive en la segunda planta.
5 – ¿Dónde vive la familia Pardo González?
– Vive en la planta baja.
6 – ¿Dónde vive doña Pérez de Santos?
– Vive en la primera planta.
7 – ¿Dónde vive la señorita Urdangarín?
– Vive en la cuarta planta.
8 – ¿Y dónde vive el señor Aguirre Castro?
– Vive en la cuarta planta también.

3c Con tu compañero/a, pregunta y contesta. (AT2/2) [W1,5; S4,9; L4]

✉ *Speaking and interacting with others – Level D*

Speaking. Pupils take it in turns to ask their partner questions about where the people from activity 3a live.

4a Copia y completa. (AT3/4, AT4/2) [W1, T1]

✉ *Knowing about language*

Reading/Writing. Pupils copy the description of a house, replacing the pictures with the appropriate words.

Answers

casa, comedor, cocina, aseo, pasillo, escaleras, cuarto de baño, hermanas, despacho, dormitorio, jardín, terraza, garaje

4b Escribe una descripción de la casa de tus sueños. (AT4/3–4) [W1,2,5; S9; T5]

✉ *Writing to exchange information and ideas – Level D/E/F*

Writing. Pupils write a description of their dream house.

🖱 ICT activity

Pupils could use the Internet to find pictures and descriptions of houses, and then use either a word-processing package or desk-top publishing software to write a description of the house as in activity 4a, or write a more factual description as in an estate agent's description.

Plenary

At the beginning of the lesson explain to two students (of similar ability) that you will be asking them to summarise the main points of the lesson at the end of the class. They take it in terms to cover what has been learned, using the board or projector. The rest of the class discusses the summary and corrects any mistakes and adds any information that may have been omitted.

Cuaderno A, page 37

1 Completa los nombres de las habitaciones con *a, e, i, í, o, ó o u*. (AT3/1, AT4/1) [W1,4,7; S8]

✉ *Knowing about language*

Reading/Writing. Pupils complete the names of the rooms by filling in the missing vowels.

Answers

1 la cocina	**2** el salón	**3** el comedor
4 el cuarto de baño	**5** el dormitorio	**6** el despacho
7 el aseo	**8** el pasillo	**9** la escalera
10 la terraza	**11** el garaje	**12** el jardín

2 Lee la descripción y escribe los nombres de las habitaciones en el plano. (AT3/3) [W1,4,5; T3]

✉ *Reading for information and instructions – Level C/D*

Reading. Pupils read the description of the house and use the information to label the rooms on the plan.

Answers

a el despacho	**b** el dormitorio	**c** el dormitorio	
d el aseo	**e** el comedor	**f** el pasillo	**g** las escaleras
h el dormitorio	**i** el cuarto de baño	**j** la cocina	
k el jardín	**l** la terraza	**m** el salón	**n** el garaje

3 Dibuja un plano de tu casa y escribe una descripción. (AT4/2–3) [W1,2,5; S9; T6]

✉ *Writing to establish and maintain personal contact – Level C*

Writing. Pupils draw and label a plan of their own home and write a description of it, using the writing frame.

módulo 4 — En casa

Cuaderno B, page 37

1 Completa los nombres de las habitaciones con *a, e, i, í, o, ó o u*. (AT3/1, AT4/1) [W1,4,7; S8]

✉ *Knowing about language*

Reading/Writing. Pupils complete the names of the rooms by filling in the missing vowels.

Answers

1 la cocina	**2** el salón	**3** el comedor
4 el cuarto de baño	**5** el dormitorio	**6** el despacho
7 el aseo	**8** el pasillo	**9** la escalera
10 la terraza		

2 Lee la descripción y escribe los nombres de las habitaciones en el plano. (AT3/4) [W1,4,5; T3]

✉ *Reading for information and instructions – Level D*

Reading. Pupils read the description of the house and use the information to label the rooms on the plan.

Answers

a el despacho	**b** el dormitorio	**c** el dormitorio
d el aseo	**e** el comedor	**f** el pasillo
g las escaleras	**h** el dormitorio	**i** el cuarto de baño
j el jardín	**k** la terraza	**l** la cocina
m el salón	**n** el garaje	

3 Dibuja un plano de tu casa y escribe una descripción. (AT4/2–4) [W1,2,5; S9; T6]

✉ *Writing to establish and maintain personal contact – Level D/E/F*

Writing. Pupils draw and label a plan of their own home and write a description of it.

Hoja de trabajo 1, page 67 [W5; L4]

Pairwork activity for pupils to practise asking what floor people live on, and answering using ordinal numbers. Pupils need to use the questions and names on their pairwork card to complete their floor plan of a block of flats.

módulo 4

4 Mi dormitorio

(Pupil's Book pages 68–69)

Main topics
- Describing your bedroom

Key Framework Objectives
- Everyday words 7W1 (Reinforcement)
- Letters and sounds 7W6 (Reinforcement)
- Stories and songs 7C4 (Reinforcement)

Grammar
- Prepositions: *delante (de), encima (de) …*

Key language
debajo (de)
delante (de)
detrás (de)
encima (de)
entre
a la derecha (de)
a la izquierda (de)
al lado (de)
¿Qué hay en tu dormitorio?
En mi dormitorio hay una cama.
la alfombra
el armario
la cama
las cortinas
el equipo de música
las estanterías
la lámpara
la mesa
el ordenador
la pared
los pósters
la puerta
la silla
la televisión
la ventana

Resources
Cassette B, side 2
CD 2, track 13
Cuaderno A and B, page 38
Starter 2, Resource and Assessment File, page 74
Hojas de trabajo 2, 3 and 4, Resource and Assessment File, pages 68, 69 and 70
OHTs 19 and 20: bedroom items, prepositions

Starter 1: ¿Qué soy yo? [T1]

Aims: To introduce the vocabulary for bedroom furniture and to develop reading skills. (Timing: 5–10 minutes)

Activity: Refer pupils to the picture at the top of page 68 of the Pupil's Book. Explain that you will describe a bedroom object in Spanish and they must work out which object it is (a–o) and write it down. Set a time limit of one to two minutes for each clue. Read out the following clues: 1 *Soy grande y rojo* (answer: *la cama*); 2 *Soy eléctrica y roja y estoy cerca de los pósters* (answer: *la lámpara*); 3 *Tengo una pantalla, un ratón y un teclado y soy amarillo* (answer: *el ordenador*). Pupils can then use the list of Spanish words for bedroom objects next to the picture on page 68 and try to pronounce these new words in Spanish.

R For less-able students, write up the clues as well as saying them and revise colours before starting the exercise.

1a Escucha y escribe las cosas en el orden correcto. (1–15) (AT1/1) [W1,2,4,6]

✶ *Knowing about language*

Listening. Pupils listen to the recording and write down the bedroom items in the order they hear them mentioned, showing that they recognise the link between sound and writing.

R Teachers may wish to introduce the names of the bedroom items first, using flashcards or OHT, or the picture and words on page 68. The question *¿Qué letra es (la silla)?* could be asked to get pupils to recognise the names of the items, and then *¿Qué cosa es la letra (h)?*

Answers

1 f	2 d	3 a	4 b	5 e	6 c	7 g
8 n	9 h	10 o	11 j	12 l	13 k	14 i
15 m						

Tapescript

1 – la cama
2 – la silla
3 – el armario
4 – las estanterías
5 – los pósters
6 – la mesa
7 – la lámpara
8 – la alfombra
9 – el ordenador
10 – las cortinas
11 – la televisión
12 – la ventana
13 – el equipo de música
14 – la puerta
15 – la pared

1b Escucha otra vez y repite. Pon atención a la pronunciación. (AT1/1, AT2/1) [W1,4; L1]

✶ *Knowing about language*

Listening/Speaking. Pupils listen to the recording for activity 1a again and repeat the names of the bedroom items. They should follow the names of the items in the box, in order to reinforce the relationship between sound and writing.

módulo 4 — En casa

Tapescript
As for activity 1a

1c Con tu compañero/a, indica un dibujo en **1a**. Tu compañero/a dice el nombre apropiado. (AT2/2) [W1,4,5]

✣ *Speaking and interacting with others – Level C/D*

Speaking. Pupils work in pairs to ask for and say the names of the items in the bedroom.

R Before attempting this activity, teachers may wish to revise *es* and *son* with the class.

1d Con tu compañero/a, pregunta y contesta. (AT2/2) [W1,2,5; S4,9; L4]

✣ *Speaking and interacting with others – Level D*

Speaking. Pupils work in pairs to ask and answer questions on what there is in their own bedroom.

R Before attempting this activity, teachers may wish to revise *hay* with the class.

2a Escucha y repite. Pon atención a la pronunciación. (AT1/1) [W1,2; L1]

✣ *Knowing about language*

Listening. Pupils listen to the recording and point to the prepositions in the order that they are mentioned, showing that they recognise the link between sound and writing. They should then listen a second time and repeat the prepositions, paying attention to pronunciation.

R Before attempting this activity, teachers may wish to introduce the prepositions in a variety of ways. Using a poster or OHT, teachers could try a 'Where's Wally?' type activity, showing the different prepositions (*delante de la mesa, entre la silla y la pared*). Alternatively, pupils could illustrate these prepositions, for example by saying where they are sitting (*Ahmed está entre Dionne y Ben*) then asking pupils to guess who is being spoken about (*está a la derecha de Lizzie*).

Tapescript
– delante de
– detrás de
– encima de
– debajo de
– al lado de
– a la derecha de
– a la izquierda de
– entre

2b Con tu compañero/a, mueve tus manos a la orden. (AT2/1) [W2; L4]

✣ *Speaking and interacting with others – Level C/D*

Speaking. In pairs, pupils take turns to give each other instructions on where to put their hands.

🎲 This could be practised as a whole-class activity, with some of the less obvious instructions, such as *entre* (pupils could put hands between their knees) first being agreed. Teachers may wish to use this as an opportunity to play a 'Simon Says' type game with the whole class.

3a Dibuja un plano del dormitorio de Emilia. (AT3/4) [W2,5; T1]

✣ *Reading for enjoyment – Level E*

Reading. Pupils read the description of Emilia's bedroom and draw a plan based on the details and locations given.

Teachers may wish pupils to compare their plans with their partner and discuss any differences, referring back to the text, before checking the answers with the whole class.

Answers

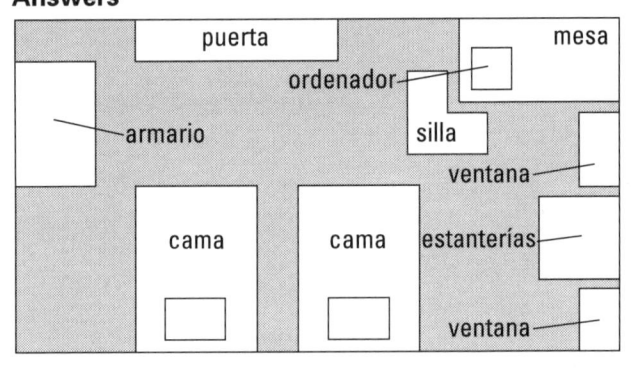

puerta		mesa
	ordenador	
armario	silla	
		ventana
cama	cama	estanterías
		ventana

Starter 2: Accents and pronunciation [W1,6,7]

Aims: To revise bedroom furniture and other vocabulary from pages 68–69 and to develop pupils' knowledge of accents and pronunciation. (Timing: 5 minutes)

Resources: Resource and Assessment File, page 74 (Starter 2)

Activity: Make an OHT using the master provided. Reveal Column 1 of the OHT, without accents, one by one and ask pupils to read out each word. If a word is pronounced incorrectly, say the word. Ask pupils if they think the words are spelled correctly. If pupils do not spot the missing accents, point them out. Ask for volunteers to come to the front and as you say the words they must try to put the accent in the correct place on the transparency. Reveal Column 2, the words with accents, and compare the two. Ask for volunteers to try and pronounce the difference in the words if the accent has been positioned incorrectly, e.g. *lampára* versus *lámpara*.

En casa — módulo 4

3b Mira el dibujo. ¿Verdad (✓) o mentira (✗)? (AT3/2) [W1,2,5; S9]

✉ *Reading for information and instructions – Level D*

Reading. Pupils use the picture to help them decide whether the sentences are true (*verdad*) or false (*mentira*).

Answers

| 1 ✓ | 2 ✗ | 3 ✓ | 4 ✗ | 5 ✓ | 6 ✗ | 7 ✗ |

3c Corrige las frases en **3b** que son falsas. (AT4/2) [W2,5; S3,9]

✉ *Reading for information and instructions – Level D*

Writing. Pupils correct the sentences that are false in activity 3b.

✚ As an extension activity, pupils could make up five sentences of their own about the picture, some true, some false, for their partner or the rest of class. [S9]

Answers

2 Encima de la mesa hay un ordenador.
4 Delante de la mesa hay una silla.
6 En las paredes hay pósters.
7 Los muebles no son todos marrones. La silla es rosa.

4a Escucha y lee la canción. Contesta a las preguntas. Busca las palabras que no conoces en el diccionario. (AT1/4, AT3/4) [W1,2,5; T4; C4]

✉ *Listening for enjoyment*

Listening/Reading. Teachers will need to decide whether to attempt this activity as a reading or listening activity first, and the sequence in which to attempt the activities. The suggested sequence is as follows.

Pupils listen to the song and follow the text to show they understand the relationship between sound and writing.

The teacher may wish to then repeat the song at this stage so that pupils can sing along.

Pupils reread the song and note down any new words, then find the meanings in a glossary or dictionary.

Pupils then answer the five comprehension questions to check they have understood the song, before singing along to the song one last time.

Answers

1 Al lado de la cama hay la butaca.
2 En las ventanas hay las persianas.
3 La televisión está delante de la cama.
4 En la estantería hay los libros.
5 Enfrente del armario hay el escritorio.

Tapescript

Enfrente del armario
Está el escritorio.
Al lado de la cama
Está la butaca.
Delante de la silla
Está la mesa.
Y en la mesa está el ordenador.

Mi lugar privado
Es mi dormitorio.
Mi lugar privado
Donde voy si estoy cansado.

En las paredes
Están los carteles.
En las ventanas
Están las persianas.
En la estantería
Están los libros míos.
Y el espejo está en el tocador.

Mi lugar privado
Es mi dormitorio.
Mi lugar privado
Donde voy para estar relajado.

Enfrente de la puerta
Está la butaca.
Delante de la cama
Está la televisión.
A la izquierda del lavabo
Está mi equipo.
Y sobre la mesilla está mi reloj.

Mi lugar privado
Es mi dormitorio.
Mi lugar privado
Donde voy para estar tranquilo.

4b Escribe una descripción de tu dormitorio. (AT4/2–4) [W1,2,5; S9; T5]

✉ *Writing to establish and maintain personal contact – Level D/E/F*

Writing. Pupils write a description of their own bedroom. Teachers may wish to provide a writing frame or list of structures to use, which should include *es, son, hay, está* + location.

Plenary

Recap on prepositions by playing *¿Dónde está el caramelo?* with the class. The class should close their eyes while you hide a sweet (or any small object). Pupils must then guess *¿Dónde está el caramelo?* using the prepositions they have learned. This can be played several times, depending on the time available. Alternatively, pupils could play the game in groups.

módulo 4 — En casa

Cuaderno A, page 38

1 Rellena los espacios en blanco con las palabras apropiadas. (AT3/3) [W1; S2]

✳ *Knowing about language*

Reading. Pupils choose the appropriate words to replace the pictures and complete the description of a bedroom.

Answers

cama, armario, televisión, mesa, ordenador, silla, paredes, ventanas, cortinas, puerta

2 ¿Verdad (✓) o mentira (✗)? (AT3/2) [W1,2; S2]

✳ *Reading for information and instructions – Level C/D*

Reading. Pupils look at the picture of the room and decide whether the sentences are true (*verdad*) or false (*mentira*).

Answers

1 ✗	2 ✗	3 ✓	4 ✓	5 ✗	6 ✗	7 ✓

3 Dibuja un plano de tu dormitorio y escribe una descripción. (AT4/2–4) [W1,2; S9; T5]

✳ *Writing to establish and maintain personal contact – Level D*

Writing. Pupils draw and label a plan of their bedroom and then write a description of it.

Cuaderno B, page 38

1a Rellena los espacios en blanco con las palabras apropiadas. (AT3/3) [W1; S2]

✳ *Knowing about language*

Reading. Pupils choose the appropriate words to replace the pictures and complete the description of a bedroom.

Answers

cama, armario, estanterías, equipo de música, televisión, mesa, ordenador, lámpara, silla, alfombra, paredes, pósters, ventanas, cortinas, puerta

1b Lee la descripción del dormitorio otra vez. Dibuja las cosas que faltan y colorea las cosas con los colores apropiados. (AT3/3) [W1; S2]

✳ *Reading for information and instructions – Level D*

Reading. Pupils reread the description of the bedroom in activity 1a, draw pictures of the missing items (e.g. *mesa*) and colour in the items where the colour is mentioned (e.g. colour the rug blue).

Answers

Items to be coloured in are as follows: rug – blue, walls – yellow, curtains – blue, door – green

1c ¿Verdad (✓) o mentira (✗)? Mira el dibujo y corrige las frases que son falsas. (AT3/2, AT4/2) [W1,2; S2,3]

✳ *Reading for information and instructions – Level D*

Reading/Writing. Pupils look at the picture of the room and decide whether the sentences are true (*verdad*) or false (*mentira*). They should then correct the sentences that are false.

Answers

1 ✗ – El armario está al lado de la ventana/de la cama.
2 ✗ – La mesa está delante de la cama.
3 ✗ – La cama está al lado de la silla/detrás de la mesa.
4 ✗ – Las cortinas están detrás de la cama.
5 ✗ – La puerta está a la derecha de la cama/silla.
6 ✓

Hojas de trabajo 2–3, pages 68–69 [W1]

15 picture cards and 15 corresponding labels which can be used for matching activities.

Hoja de trabajo 4, page 70 [L4]

Pairwork activity for pupils to practise the question ¿*Dónde está …* ? and use prepositions to find out and draw where the television is.

módulo 4

5 *Por la mañana*
(Pupil's Book pages 70–71)

Main topics
- Talking about your daily routine

Key Framework Objectives
- High-frequency words 7W2 (Reinforcement)
- Word order 7S1 (Reinforcement)
- Reading aloud 7T2 (Reinforcement)
- Sound patterns 7L1 (Reinforcement)

Grammar
- Reflexive verbs: *levantarse, despertarse, vestirse*

Key language
¿A qué hora te despiertas/te levantas?
Me despierto a las siete.
No me despierto temprano.
Me levanto tarde.
Primero me ducho y me visto.
No me peino, pero me lavo los dientes.
¿A qué hora desayunas?
Los fines de semana desayuno a las ocho y media.
Desayuno cereales, pan tostado y un vaso de leche.

Resources
Cassette B, side 2
CD 2, track 14
Cuaderno A and B, page 39
Grammar, Resource and Assessment File, page 71
OHTs 21 and 22: daily routines, times

Starter 1: Noughts and crosses [W1,2; L1,4]

Aims: To revise numbers 1–30 and how to tell the time (*y / menos cinco, diez, cuarto, media,* etc.). (Timing: 5 minutes)

Activity: Draw up a noughts and crosses grid on the board or projector. Fill the grid with times as per a digital watch (6:20, 12:30, etc.). Divide the class into two teams and play the game. If a pupil gives the correct time they get their 0 or X in that square. Replace times that pupils find easy for more difficult ones for the next game, but remember to use times that feature most for daily routine sentences. If there is sufficient time, pupils can copy the grid and play the game with a partner.

1a Escucha y repite. (AT1/1) [W1,2; L1]

✉ *Knowing about language*

Listening. Pupils listen to the recording and follow the text in their Pupil's Book to show they understand the link between sound and writing. Teachers may wish to play the recording a second time for the pupils to repeat, paying attention to their pronunciation.

R Teachers may wish to introduce the new expressions before attempting this activity. As an alternative to using flashcards or OHT, teachers could do a mime for each expression, and then get their pupils to play 'Simon Says', acting out the mimes to show they have understood the expressions.

Tapescript
a – *Me despierto.*
b – *Me levanto.*
c – *Me ducho.*
d – *Me visto.*
e – *Me peino.*
f – *Desayuno.*
g – *Me lavo los dientes.*

1b Escucha y escribe el orden. (1–7) (AT1/1) [W1,2; S7; L3]

✉ *Knowing about language*

Listening. Pupils listen to the recording and write down the letters of the expressions from activity 1a in the order they hear them. Teachers may prefer pupils to write the actual expression and use this as an opportunity to reinforce the sound and writing link.

Answers

| a, b, f, c, d, e, g |

Tapescript
1 – *Me despierto.*
2 – *Me levanto.*
3 – *Primero desayuno.*
4 – *Después me ducho.*
5 – *Me visto.*
6 – *Me peino.*
7 – *Me lavo los dientes.*

2 Con tu compañero/a, habla de tu rutina diaria. (AT2/1–2) [W1,2; S9]

✉ *Speaking to convey information – Level C/D*

Speaking. In pairs, pupils take turns to talk about their daily routine, using the expressions from activity 1a.

Before attempting this activity, teachers could ask pupils to pick out the reflexive verbs from the seven expressions, and formulate their own rule for the difference between reflexive and non-reflexive verbs.

3 Escribe la hora que se menciona en cada respuesta. (AT1/2) [W2; S4,7; L3]

✉ *Listening for information and instructions – Level D*

módulo 4 En casa

Listening. Pupils listen and write down the time at which the boy says he does each activity illustrated.

R Teachers may wish to revise the time before attempting this activity: pupils last encountered time in Module 3, in the context of talking about their school day.

Answers

| 1 6.30 | 2 6.45 | 3 7.10 | 4 7.20 | 5 7.30 |

Tapescript

1 – ¿A qué hora te despiertas por la mañana?
 – Me despierto a las seis y media.
2 – ¿A qué hora te levantas?
 – Me levanto a las siete menos cuarto.
3 – ¿A qué hora te vistes?
 – Me visto a las siete y diez.
4 – ¿A qué hora desayunas?
 – Desayuno a las siete y veinte.
5 – ¿A qué hora te lavas los dientes?
 – Me lavo los dientes a las siete y media.

Starter 10: Back-to-front sentences [W5; S1,4,9; T2; L1,6]

Aims: To develop reading skills by focusing closely on the text. (Timing: 5 minutes)

Pairwork activity: Write the following sentences on a transparency: *Me despierto a las ocho menos diez; Me levanto a las ocho; Desayuno a las ocho y media; Me ducho a las nueve menos cuarto; ¿A qué hora te levantas normalmente?*. Display this OHT with the text back-to-front and ask pupils to read the sentences in pairs. One person reads the sentence while the other listens and corrects any errors in pronunciation. Then select some pupils to read the sentences to the class and comment on pronunciation.

4 Con tu compañero/a, pregunta y contesta sobre tu rutina diaria. (AT2/2) [W1,2; S4,7,9; L4]

✉ *Speaking and interacting with others – Level D/E*

Speaking. Pupils work in pairs to ask and answer questions about their daily routine.

Before attempting this activity, teachers may wish to practise the questions and answers from the boxes with the whole class. It may help some pupils to write their answers first (*Me despierto a las …*, etc.) to use as support for the pairwork activity.

Teachers may also wish to build on the discussion about reflexive verbs suggested after activity 2. Pupils can now see the *tú* form of reflexive verbs, and they could be referred to the **Gramática** box on page 71 at this stage.

5 Mira el dibujo. ¿Qué dice Pablo? Elige las frases apropiadas. (AT3/2) [W1,2; S5,7]

✉ *Reading for information and instructions – Level D*

Reading. Pupils use the clues in the picture to help them work out which of the sentences Pablo would say.

✚ Teachers may wish to use checking the answers as an opportunity to introduce and practise the 3rd person form of reflexive verbs (*Pablo se despierta tarde*, etc.).

Answers

| a, b, f, g, h, i |

6 Escribe cuatro frases sobre lo que haces por la mañana los fines de semana. (AT4/2–4) [W1,2; S6,9; T5]

✉ *Writing to establish and maintain personal contact – Level D/E*

Writing. Pupils write at least four sentences about what they do in the morning at the weekend. They may wish to use their notes from activity 4 to help them. Teachers may wish to use this opportunity to revise connectives (linking words) and opinions with the class, which would greatly enhance the quality of pupils' writing.

Plenary

Throw-and-catch game, using a soft ball or object. Throw the object to a pupil and ask a question in Spanish from those introduced on the daily routine. The pupil answers and throws the ball back to you. When you have asked the questions a number of times, a pupil can replace you and throw the ball and ask the questions. Eventually the ball can be thrown to a pupil who will answer a question and then pose another question while throwing the ball to another pupil.

Cuaderno A, page 39

1 Elige la frase apropiada para cada dibujo. (AT3/2) [W1,2,5; S7,9]

✉ *Reading for information and instructions – Level C*

Reading. Pupils choose the correct sentence for each picture.

Answers

| 1 a | 2 a | 3 b | 4 b | 5 b | 6 b |

2a Rellena el cuadro para Gregorio. (AT3/4) [W5; S2,6,7]

✉ *Reading for information and instructions – Level C/D*

En casa **módulo 4**

Reading. Pupils read the description of Gregorio's daily routine and complete the grid with the times, and answer *sí* or *no* to the questions.

Answers

	Sergio	Gregorio
¿A qué hora se despierta los sábados?	9.00	10.30
¿A qué hora se levanta?	9.10	10.45
¿Se ducha?	sí	sí
¿Desayuna?	sí	sí
¿Se lava los dientes?	sí	sí
¿Se viste?	sí	sí
¿Se peina?	sí	no

2b Completa las frases para Sergio. (AT3/3) [W1,2,5; S2,6,7]

✖ *Knowing about language*

Reading. Pupils use the information in the grid for activity 2a to complete Sergio's description.

Answers

Los sábados me despierto a las nueve. Me levanto a las nueve y diez. Me ducho y desayuno. Me lavo los dientes. Me visto y me peino.

Cuaderno B, page 39

1 Empareja las frases con los dibujos. (AT3/1) [W1,2,5; S9]

✖ *Knowing about language*

Reading. Pupils match up the sentences with the pictures.

Answers

| 1 d | 2 b | 3 a | 4 f | 5 g | 6 c | 7 e |

2a Rellena el cuadro para Gregorio. (AT3/4) [W5; S6,7; T3]

✖ *Reading for information and instructions – Level D*

Reading. Pupils read the description of Gregorio's daily routine and complete the grid with the times, and answer *sí* or *no* to the questions.

Answers

	Sergio	Inés	Gregorio
¿A qué hora se despierta los sábados?	9.00	11.00	10.30
¿A qué hora se levanta?	9.10	11.30	10.45
¿Se ducha?	sí	no	sí
¿Desayuna?	sí	sí	sí
¿Se lava los dientes?	sí	no	sí
¿Se viste?	sí	no	sí
¿Se peina?	sí	no	no

2b Completa las frases para Sergio. (AT3/3) [W1,2,5; S2,6,7]

✖ *Knowing about language*

Reading. Pupils use the information in the grid for activity 2a to complete Sergio's description.

Answers

Los sábados me despierto a las nueve. Me levanto a las nueve y diez. Me ducho y desayuno. Me lavo los dientes. Me visto y me peino.

2c Escribe un texto similar para Inés. (AT4/3) [T6]

✖ *Writing to exchange information and ideas – Level D*

Writing. Pupils use the information in the grid for activity 2a to write a similar description for Inés.

Answers

Los sábados me despierto a las once. Me levanto a las once y media. No me ducho, no me lavo los dientes, no me visto y no me peino, pero desayuno.

Grammar, Resource and Assessment File, page 71

Activities to practise reflexive verbs in first, second and third person (singular) forms.

1 [W2; S9]

Answers

| 1 c | 2 f | 3 a | 4 e | 5 d | 6 b |

módulo 4

6 Por la tarde

(Pupil's Book pages 72–73)

Main topics

- Talking about what you do after school

Key Framework Objectives

- Checking before reading 7T3 (Reinforcement)
- Using resources 7T4 (Reinforcement)
- Improving speech 7L6 (Reinforcement)

Grammar

- Reflexive verbs: *acostarse, divertirse*

Key language

¿Comes en el instituto o en casa?
Como en casa a la una.
¿A qué hora meriendas/cenas?
Meriendo/Ceno a las ...
¿Cuándo haces los deberes?
Hago los deberes a las ...
¡Me divierto con mis amigos!
¿Qué haces después de cenar?
Después de cenar, veo la televisión.
¿A qué hora te acuestas?
Me acuesto a las once.

Resources

Cassette B, side 2
CD 2, track 15
Cuaderno A and B, page 40
Starter 2, Resource and Assessment File, page 74
OHTs 21 and 22: daily routines, times

Starter 1: **Odd one out** [W1,2,5]

Aims: To reinforce the understanding and knowledge of verbs and meaning with daily routine language, and to use thinking skills. (Timing: 5–10 minutes)

Pairwork activity: Copy the following words onto a grid with three columns and three rows: (Row 1) 1 *me acuesto* 2 *tengo* 3 *soy* (Row 2) 4 *me gusta* 5 *me levanto* 6 *me ducho* (Row 3) 7 *odio* 8 *veo la televisión* 9 *hago los deberes*. Pupils must locate the odd one out in each row. Encourage use of the target language by giving an example and putting keywords on the board (regular, irregular, *verbo reflexivo, diferente, número tres es la excepción porque ...*), but allow pupils to communicate in English for more complex ideas. Pairs feed back to the whole class and justify their decision (in English). Accept all valid suggestions. If there is time, repeat the process using the columns, or ask pupils to construct sentences using the verbs, e.g. *hago los deberes en mi dormitorio.*

1a Empareja las frases con las fotos. (AT3/2) [W1,5; S2]

✖ *Knowing about language*

Reading. Pupils match up the sentences with the photos of Eduard's routine after school.

Teachers will probably not want to introduce any new expressions before pupils attempt this activity, since the meanings of all the verbs encountered are given at the bottom of page 72.

Teachers may, however, wish to introduce these expressions orally before pupils open their books, either using flashcards or OHT pictures, or miming the activities. In this way, pupils will make the connection between sound and writing in advance of listening to the expressions in activity 1b.

Answers

| 1 b | 2 a | 3 c | 4 e | 5 g | 6 f | 7 d |

1b Escucha y comprueba tus respuestas. (AT1/2) [W1,5; L1]

✖ *Knowing about language*

Listening. Pupils listen to the recording to check their answers to activity 1a.

Teachers may wish to play the recording a second time for pupils to repeat, paying attention to their pronunciation.

Tapescript

1 – *Como en casa a las dos y media.*
2 – *Hago los deberes a las tres y cuarto.*
3 – *Meriendo a las cinco: un yogur, galletas y un vaso de leche.*
4 – *Luego, a las seis me divierto un rato con mis amigos.*
5 – *Ceno a las nueve.*
6 – *Después de cenar, a las nueve y media, veo la televisión.*
7 – *Me acuesto a las once.*

1c ¿Qué contesta Eduard a estas preguntas? Escribe sus respuestas. (AT3/2, AT4/2) [W2,4,5; S9]

✖ *Reading for information and instructions – Level D*

Reading/Writing. Pupils reread the sentences in activity 1a in order to answer the questions about Eduard's routine.

Before attempting this activity, which practises the 2nd person of verbs, teachers may wish to revise the verbs encountered on pages 70–71, and read through the *Gramática* box with their pupils.

En casa módulo 4

Answers

1 Como en casa.
2 Como a las dos y media.
3 Hago los deberes a las tres y cuarto.
4 Meriendo a las cinco.
5 Ceno a las nueve.
6 Después de cenar veo la televisión.
7 Me acuesto a las once.

1d Con tu compañero/a, haz y contesta a las preguntas en **1c**. (AT2/2–3) [W2,5; S4,9; L4]

✳ *Speaking and interacting with others – Level D/E*

Speaking. Pupils take turns to ask one another the questions from activity 1c about their own routines.

Teachers may wish to ask pupils to write out their answers to help prepare for the writing activity 2b.

> *Starter 2:* **Vowel combinations** [W5,6; L1,6]
>
> *Aims:* To develop pupils' pronunciation skills (*ie, io, ia, ue, ua*); to reinforce knowledge of reflexive verbs and vocabulary from this topic. (Timing: 5–10 minutes)
>
> *Resources:* Resource and Assessment File, page 74 (Starter 2)
>
> *Activity:* Make an OHT using the master provided. Display the OHT with the Spelling column visible and ask pupils to try to pronounce the vowel strings. Then display the Sound column and ask pupils to improve on their previous attempts. Encourage whole-class repetition of the sounds, with just the Spelling column at first, and then with the Sound column. Reveal the four words below the grid (all new words) and ask pupils to try to pronounce them. Then reveal the tongue-twisters, which contain words from this unit, and ask pupils to practise them in pairs to prepare for a class competition against the clock.

2a Lee la carta. Decide si las frases son verdad (✓) o mentira (✗). Busca las palabras que no conoces en el diccionario. (AT3/4) [W5; S9; T1,3,4]

✳ *Reading for information and instructions – Level E*

Reading. Pupils read the letter from Felipe and decide whether the statements about his routine are true (*verdad*) or false (*mentira*).

Before attempting this activity, which practises the 3rd person of verbs, teachers may wish to revise the verbs encountered on pages 70–71, and read through the *Gramática* box with their pupils.

Answers

1 ✓	2 ✗	3 ✓	4 ✓	5 ✗	6 ✓	7 ✓
8 ✗						

2b Escribe una carta a Felipe y contesta a sus preguntas. (AT4/3–4) [W2,5; T5]

✳ *Writing to establish and maintain personal contact – Level E/F*

Writing. Pupils write a reply to Felipe. Teachers should make sure that their pupils have understood all the questions that Felipe asks, and that they should include answers to all of them in their letters. Pupils may find their notes from speaking activity 1d provide a helpful starting point to writing about their own routines.

💻 ICT activity

If the school has a Spanish-speaking partner school, this would be an ideal activity for an e-mail exchange. If this is not possible, go to www.heinemann.co.uk/hotlinks for a good starting point.

> *Plenary*
>
> Use the letter from exercise 2a on page 73 of the Pupil's Book as a basis for a discussion on reading skills. Encourage pupils to tell you what they find easy or difficult about tackling a long text written in Spanish. Use a brainstorming activity, on the board, to find out how they would read a text of similar length in English. Discuss whether the following skills are suitable for Spanish: scanning, reading quickly for gist, etc. Ask pupils how punctuation can be an aid to understanding a text, encouraging them to find questions and exclamations in the text. You can also revisit ways of understanding new vocabulary (cognates, guessing in context, using pictures as clues, etc.).

Cuaderno A, page 40

1 Escribe las frases en los globos apropiados. (AT3/2) [W2,5; S9]

✳ *Reading for information and instructions – Level C*

Reading. Pupils match up the sentences with the speech bubbles.

Answers

1 e	2 a	3 d	4 g	5 b	6 f	7 c

2 Lee los globos y escribe P (Pili) o F (Francisco) para cada frase. (AT3/3) [W5; S6,7; T3]

✳ *Reading for information and instructions – Level D*

módulo 4 — En casa

Reading. Pupils read the texts in the speech bubbles and decide whether the statements below refer to Pili (P) or Francisco (F).

Answers

F, F, P, F, P, P, F

Cuaderno B, page 40

1 Empareja las frases. (AT3/2) [W1,5; S2]

✉ *Knowing about language*

Reading. Pupils match up the sentence halves.

Answers

1 d	2 f	3 e	4 g	5 b	6 c	7 a

2 Lee los globos y escribe P (Pili) o F (Francisco) para cada frase. (AT3/3) [W5; S6,7; T3]

✉ *Reading for information and instructions – Level D*

Reading. Pupils read the texts in the speech bubbles and decide whether the statements below refer to Pili (P) or Francisco (F).

Answers

a F	b F	c P	d F	e P	f P	g F

3 Escribe una frase para cada dibujo. (AT4/2) [W2,5; S9]

✉ *Writing to exchange information and ideas – Level D*

Writing. Pupils write a sentence about each picture, including the time and activity.

Suggested answers

1. A la una y media como en la cafetería.
2. A las siete me divierto con mis amigos.
3. A las cuatro y media hago mis deberes.
4. Ceno a las nueve.
5. A las diez veo la televisión.
6. Me acuesto a las diez y media.

módulo 4 — Resumen y Prepárate

(Pupil's Book pages 74–75)

Resumen

This is a checklist of language covered in Module 4. There is a comprehensive **Resumen** list for Module 4 in the Pupil's Book (page 74) and a **Resumen** test sheet in Cuaderno A and B (page 44).

Key Framework Objectives

- Adapting sentences 7S3 (Reinforcement)
- Basic questions 7S4 (Reinforcement)
- Reading using cues 7T1 (Reinforcement)
- Assembling text 7T5 (Reinforcement)

Prepárate

A revision test to give practice for the test itself at the end of the module.

Resources

Cassette B, side 2
CD 2, track 16
Cuaderno A and B, Repaso (previously ¡Extra!), pages 41–42; Gramática, page 43

---

1 Escucha y completa las frases con las palabras apropiadas. (AT1/2) [W1,5; S7; L3]

Listening for information and instructions – Level C

Listening. Pupils listen to the recording and complete the sentences with the appropriate ending.

Answers

| 1 a | 2 b | 3 a | 4 b | 5 b | 6 b |

Tapescript

1 – Hola, Martín. ¿A qué hora te levantas de lunes a viernes?
 – Pues, normalmente me levanto a las siete.
2 – ¿A qué hora empiezan las clases?
 – Empiezan a las ocho y media.
3 – ¿Hay clases por la tarde?
 – No, las clases terminan a la una.
4 – ¿Qué haces por la tarde?
 – Hago los deberes.
5 – ¿Qué haces después de cenar?
 – Veo un poco la televisión.
6 – ¿A qué hora te acuestas?
 – Normalmente me acuesto a las 11.00.

2 Con tu compañero/a, empareja las preguntas con las respuestas. (AT2/2, AT3/2) [W2,4,5; S9]

Speaking to convey information – Level D

Speaking/Reading. Pupils work in pairs to match up the questions and answers.

Answers

| 1 e | 2 b | 3 f | 4 a | 5 d | 6 c |

3 Pregunta y contesta para ti. (AT2/3) [W2,4,5; S3,4,9; L4]

Speaking and interacting with others – Level D

Speaking. Pupils work in pairs and take turns to ask the questions from activity 2 and answer for themselves.

4 Lee la carta de Patricio y contesta a las preguntas en inglés. (AT3/4) [W2,5; T1]

Reading for information and instructions – Level D

Reading. Pupils read the letter from Patricio and answer the questions in English.

Answers

1. He lives in a flat.
2. His block has 10 floors.
3. His flat is on the third floor.
4. The district he lives in is on the outskirts of Málaga.
5. The flat is big.
6. It has four bedrooms.
7. It has a bathroom, a lounge/diner, a kitchen and a toilet.
8. He likes it very much because is it very pretty.

5 Escribe una respuesta a la carta de Patricio. (AT4/2–4) [W2,5; T5,6]

Writing to establish and maintain personal contact – Level D/E/F

Writing. Pupils write a reply to Patricio, telling him about their own home. They can use the writing frame and Patricio's letter as a model.

Cuaderno A, pages 41–42

Repaso (previously ¡Extra!)

1 Completa el crucigrama. (AT3/1, AT4/1) [W1,2,5,7; S2]

Reading for enjoyment

Reading/Writing. Pupils fill in the gaps in each sentence to find the words to complete the crossword.

módulo 4 — En casa

Answers

(Crossword grid with answers:)
- ORDENADOR
- ACUESTO
- PLANTAS
- DEBAJO
- LEVANTA
- HABITACIONES
- ALFOMBRA
- MESA
- PÓSTERS
- ASEO
- TELEVISIÓN

2 Rellena los espacios en blanco con las palabras apropiadas. (AT3/1, AT4/1) [W1]

✖ *Knowing about language*

Reading/Writing. Pupils choose the correct words from the list to replace the pictures and complete the text.

Answers

pueblo, sur, jardín, garaje, cocina, salón, comedor, aseo, cuarto de baño, dormitorio

3 ¿Verdad (✓) o mentira (✗)? (AT3/3) [W2,5; S2; T3]

✖ *Reading for information and instructions – Level D*

Reading. Pupils read the letter from Santi and decide whether the statements below are true (*verdad*) or false (*mentira*).

Answers

| 1 ✗ | 2 ✗ | 3 ✓ | 4 ✓ | 5 ✗ | 6 ✓ | 7 ✗ |
| 8 ✗ | 9 ✗ | 10 ✓ | | | | |

Cuaderno B, pages 41–42

Repaso (previously ¡Extra!)

1 Completa el crucigrama. (AT3/1, AT4/1) [W1,2,5,7; S2]

✖ *Reading for enjoyment*

Reading/Writing. Pupils fill in the gaps in each sentence to find the words to complete the crossword.

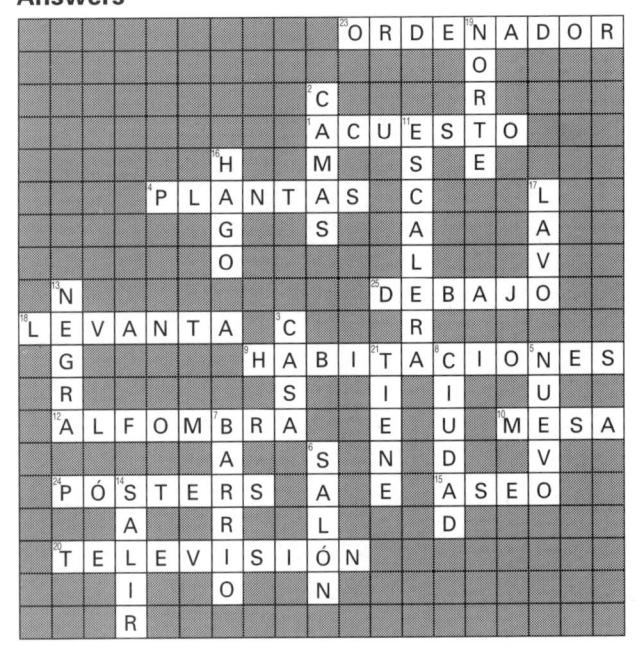

2 Contesta a las preguntas. (AT3/4) [W2,5; S4; T1,3]

✖ *Reading for information and instructions – Level F*

Reading. Pupils read the letter from Santi and answer the questions on it in Spanish.

Answers

1. Santi vive en el sur de España.
2. Su casa es grande.
3. Su casa tiene seis habitaciones, un jardín, una terraza y un garaje.
4. Hay cuatro personas en la familia de Santi.
5. En la planta baja hay una cocina, un salón, un comedor, un aseo y un pasillo con una escalera.
6. Hay tres dormitorios.
7. El cuarto de baño está en el primer piso.
8. El despacho está en el ático.
9. Su dormitorio tiene una ventana.
10. La mesa está entre las camas.
11. En la estantería hay su equipo de música y sus libros.
12. Las paredes son blancas.
13. Normalmente se levanta a las seis y media.
14. Desayuna a las siete.
15. Come en la cafetería.
16. Merienda galletas y fruta.
17. Después de hacer los deberes se divierte con sus amigos.
18. Cena a las nueve.
19. Se acuesta a las once.

En casa — módulo 4

Cuaderno A, page 43

Gramática

1 Mira el dibujo y completa las frases con las palabras apropiadas. (AT3/2) [W1,2]

✉ *Knowing about language*

Reading. Pupils complete the sentences using the correct preposition to describe where the objects are in the picture above.

Answers

1 encima	**2** debajo	**3** al lado	**4** a la derecha
5 entre	**6** enfrente	**7** a la izquierda	

2 Escribe *me, te* o *se*. (AT3/2) [W2,5]

✉ *Knowing about language*

Reading. Pupils read the box to revise reflexive verbs, and then write *me, te* or *se* to complete the sentences.

Answers

1 te	**2** se	**3** Me	**4** Te	**5** se	**6** Me

Cuaderno B, page 43

Gramática

1 Mira el dibujo y completa las frases con las palabras que faltan. (AT3/2) [W1,2]

✉ *Knowing about language*

Reading. Pupils complete the sentences using the correct preposition to describe where the objects are in the picture above.

Answers

1 encima	**2** debajo	**3** al lado	**4** a la derecha
5 entre	**6** enfrente	**7** a la izquierda	

2 Escribe *me, te* o *se*. (AT3/2) [W2,5]

✉ *Knowing about language*

Reading. Pupils read the box to revise reflexive verbs, and then write *me, te* or *se* to complete the sentences.

Answers

1 te	**2** se	**3** Me	**4** Te	**5** se	**6** Me

3 Completa las frases con la forma apropiada del verbo. (AT3/2, AT4/1) [W2,5]

✉ *Knowing about language*

Reading/Writing. Pupils complete the sentences with the correct form of the reflexive verbs in brackets. They should use the information in the box to help make sure they spell the verbs correctly, paying particular attention to the middle letters.

Answers

1 me acuesto	**2** te despiertas/se despierta usted
3 se divierte **4** te vistes **5** me despierto **6** se divierte	

módulo 4

¡Extra! 7 Mi casa

(Pupil's Book pages 76–77)

Main topics

This is an optional unit which reviews some of the key language of the module: it focuses on activities about houses.

Key Framework Objectives

- Checking before reading 7T3 (Reinforcement)
- Using resources 7T4 (Reinforcement)

Resources

Cassette B, side 2
CD 2, track 17

Starter 1: **Text scanning [W2,4; T1,3]**

Aims: To develop pupils' confidence in reading longer texts in Spanish; to build on reading skills by getting pupils to focus on specific aspects of a text; to revise knowledge of adjectives and gender and to develop dictionary/glossary skills. (Timing: 5–10 minutes)

Activity: Ask pupils to look at the text on page 76 of the Pupil's Book and give them 90 seconds to scan the text for adjectives (*moderna, grande, pequeño, cómodo, amarillas, azul, azules, alta*). Give them one example to start them off. Ask pupils how many adjectives they have found. Compile a list on the board and ask pupils to write the masculine singular form of these adjectives as they would be found in the dictionary. If there is time, divide the class into seven groups and ask them to check one adjective each in the dictionary to see if they have written the masculine singular form correctly.

1a Escucha y lee el texto. Busca las palabras que no conoces en el diccionario. (AT1/4, AT3/4) [T1,4]

✉ *Knowing about language*

Listening/Reading. Pupils listen to the recording and follow the text of Marina's e-mail. They should then look up any words that they do not understand.

Tapescript

Vivo en Mataró, en el noreste de España. Está en la costa, a 30 kilómetros al norte de Barcelona.

Vivimos en una casa. Está en el centro de la ciudad. Es moderna y bastante grande. Es de dos plantas. En la planta baja tenemos una cocina, un salón-comedor y un despacho. Arriba, en el primer piso hay dos dormitorios y un cuarto de baño.

Abajo, tenemos una terraza, un garaje y un jardín.

Mi dormitorio es pequeño y cómodo. Las paredes son amarillas y la alfombra es azul. Las cortinas son azules. Hay una cama alta con una escalera. Debajo de la cama hay un escritorio, una silla y una librería. En el escritorio hay una lámpara y un ordenador. Entre el armario y la cama hay un tocador y encima del tocador hay un espejo. También tengo un equipo de música, unos pósters, muchos discos compactos ¡y una gran colección de peluches!

Los fines de semana y durante las vacaciones, me despierto bastante tarde. Me levanto pero no me visto. Desayuno y luego escucho música en mi dormitorio.

1b Dibuja un plano de la casa de Marina o de su dormitorio. Escribe los nombres de los cuartos/muebles en el plano. (AT3/4) [W1; T1]

✉ *Reading for enjoyment*

Reading. Pupils draw and label a picture either of Marina's house or her bedroom. Teachers may wish to suggest that pupils work in groups of four, one pair drawing the house, the other pair drawing the bedroom, and then swap over and compare drawings.

Answers

Pupils' drawings should contain the following details:
La casa de Marina
Two floors; Ground floor: kitchen, lounge/diner, office;
First floor: 2 bedrooms, bathroom;
Outside: terrace, garage, garden.
El dormitorio de Marina
Rug; curtains; raised bed with ladder;
Below bed: writing desk (with computer and lamp), chair, bookcase;
Between bed and wardrobe: dressing table with mirror above;
Hi-fi, posters, cuddly toys.

1c Con tu compañero/a, haz y contesta a las preguntas. (AT2/3–4) [W2,5; S4,9; L4]

✉ *Speaking and interacting with others – Level E/F*

Speaking. Pupils take turns to ask and answer the questions about Marina.

1d Escribe las respuestas a las preguntas en **1c**. (AT4/2–4) [W2,5; S9]

✉ *Writing to exchange information and instructions – level E/F*

En casa — módulo 4

Writing. Pupils write answers to the questions from activity 1c, either in individual sentences, or as a paragraph reporting back information about Marina.

Answers

1. Marina vive en Mataró, en el noreste de España.
2. Vive en la costa.
3. Vive en una casa.
4. No, la casa está en el centro de la ciudad.
5. La casa es moderna y bastante grande.
6. Tiene dos plantas.
7. En la planta baja hay una cocina, un salón-comedor y un despacho.
8. Sí, tiene una terraza.
9. El dormitorio de Marina está en el primer piso/la primera planta. Es pequeño y cómodo.
10. Los fines de semana Marina se despierta bastante tarde. Se levanta pero no se viste. Desayuna y luego escucha música en su dormitorio.

Starter 2: Vocabulary hunt [S1,3; T4,5]

Aims: To encourage pupils to use the vocabulary lists in the Pupil's Book; to teach strategies to aid comprehension. (Timing: 5 minutes)

Pairwork activity: Using the vocabulary lists on pages 78–79 of the Pupil's Book, pupils find language that can describe the top three pictures in the bubble on page 77. There is a strict time limit for pupils to collect the phrases, such as *en la montaña, la ciudad, un bloque antiguo*, which they then feed back orally. Then ask pupils to put these words into longer phrases (e.g. *Vivo encima de la montaña; Mi piso está en la ciudad; Hay un bloque antiguo detrás de mi casa*). Reward interesting and inventive sentences as well as accurate ones.

1e Escribe una descripción similar de tu casa. (AT4/2–4) [W2,5; S9; T5,6]

✕ *Writing to establish and maintain personal contact – Level E/F*

Writing. Pupils write a similar description of their own home.

2 Unos amigos de tus padres buscan una casa en España. Lee los anuncios y elige la casa ideal para ellos. (AT3/4) [T1,3]

✕ *Reading for information and instructions – Level E*

Reading. Pupils read the four estate agents' adverts and choose the ideal home for their parents' friends.

Before attempting this activity, teachers may wish to go through orally with the whole class what sort of home the parents' friends want.

Answers

3

3 Con tu compañero/a, haz y contesta a las preguntas y elige la casa ideal de los anuncios en **2** para él/ella. (AT2/3–4) [W2,5; S4,9; T1; L4]

✕ *Speaking and interacting with others – Level D*

Speaking. Pupils take turns to interview their partner to choose and recommend an ideal home from the adverts.

Plenary

Ask pupils to use the *Resumen* section on page 74 in the Pupil's Book to test each other orally on the language that has been introduced during the module. Encourage pupils to monitor the pronunciation and meaning of their partner's replies. Then each pair can look at the advert on page 74 and write a description of it, using a dictionary if necessary.

Optional Thinking Skills lesson

Aims
To develop reading skills and to revise types of houses, rooms in the house and description language; to help pupils think laterally. (Timing: 40 minutes)

Resources
Resource and Assessment File, page 75 (Thinking Skills)

Map from memory: Logic problem [S2; T1,3]

Pairwork activity: Make worksheets and an OHT using the master provided. Give each pair of pupils a copy of the blank grid and answer options and explain that they must read the ten clues you are about to show them and work out the information to complete the grid for each person. Explain that each person on the grid needs one piece of information for each category: *¿Casa?, ¿Cómo es?, ¿Habitaciones?*, and that the options listed below the grid can only be used once. Check that pupils can identify which are boys and which are girls from the names in the grid. Reveal the first clue on the OHT and give pupils two minutes to fill in the grid. Pupils must also decide what other incomplete information they have received. One by one, reveal the ten sentences. Pupils must not ask you for the answer. If pupils run into difficulties, stop, go back to the first two or three clues and go through them with the class.

módulo 4 En casa

Answers

Estela: chalet, pequeño, cuatro dormitorios;
Alberto: granja, moderna tres salones;
Isabel: casa, grande, un jardín;
Eduardo: piso, antiguo, dos cuartos de baño;
Adela: bloque, bonito, dos aseos.

Pairs then feed back their answers. Select the least-able pupils to feed back first, as they will give the most straightforward answers. Then discuss with pupils how this technique helped them to work out the language and how it made them think. Try to ask open questions, such as: 'What did you learn? What did you find easy/difficult? How did you tackle the task? How might you approach it differently next time? How does a task like this help you learn Spanish? What skills have you developed/used? Where else might you use these skills?'.

módulo 4

Te toca a ti
(Pupil's Book pages 122–123)

- Self-access reading and writing at two levels.

A Reinforcement

1 Empareja las frases. (AT3/2) [W1,5; S1,2]

✉ *Knowing about language*

Reading. Pupils match up the sentence halves.

Answers

| 1 c | 2 b | 3 a | 4 g | 5 f | 6 e | 7 d |

2a Mira el dibujo. Completa las frases con el color correcto. (AT3/2) [W1,4; S2]

✉ *Reading for information and instructions – Level C*

Reading. Pupils use the picture to help them pick the correct colour for each of the statements.

Answers

| 1 marrón | 2 azul | 3 amarillas | 4 azules | 5 verdes |
| 6 azul | | | | |

2b Mira el dibujo otra vez. Copia y completa las frases con las palabras apropiadas. (AT3/2, AT4/1) [W2,5; S2]

✉ *Knowing about language*

Reading/Writing. Pupils use the picture from activity 2a to help them choose the correct preposition from the list to describe where the objects are in the bedroom.

Answers

| 1 debajo | 2 encima | 3 encima | 4 delante | 5 al lado |
| 6 al lado | 7 entre | 8 delante | | |

B Extension

1 Empareja cada descripción con el dibujo apropiado. (AT3/3) [W2,5; T1]

✉ *Reading for information and instructions – Level D*

Reading. Pupils match up the descriptions with the pictures.

Answers

| 1 e | 2 c | 3 a | 4 d | 5 b |

2 Pon las frases en el orden correcto. (AT3/2) [W2,5; S7,9]

✉ *Reading for information and instructions – Level D*

Reading. Pupils put the sentences in the appropriate order to describe daily routine.

Answers

| l, d, b, e, j, g, i, f, k, a, h, c |

3 Escribe una frase para cada dibujo. (AT4/2) [W2,5; S9]

✉ *Writing to exchange information and ideas – Level D*

Writing. Pupils write a sentence for each picture, including times as appropriate, and activities.

Answers

a	Me levanto a las nueve y media.
b	Desayuno cereales.
c	Después de desayunar veo la televisión.
d	Como a la una.
e	Por la tarde me divierto en el jardín.
f	Ceno a las diez.

módulo 5 *Mi pueblo*

(Pupil's Book pages 80–97)

Unit/topics	Framework objectives	PoS	Key language and Grammar
1 Voy al polideportivo (pp. 80–81) Saying where you are going	7W5 Verbs present (R) 7W8 Finding meanings (R) 7S9 Simple sentences (R) 7L5 Spontaneous talk (R)	1b grammar and how to apply it 1c how to express themselves 2c ask/answer questions 2e adapt language	Consolidation of *ir* *al, a la* Locations in a town *¿Adónde vas/vais?* *Voy al centro comercial.* *Vamos a la playa.* *Marina va al polideportivo.*
2 ¿Por dónde se va al Corte Inglés? (pp. 82–83) Giving directions Understanding directions	7W2 High-frequency words (R) 7W4 Gender/plural (R) 7W6 Letters and sounds (R) 7W7 Learning about words (R)	1b grammar and how to apply it 2c ask/answer questions	Imperatives Directions More locations *Toma/Tome la primera a la izquierda.* *Sigue/Siga todo recto.* *la catedral* *la oficina de turismo*
3 Sube la avenida y cruza la plaza … (pp. 84–85) Describing the location of places in a town Giving more detailed directions	7S1 Typical word order (R) 7T1 Reading using cues (R) 7L2 Following speech (R) 7C5 Social conventions (R)	1b grammar and how to apply it 1c how to express themselves 5a communicating in the target language	Consolidation of prepositional phrases More imperatives *al final de* *al lado de* *del, de la* *Sube la Calle Sevilla.* *Cruza la plaza.*
4 ¿Está cerca? (pp. 86–87) Talking about distance	7S4 Basic questions (R) 7T1 Reading using cues (R) 7T3 Checking before reading (R)	1a sounds and writing 3a memorising	Numbers 32–100 *¿Dónde está …?* *Está (muy) cerca.* *Está (bastante) lejos.* *Está a 10 kilómetros.* *Está a 5 minutos andando/ en coche.*
5 ¿Cómo es tu ciudad? (pp. 88–89) Talking about what your town is like	7S6 Compound sentences (R) 7C1 Geographical facts (R) 7C3 Contact with native speakers (R) 7C4 Stories and songs (R)	1b grammar and how to apply it 1c how to express themselves 2c ask/answer questions 3b use context to interpret meaning	Consolidation of adjective agreement More locations *¿Cómo es tu ciudad?* *Es antigua/pequeña/ grande/industrial.* *¿Qué hay en tu pueblo?* *Hay/Tiene un castillo.*
6 ¿Qué tiempo hace? (pp. 90–91) Talking about the weather	7S7 Time and tenses (Part-L) 7W6 Letters and sounds (R) 7T7 Improving written work (R) 7L1 Sound patterns (R)	1a sounds and writing 2i report main points 3b use context to interpret meaning	Weather vocabulary The seasons *En primavera llueve y hace viento.* *En verano hace (mucho) calor y a veces hace tormenta.*
Resumen y Prepárate (pp. 92–93) Pupils' checklist and practice test	7S9 Simple sentences (R) 7L3 Gist and detail (R) 7L4 Classroom talk (R)	3a memorising 3e develop their independence	
¡Extra! 7 Un paseo por Barcelona (pp. 94–95) Optional extension unit: About Barcelona	7W8 Finding meanings (R) 7C2 Everyday culture (R)	2h scan texts 4d consider experiences in other countries	
Te toca a ti (pp. 124–125) Self-access reading and writing at two levels		1b grammar and how to apply it 2f adapt language for different contexts	

módulo 5

1 Voy al polideportivo

(Pupil's Book pages 80–81)

Main topics
- Saying where you are going

Key Framework Objectives
- Verbs present 7W5 (Reinforcement)
- Finding meanings 7W8 (Reinforcement)
- Simple sentences 7S9 (Reinforcement)
- Spontaneous talk 7L5 (Reinforcement)

Grammar
- Present tense of *ir*
- *a + el = al*
- *a + la = a la*

Key language
¿Adónde vas/vais?
Voy al centro comercial.
Vamos a la playa.
Marina va al polideportivo.
Van al cine.

el centro comercial	el parque
el cine	la playa
la estación (de autobuses)	la plaza de toros
la estación (de trenes/de RENFE)	el polideportivo
el estadio	la tienda (de regalos)

Resources
Cassette C, side 1
CD 3, track 2
Cuaderno A and B, page 45
Starter 2, Resource and Assessment File, page 92
OHTs 23 and 24: places in town, directions

Starter 1: Cognates [W1,8]

Aims: To show pupils that there are many words in Spanish that are very similar to English and build confidence in their learning. (Timing: 5 minutes)

Activity: Write the following words on the board or a transparency: *el centro comercial, el cine, el parque, la plaza de toros, el polideportivo, la tienda de regalos, el estadio, la playa, la estación de autobuses, la estación de trenes*. Ask pupils to identify what they think the topic might be. In groups, pupils then have to try to work out the equivalents for these words in English. Groups feed back and justify their answers.

1 Escribe las letras de los lugares en el orden correcto. (1–10) (AT1/1) [W1,4,6]

✶ *Knowing about language*

Listening. Pupils listen to the recording and write down the letters of the places in town in the order they hear them mentioned.

Before attempting this activity, teachers may wish to introduce the names of places in town using an OHT or flashcards. A different context may make these new words more memorable: for example, using an OHT of a basic street map containing all the places on page 80, and putting a cut out 'you' on the map, to 'go' to all the places. In this way *voy a …* can also be introduced.

Teachers may wish to ask pupils to follow the words on page 80 the first time they hear the recording and repeat the words, in order to reinforce the link between sound and writing.

Answers
b, c, d, a, e, h, i, j, f, g

Tapescript
1 – el cine
2 – el parque
3 – la plaza de toros
4 – el centro comercial
5 – el polideportivo
6 – la playa
7 – la estación de autobuses
8 – la estación de RENFE
9 – la tienda de regalos
10 – el estadio

2 Escucha y elige el lugar apropiado. (1–10) (AT3/1) [W1,4]

✶ *Knowing about language*

Reading. Pupils listen to the recording and find the name of the place from activity 1 to match the sound effect.

Answers
| 1 h | 2 e | 3 c | 4 b | 5 a | 6 d | 7 i |
| 8 f | 9 j | 10 g | | | | |

Tapescript
(sound effects only on recording)
1 – (sound of waves on shore)
2 – (sound of sport being played indoors)
3 – (sound of birds, etc.)
4 – (sound effect for Western)
5 – (shop noises)
6 – (sound of paso doble and crowd shouting 'olé')
7 – (sound of buses backing)

módulo 5 — Mi pueblo

8 – (sound of till)
9 – (sound of trains arriving or leaving station)
10 – (noise of crowd at football match)

3 Escucha y escribe los destinos. (1–8) (AT1/2) [W1,2,4,5; S4,9]

Listening for information and instructions – Level C

Listening. Pupils listen to the recording and write the letter of the destination for each conversation.

Answers

1 a	2 b	3 c	4 g	5 j	6 f	7 i
8 e						

Tapescript

1 – ¿Adónde vas?
 – Voy al centro comercial.
2 – ¿Adónde vais?
 – Vamos al cine.
3 – Oye, ¿adónde vas?
 – Voy al parque.
4 – ¿Adónde vais?
 – Al estadio.
5 – ¿Adónde va usted?
 – A la estación de trenes, por favor.
6 – ¿Adónde vamos ahora?
 – Vamos a la tienda de regalos.
7 – A la estación de autobuses, por favor.
8 – ¿Adónde vas, Pablo?
 – Voy al polideportivo.

4 ¿Adónde van las personas en los dibujos? Copia y completa las frases. (AT4/2) [W2,4,5; S9]

Knowing about language

Writing. Pupils copy and complete the phrases to say where the people are going.

Teachers may wish to use this opportunity to introduce the verb *ir* using the *Gramática* box, as well as the structures *al* and *a la*.

Answers

a Vamos a la playa.   b Voy a la estación de trenes.
c Voy al polideportivo.   d Vamos al estadio.
e Voy a la plaza de toros.

5a Mira los lugares en 1. Con tu compañero/a, pregunta y contesta. (AT2/2) [W2,4,5; S4,9; L4]

Speaking and interacting with others – Level D

Speaking. Working in pairs, pupils take turns to choose a place from activity 1 and practise the question and answer ¿Adónde vas? Voy al … Pupils may wish to use the model question and answer in the box on page 81 to help them.

Alternatively, pupils could play a guessing game, taking it in turns to choose a destination from activity 1, while their partner tries to guess the destination by asking ¿Vas a (la playa)? until they guess correctly and then swap roles.

Starter 2: Battleships [W2,5; S9; L1,5]

Aims: To revise places in a town (*el centro comercial, el cine, el parque, la plaza de toros, el polideportivo, la tienda de regalos, el estadio, la playa, la estación de autobuses, la estación*) and the verb *ir* in the present tense; to develop pupils' memory skills. (Timing: 10 minutes)

Resources: Resource and Assessment File, page 92 (Starter 2)

Pairwork activity: Make game cards using the master provided. Give a copy of the game card to each pupil to play battleships in pairs. One person has the ship (Pupil A) and the other tries to destroy it (Pupil B). Pupil A secretly marks out five squares to represent the position of their battleship. These can be horizontal, vertical or diagonal. Pupil B then reads out sentences in Spanish using part of the verb *ir* followed by a place in the town and Pupil A must say *golpe* (hit) or *nada* (miss) until the ship is found.

➕ Pupils who finish quickly can be given more copies of the worksheet and swap roles.

🅁 For lower-ability students, create a transparency with the key language in Spanish to display on the projector.

5b Escribe una frase para cada lugar en 1. (AT4/2) [W2,4,5; S9]

Writing to exchange information and ideas – Level D

Writing. Pupils write a sentence to say they are going to each destination in activity 1. Teachers should remind pupils to use the *Gramática* box to check they are using the correct form of *ir*, as well as *al* or *a la*.

Answers

a Voy al centro comercial.	b Voy al cine.
c Voy al parque.	d Voy a la plaza de toros.
e Voy al polideportivo.	f Voy a la tienda de regalos.
g Voy al estadio.	h Voy a la playa.
i Voy a la estación de autobuses.	
j Voy a la estación de trenes/de RENFE.	

Mi pueblo — módulo 5

6 Mira los dibujos y escribe frases. (AT4/2) [W2,4,5; S9]

✠ *Writing to exchange information and ideas – Level D*

Writing. Pupils work out where the people in activity 6 are going and then write a sentence using the appropriate form of *ir*. Teachers should remind pupils that sentences about one person will require *va*, while sentences about more than one person will take *van*.

Answers

| Marina va al polideportivo. |
| José y Carlos van al cine. |
| Julio va al parque. |
| Sofía va al estadio. |
| Inés y Carla van a la playa. |
| Ricardo va a la estación de trenes/de RENFE. |

7 Lee el diálogo. Con tu compañero/a, escribe un diálogo similar. (AT2/3, AT3/3, AT4/3) [W2,4,5; S3; T6]

✠ *Speaking and interacting with others – Level D*

Speaking/Reading/Writing. Pupils read the dialogue in pairs. Teachers may wish to encourage pupils to act out the dialogue. Pupils should then write their own dialogue, based on the model.

> **Plenary**
> Ask pupils to work in pairs for four minutes to memorise the different endings for the verb *ir* and the places in the town introduced on pages 80–81 in the Pupil's Book. Test pupils' knowledge of the language by asking them to translate different sentences orally, e.g. *¿Cómo se dice* 'They go to the bullring' *en español?*. You can make this exercise into a game by dividing the class into small groups and awarding points.

Cuaderno A, page 45

1a Mira los dibujos y completa las palabras. (AT3/1) [W1,7]

✠ *Knowing about language*

Reading. Pupils use the pictures to help them complete the words.

Answers

| a el cine | b el parque | c la playa | d el polideportivo |
| e el estadio | f el centro comercial | | |

1b Escribe una frase para cada dibujo en **1a**. (AT4/2) [W2,4,5; S9]

✠ *Knowing about language*

Writing. Pupils write sentences to say that they are going to each of the places in activity 1.

Answers

a Voy al cine.	d Voy al polideportivo.
b Voy al parque.	e Voy al estadio.
c Voy a la playa.	f Voy al centro comercial.

2 Empareja las frases y escribe una frase para cada dibujo. (AT3/2, AT4/2) [W2,4,5; S9]

✠ *Knowing about language*

Reading/Writing. Pupils use the words in boxes to write a sentence for what the people in each speech bubble would say, taking care to use the appropriate part of *ir*.

Answers

a Voy al parque.	d Voy a la estación de autobuses.
b Vamos a la playa.	e Va al cine.
c Van a la tienda de regalos.	

Cuaderno B, page 45

1a Mira los dibujos y completa las palabras. (AT3/1) [W1,7]

✠ *Knowing about language*

Reading. Pupils use the pictures to help them complete the words.

Answers

| a el cine | b el parque | c la estación de trenes/de RENFE |
| d la playa | e la estación de autobuses | f el estadio |

1b Escribe una frase para cada dibujo en **1a**. (AT4/2) [W2,4,5; S9]

✠ *Knowing about language*

Writing. Pupils write sentences saying that they are going to each of the places in activity 1.

Answers

a Voy al cine.	b Voy al parque.
c Voy a la estación de trenes/de RENFE.	
d Voy a la playa.	e Voy a la estación de autobuses.
f Voy al estadio.	

módulo 5 Mi pueblo

2 Empareja las frases y escribe una frase para cada dibujo. (AT3/2, AT4/2) [W2,4,5; S9]

Knowing about language

Reading/Writing. Pupils use the words in boxes to write a sentence for what the people in each speech bubble would say, taking care to use the appropriate part of *ir*.

Answers

a Voy al parque.
b Vamos a la playa.
c Van a la tienda de regalos.
d Voy a la estación de autobuses.
e Va al cine.

módulo 5

2 ¿Por dónde se va al Corte Inglés?

(Pupil's Book pages 82–83)

Main topics
- Giving directions
- Understanding directions

Key Framework Objectives
- High-frequency words 7W2 (Reinforcement)
- Gender/plural 7W4 (Reinforcement)
- Letters and sounds 7W6 (Reinforcement)
- Learning about words 7W7 (Reinforcement)

Grammar
- Imperatives: *toma/tome, sigue/siga*

Key language
¿Por dónde se va a la oficina de turismo?
Toma la primera/segunda a la derecha.
Tome la tercera a la izquierda.
Sigue/Siga todo recto/todo derecho.
el café de Internet
la catedral
el Corte Inglés
el mercado
la piscina
la oficina de turismo

Resources
Cassette C, side 1
CD 3, track 3
Cuaderno A and B, page 46
Starter 2, Resource and Assessment File, page 92
Hoja de trabajo 1, Resource and Assessment File, page 87
OHTs 23 and 24: places in town, directions

Starter 1: Guess the gender [W1,4,8]

Aims: To introduce new vocabulary and to develop knowledge of gender patterns; to develop thinking skills. (Timing: 5 minutes)

Activity: Write the following words on the board or a transparency: *piscina, catedral, oficina de turismo, mercado, Corte Inglés, café de Internet.* Explain to pupils that they will read a list of words in Spanish and they must identify if the words are masculine or feminine. For some classes, it may be appropriate to give a couple of examples. The response can be written on a whiteboard (M or F) or pupils can give a physical response, such as stay seated for masculine and stand up for feminine. Reveal one word at a time and await the response. Discuss with the class which words are feminine or masculine and why. Explain why *oficina de turismo* is feminine and draw pupils' attention to words that do not end in either 'o' or 'a' as these have to be learned carefully in terms of gender. Then ask pupils if they can work out or guess the meaning of the words.

1a Escucha y repite. (AT1/1) [W1,4; L1]

✎ *Knowing about language*

Listening. Pupils listen to the recording and repeat the names of the places pictured. Teachers may wish to encourage pupils to point to the words in the box to reinforce the relationship between sound and writing.

Tapescript
a – *la piscina*
b – *la catedral*
c – *la oficina de turismo*
d – *el mercado*
e – *el Corte Inglés*
f – *el café de Internet*

1b Con tu compañero/a, pregunta y contesta. (AT2/2) [W1,4,5; S4,9]

✎ *Speaking and interacting with others – Level D*

Speaking. Pupils take turns to ask their partner the names of each of the places pictured in activity 1a.

2 Escucha e indica la dirección con la mano. (AT1/1) [W1,2; L4]

✎ *Listening for information and instructions – Level D*

Listening. Pupils listen to the recording and indicate the directions with their hands.

Teachers may wish to revise vocabulary covered in Module 4 for describing where things are. Pupils have already encountered *izquierda* and *derecha*.

Tapescript
a la izquierda
todo recto / todo derecho
a la derecha
a la izquierda
todo recto / todo derecho
a la derecha

a la derecha
a la izquierda
todo recto

a la izquierda
a la derecha
a la derecha
todo recto
a la izquierda
todo derecho

módulo 5 — Mi pueblo

3 Con tu compañero/a, dibuja una flecha y dice la dirección. (AT2/1) [W1,2; L4]

✄ *Speaking and interacting with others – Level D*

Speaking. Pupils take turns to draw an arrow and their partner says the direction in which it is pointing.

🎲 Teachers may wish to play a game to consolidate giving directions. One pupil stands by the entrance to the classroom with their eyes shut. Volunteers from the class take it in turns to give the pupil directions to navigate safely from the classroom entrance to the board. Teachers who are concerned about the health and safety risks of this activity may prefer to attempt a similar activity using the OHT map and cut out person suggested in Unit 1.

4 ¿Adónde van? Escucha y escribe el lugar y la dirección. (1–6) (AT1/2) [W1,2,4; S9; L3]

✄ *Listening for information and instructions – Level D*

Listening. Pupils listen to the recording and write the letter of the destination and draw an arrow to indicate the direction.

Answers

| 1 a ↑ | 2 d ← | 3 b → | 4 e ← | 5 f → | 6 c ↑ |

Tapescript

1 – ¿Por dónde se va a la piscina?
 – La piscina, pues todo derecho.
2 – ¿Dónde está el mercado?
 – El mercado está a la izquierda.
3 – La catedral, por favor.
 – ¿La catedral? Vamos a ver … la catedral está allá, a la derecha.
4 – ¿Por dónde se va al Corte Inglés?
 – ¿El Corte Inglés? Está allá, a la izquierda.
5 – ¿El café de Internet? Ah, sí, mire, a la derecha.
6 – ¿Hay una oficina de turismo?
 – Sí señor, siga todo recto.

Starter 2: **Unjumble sounds** [W1,6; L1,6]

Aims: To develop pupils' ability to pronounce key letters (c, z) and letter strings in Spanish and to consolidate knowledge of directions and places in a town (*izquierda, lugar, plaza, estación, sigue*). (Timing: 10 minutes)

Resources: Resource and Assessment File, page 92 (Starter 2)

Pairwork activity: Make an OHT using the master provided. Ask pupils to pronounce the letter strings on the OHT, drawing attention to the pronunciation of the letters 'c' and 'z'. Then reveal the list of jumbled-up words that use these strings (*lugar, izquierda, plaza, estación, sigue*). Pupils must unjumble the sounds and say the words correctly. Reveal the list of new words that contain some of the same sounds and get different pairs of pupils to pronounce these correctly (*Zaragoza, Guérnica, tradición, garbanzos, sierra, José María Áznar*). Then reveal the rhyme and give pupils three minutes to practise this, again in pairs (they can read alternate lines). Pupils then say the rhyme to the others. Award points for accurate pronunciation.

5a Mira el mapa. Escucha y escribe la letra apropiada para cada lugar. (1–7) (AT1/2) [W1,2,5; S4,9; L3]

✄ *Listening for information and instructions – Level D*

Listening. Pupils listen to the recording and write the correct letter from the map for each place on the signpost.

Before attempting this activity, teachers should introduce *primera, segunda, tercera (a la izquierda, derecha)*. The *Gramática* box gives the different command forms.

Answers

la oficina de turismo G, el Corte Inglés A, la estación de autobuses F, la piscina E, el mercado D, el estadio C, la catedral B

Tapescript

1 – ¿Para ir a la oficina de turismo, por favor?
 – Tome la primera a la derecha.
2 – ¿Por dónde se va al Corte Inglés?
 – Toma la primera a la izquierda.
3 – ¿Por dónde se va a la estación de autobuses?
 – Toma la segunda a la derecha.
4 – ¿Dónde está la piscina, por favor?
 – Toma la tercera a la derecha.
5 – ¿Por dónde se va al mercado?
 – Siga todo recto y al final está el mercado.
6 – ¿Por dónde se va al estadio?
 – Tome la tercera a la izquierda.
7 – ¿Dónde está la catedral?
 – ¿La catedral? Pues, tome usted la segunda a la izquierda.

5b Con tu compañero/a, pide y da direcciones para llegar a los lugares en el mapa. (AT2/2) [W2,5; S4,9]

✄ *Speaking and interacting with others – Level D*

Speaking. Working in pairs, pupils take turns to ask for and give directions to the places on the map in activity 5a. They will need to use the answers from the listening activity to remind them what the places A–G on the map are.

Mi pueblo — módulo 5

Before attempting this activity, teachers will want to draw their pupils' attention to the vocabulary box below the example question and answer, and explain, or see if pupils can come up with suggestions for a rule about, the imperative form.

5c Escribe direcciones para cinco lugares en **5a**. (AT4/2) [W2,5; S9]

✉ *Writing to exchange information and ideas – Level D*

Writing. Pupils write directions to five of the places in activity 5a. Pupils should be reminded to use the vocabulary practised in the speaking activity.

> **Plenary**
> Start with a discussion of verbs in the present tense, and in particular the verb *ir*. Ask pupils to tell you if the verb is irregular or regular, and why. Then ask pupils in pairs to write down as many sentences as they can which use the verb *ir* from other topics covered so far. They can use their exercise books and textbooks. Pupils can also try to invent new sentences using previous language introduced, e.g. *Vamos a mi casa a las doce.* Remind pupils about *al* and *a la* if following a verb with places in a town.

Cuaderno A, page 46

1 Empareja las palabras con los dibujos apropiados. (AT3/1) [W1,4]

✉ *Knowing about language*

Reading. Pupils match up the words with the correct pictures.

Answers

| a la piscina | b el mercado | c la oficina de turismo |
| d la catedral | e el café de Internet | f El Corte Inglés |

2 Empareja las flechas con las direcciones. (AT3/1) [W2]

✉ *Knowing about language*

Reading. Pupils match up the arrows with the directions.

Answers

a la izquierda 3, la primera a la derecha 4, a la derecha 2, todo derecho 1, la segunda a la izquierda 5, la tercera a la izquierda 6

3 Mira el mapa y completa las direcciones. (AT3/2, AT4/1) [W2,5; S2,4,9]

✉ *Knowing about language*

Reading/Writing. Pupils use the map to help them fill in the gaps in the directions.

Answers

a Sigue todo derecho/recto.
b Toma la primera a la izquierda.
c Toma la segunda a la derecha.
d Toma la tercera a la izquierda.

Cuaderno B, page 46

1 Descifra los anagramas y empareja las palabras con los dibujos apropiados. (AT3/1) [W1,7]

✉ *Knowing about language*

Reading. Pupils unjumble the anagrams and match up the words with the appropriate pictures.

Answers

| 1 la catedral d | 2 la piscina a | 3 el café de Internet e |
| 4 El Corte Inglés f | 5 el mercado b | 6 la oficina de turismo c |

2 Empareja las flechas con las direcciones. (AT3/1) [W2]

✉ *Knowing about language*

Reading. Pupils match up the arrows with the directions.

Answers

a la izquierda 3, la primera a la derecha 4, a la derecha 2, todo derecho 1, la segunda a la izquierda 5, la tercera a la izquierda 6

3 Mira el mapa y completa las direcciones. (AT3/2, AT4/1) [W2,5; S2,4,9]

✉ *Knowing about language*

Reading/Writing. Pupils use the map to help them fill in the gaps in the directions.

Answers

a Sigue todo derecho/recto.
b Toma la primera a la izquierda.
c Toma la segunda a la derecha.
d Toma la tercera a la izquierda.

Hoja de trabajo 1, page 87 [L4]

Pairwork activity for pupils to practise asking for and giving directions.

módulo 5

3 Sube la avenida y cruza la plaza …

(Pupil's Book pages 84–85)

Main topics
- Describing the location of places in a town
- Giving more detailed directions

Key Framework Objectives
- Typical word order 7S1 (Reinforcement)
- Reading using cues 7T1 (Reinforcement)
- Following speech 7L2 (Reinforcement)
- Social conventions 7C5 (Reinforcement)

Grammar
- *de + la = de la*
- *de + el = del*
- Prepositional phrases: *al final de, al lado de*

Key language

¿Dónde está …?
La piscina está al lado del estadio.
El hospital está al final de la calle.
La Plaza Mayor está delante de la catedral.
La estación está enfrente del parque.

el aeropuerto	
la calle	el hospital
la plaza	la Plaza Mayor
el puente	el río
Baja	Cruza
Dobla	Sube
Tuerce	aquí

Resources
Cassette C, side 1
CD 3, track 4
Cuaderno A and B, page 47
Grammar, Resource and Assessment File, page 90
OHTs 23 and 24: places in town, directions

Starter 1: Squashed sentences [S1,8; L1,6]

Aims: To write simple sentences accurately and to reinforce knowledge of punctuation and spelling. (Timing: 5–10 minutes)

Pairwork activity: Write up the following sentences with no punctuation, accents or spaces: *Toma la primera a la derecha, Vamos a la playa, ¿Por dónde se va al mercado?, Váis al cine, Sigue todo recto,* (e.g. *tomalaprimeraaladerecha*). Give pupils two minutes with their partner to say the sentences to each other. Ask different pupils to read out the sentences to the class. Pupils write down the sentences with the correct word-spacing and punctuation.

1a Completa las frases con *del* o *de la*. (AT3/2) [W2,4,5; S2]

✂ *Knowing about language*

Reading. Pupils should read through the *Gramática* box in order to complete the sentences with *de la* or *del* to describe where the places are on the map.

Pupils may already be familiar with this grammatical concept and be able to work out the rule for themselves before reading the *Gramática*. Teachers may wish to revise *a la* and *al*, encountered in Unit 2 which may help to reinforce the pattern. It would also be useful at this stage to revise the pronouns of location encountered in Module 4, Unit 4.

Answers

1 del	2 del	3 de la	4 del	5 de la	6 del	7 de la

1b Escucha y comprueba tus respuestas. (AT1/2) [W2,4,5; L1]

✂ *Knowing about language*

Listening. Pupils listen to the recording to check their answers to activity 1a. Teachers may wish to ask volunteers to read out their answers before playing the recording to reinforce the grammatical point and discuss any difficulties pupils may have.

Tapescript

1 – La piscina está delante del estadio.
2 – El cine está enfrente del mercado.
3 – El hospital está al final de la Calle Mallorca.
4 – La estación de trenes está al lado del parque.
5 – Toma la primera a la derecha. La estación de autobuses está enfrente de la estación de trenes.
6 – El instituto está al lado del río.
7 – El café de Internet está a la izquierda, enfrente de la oficina de turismo.

2 Con tu compañero/a, describe lugares en el mapa. (AT2/2) [W2,4,5; S4; L4]

✂ *Speaking and interacting with others – Level D*

Speaking. Pupils work in pairs to ask and answer questions about the location of places on the map.

3a Escucha y escribe el orden correcto. (AT1/1, AT3/1) [W1; L1]

✂ *Knowing about language*

Listening/Reading. Pupils listen to the recording and match up the directions they hear with the words. This is a good opportunity to reinforce the relationship between sound and writing.

Mi pueblo — módulo 5

Before attempting this activity, teachers may wish to introduce the directions using mimes, for example pointing up for *sube*. In this way, teachers can ask pupils to do the mimes in response to hearing the directions.

Teachers may wish to revise the imperative tense encountered in Unit 2 (*toma* and *sigue*) before reading through the *Gramática*. Some pupils may wish to attempt to make up the rule for *tú* and *usted* endings.

Answers

d, a, e, b, c

Tapescript

– Tuerce
– Sube
– Cruza
– Baja
– Dobla

3b Escucha y escribe la dirección. (1–8) (AT1/1) [W1; L1; C5]

✉ *Knowing about language*

Listening. Pupils listen to the recording and either draw the symbol or write the letter from activity 3a for the directions they hear.

Answers

| 1 ↑ | 2 ↰ | 3 ↓ | 4 ↰ | 5 ↑ | 6 ↓ | 7 ↰ |
| 8 ↰ | | | | | | |

Tapescript

1 – Sube.
2 – Dobla.
3 – Baja.
4 – Tuerce.
5 – Suba.
6 – Baje.
7 – Doble.
8 – Tuerza.

3c Con tu compañero/a, da e indica las direcciones. (AT2/1) [W1; L4]

✉ *Speaking to convey information – Level D*

Speaking. Pupils give each other directions, using the list in activity 3a, and indicate the direction. Teachers may wish to agree mimes with the class before attempting this activity, as suggested in activity 3a.

Starter 2: Preposition revision [W2,4; S1; L2]

Aims: To revise *al*, *a la* and *del*, *de la*, and locations in a town (*al final de, al lado de, cerca de, delante de, enfrente de*). (Timing: 5 minutes)

Activity: Explain to pupils that they must complete the sentence with the correct preposition (*al, a la, del or de la*). Read out the following sentences, taken from Module 5, Units 1–3, saying 'beep' each time you would like pupils to add in a preposition: 1 *Vamos (a la) playa*; 2 *Tomo la segunda (a la) izquierda*; 3 *El hospital está enfrente (del) aeropuerto*; 4 *El instituto está al lado (del) río*; 5 *José y Carlos van (al) polideportivo*. Pupils can either write their answers down or give them orally.

4 ¿Adónde vamos? Lee las direcciones y mira el mapa. Escribe los lugares. (AT3/3) [W1,2; T1]

✉ *Reading for information and instructions – Level D*

Reading. Pupils follow the directions and trace the route on the map on page 84 to find out where the people are going.

Answers

| a café de Internet | b estación de autobuses |
| c el centro comercial | d la plaza de toros |

5a Mira el mapa en la página 84. Con tu compañero/a, pide y da direcciones para llegar a los lugares. (AT2/3) [W1,2; S4; L4]

✉ *Speaking and interacting with others – Level D/E*

Speaking. Pupils work in pairs to ask and give directions to the places illustrated, using the map on page 84.

5b Escribe direcciones para cada lugar en **5a**. (AT4/2–3) [W1,2; S9; T5]

✉ *Writing to convey information and ideas – Level D/E*

Writing. Pupils write out the directions to the places in activity 5a. Teachers may prefer pupils to write out the directions in pairs as a conversation.

módulo 5 — Mi pueblo

Suggested answers

Sube por la Avenida de la República y toma la tercera a la izquierda. Cruza la Avenida Vía Augusta y la piscina está a la derecha, delante del estadio.

Sube por la Avenida de la República. Toma la primera a la derecha. Baja por la Calle Sevilla. La estación de autobuses está a la izquierda.

Toma la primera a la izquierda. Sigue todo recto. La plaza de toros está al final de la calle.

Sube por la Avenida de la República. Cruza la Calle Sevilla. La oficina de turismo está a la derecha, enfrente del café de Internet.

Sube por la Avenida de la República. Toma la tercera a la derecha. El instituto está a la izquierda, entre el Corte Inglés y el puente.

Plenary

Recap on prepositions by playing ¿*Dónde está el caramelo?* with the class. The class should close their eyes while you hide a sweet (or any small object). Pupils must then guess ¿*Dónde está el caramelo?*, using the prepositions they have learned. Include *a la derecha de* and *a la izquierda de* as well as other prepositions of place. This can be played several times, depending on the time available. Alternatively, pupils could play this game in groups.

Cuaderno A, page 47

1a Completa las palabras con *a, b, c* o *e*. (AT3/1) [W7]

✉ *Knowing about language*

Reading. Pupils complete the words with the letters *a, b, c* or *e*.

Answers

| a tuerce | b dobla | c baja | d cruza | e sube |

1b Escribe la palabra apropiada para cada dibujo. (AT4/1) [W1]

✉ *Knowing about language*

Writing. Pupils write the appropriate word for each picture.

Answers

| a baja | b sube | c cruza | d dobla/tuerce |

2a Mira el mapa y elige los números apropiados. (AT3/2) [W2,5; S2]

✉ *Reading for information and instructions – Level C*

Reading. Pupils read the directions and write the number of the place on the map.

Answers

| a 4 | b 5 | c 1 | d 3 | e 2 |

2b Mira el mapa en **2a** otra vez y completa las frases con las palabras apropiadas. (AT3/2) [W2; S2]

✉ *Reading for information and instructions – Level C*

Reading. Pupils use the map in activity 2a to help them choose the appropriate word to complete the sentences.

Answers

| a delante de | b al lado de | c entre |

Cuaderno B, page 47

1a Completa las palabras con *a, b, c* o *e*. (AT3/1) [W7]

✉ *Knowing about language*

Reading. Pupils complete the words with the letter *a, b, c* or *e*.

Answers

| a tuerce | b dobla | c baja | d cruza | e sube |

1b Escribe la palabra apropiada para cada dibujo. (AT4/1) [W1]

✉ *Knowing about language*

Writing. Pupils write the appropriate word for each picture.

Answers

| a baja | b sube | c cruza | d dobla/tuerce |

2a Escribe las letras de los lugares en el mapa. (AT3/3) [W2,5; T1]

✉ *Reading for information and instructions – Level D*

Reading. Pupils read the directions to find out the names of the places numbered on the map.

Answers

| b 4 | c 5 | d 1 | e 3 | f 2 |

Mi pueblo — módulo 5

2b Mira el mapa en **2a** otra vez y contesta a las preguntas. (AT4/2–3) [W2,5; S9]

✉ *Writing to exchange information and ideas – Level D*

Writing. Pupils use the map from activity 2a to answer the questions.

Answers

a Sube la Avenida de Argentina. El cine está a la izquierda, al lado de/a la derecha de la oficina de turismo.
b Sube la Avenida de Argentina. La tienda de regalos está a la izquierda de la oficina de turismo, enfrente de la piscina.
c Sube la Avenida de Argentina y toma la primera a la derecha. El mercado está a la izquierda, detrás de la piscina.

Grammar, Resource and Assessment File, page 90 [W2, 5; S9]

Activities to practise the verb *ir*, as well as reinforce prepositions, *a la, al, de la, del*.

1 Answers

1 la	**2** el	**3** el	**4** la	**5** la
6 el	**7** la	**8** el	**9** la	**10** el

2 Answers

b Va a la piscina.
c Voy a la tienda.
d Va a la oficina de turismo.
e Vamos al polideportivo.
f Van a la plaza de toros.

3 Answers

a El instituto está al lado del mercado.
b La plaza de toros está enfrente del hospital.
c La estación de trenes está delante del aeropuerto.
d El hospital está al lado del polideportivo.
e La estación de trenes está al lado del aeropuerto.
f La oficina de turismo está delante del mercado.

módulo 5

4 ¿Está cerca?

(Pupil's Book pages 86–87)

Main topics

- Talking about distance

Key Framework Objectives

- Basic questions 7S4 (Reinforcement)
- Reading using cues 7T1 (Reinforcement)
- Checking before reading 7T3 (Reinforcement)

Key language

Numbers 32–100
¿Dónde está …?
¿Está lejos la playa?
¿Está cerca la estación de servicio?
Está (muy) cerca.
Está (bastante) lejos.
Está a 10 kilómetros.
Está a 5 minutos andando.
Está a 10 minutos en coche.
treinta (y dos)
cuarenta
cincuenta
sesenta
setenta
ochenta
noventa
cien

Resources

Cassette C, side 1
CD 3, track 5
Cuaderno A and B, page 48
Starter 1, Resource and Assessment File, page 93
Skills, Resource and Assessment File, page 91

Starter 1: Question-making [S1,4,8]

Aims: To reinforce pupils' knowledge of forming questions and using correct punctuation (*¿Dónde está … ? ¿Por dónde se va al/ a la … ?*). (Timing: 10 minutes)

Resources: Resource and Assessment Pack, page 93 (Starter 1)

Pairwork activity: Make copies of the game-card master. Give each pair of pupils a copy to cut out and shuffle. They then place the cards face-up on the table. Ask pupils to now categorise the cards in terms of verbs, question words and nouns (masculine and feminine). Go through each category and check that pupils have identified the correct words. Ask pupils to use the categories to construct a question. Complete one example as a class. End by discussing the importance of word order in questions and how this compares to English.

1a Escucha y lee. (AT1/2, AT3/2) [W2,5; S2,4; T2]

✳ *Knowing about language*

Listening/Reading. Pupils listen to the recording and read the conversations. Teachers may wish to get pupils to repeat after the recording, and/or act out the conversations in order to reinforce the relationship between sound and writing.

Before attempting this activity, teachers may wish to revise the structure *¿Dónde está …?* encountered in Unit 3 and use this to introduce *cerca* and *lejos*.

Teachers may also wish to use this opportunity to introduce the structures *está a … minutos* and *está a … kilómetros*.

Tapescript

1 – ¿Dónde está la playa? ¿Está lejos?
   – No, está cerca.
2 – ¿Dónde está la estación de servicio?
   – Está lejos.
3 – Al aeropuerto, por favor. ¿Está lejos?
   – No, está a cinco minutos en coche.
4 – ¿Está lejos el hospital?
   – Sí, está bastante lejos.
5 – ¿Hay un café de Internet por aquí?
   – Sí, hay. Está muy cerca, a 5 minutos andando.

1b Elige la respuesta apropiada a cada pregunta. (AT3/2) [W2,5; S2,4,5]

✳ *Knowing about language*

Reading. Pupils match up the questions and answers using the information from activity 1a.

Answers

1 b, No, está cerca.
2 a, No, está lejos.
3 e, No está cerca, a cinco minutos en coche.
4 d, Sí, está bastante lejos.
5 c, Sí, está muy cerca, a cinco minutos andando.

2a ¿Está cerca o lejos? Con tu compañero/a, pregunta y contesta. (AT2/2–3) [W2,5; S4,9; L4]

✳ *Speaking and interacting with others – Level D*

Speaking. Working in pairs, pupils take turns to ask and answer whether the places indicated on the signs are near or far. Teachers may wish to encourage pupils to add *está a … minutos* or *está a … kilómetros*.

R Before attempting this activity, teachers may wish to check that pupils understand all the places named on the signs.

Mi pueblo — módulo 5

2b ¿Dónde está? Tu compañero/a tiene que adivinar el lugar en **2a** que describes. (AT2/2) [W2,5; S9; L4]

✳ *Speaking and interacting with others – Level D*

Speaking. Pupils can play this guessing game in pairs or small groups. One pupil describes where one of the places from activity 2a is, and the other pupil(s) has/have to guess which place is being described.

Teachers may wish to play this guessing game as a whole-class activity before pupils work in pairs, in order to consolidate the new structures.

Starter 8: Text scanning [W1,2,5; T1,3]

Aims: To develop pupils' confidence in reading longer texts in Spanish; to build on reading skills by getting pupils to focus on specific aspects of a text; to revise knowledge of prepositions and the present tense (of verbs *vivir, estar, ir*). (Timing: 5–10 minutes)

Activity: Pupils look at the texts on page 87 of the Pupil's Book and are given 90 seconds to scan the text for prepositions of place. Give one example to start them off. Ask pupils how many they have found. Compile a list on the board, with a tally. Give pupils 90 seconds to find verbs (including *hay*) and repeat the process.

---

3 Empareja las descripciones con los mapas. (AT3/3) [W2,5; T1]

✳ *Reading for information and instructions – Level D*

Reading. Pupils read the texts describing where Alba and Laura live, and write down the letter of the map that is being described.

Answers

Alba c, Laura b

Literacy activity [T5]

There is no description for map **a**. Teachers may wish to use this opportunity to undertake a shared writing activity with the class to describe map **a**. One way in which to approach this activity may be to conduct a brainstorm of all the places and features on the map, and the structures that could be used to describe the location of these features. Pupils could then be given time to work in pairs or small groups to work on a description, before feeding back to the class. The teacher could note down the suggestions, before editing them into a final description that pupils copy into their books.

4 Dibuja un mapa de tu ciudad o pueblo y escribe una descripción. (AT4/2–4) [W2,5; T5]

✳ *Writing to establish and maintain social contact – Level D/E*

Writing. Pupils draw and label a map of their own town or village and write a description, giving details of the location of the places on their map.

Plenary

Use the three illustrations on page 87 of the Pupil's Book as a basis for recapping the language introduced in the module. Working in groups of three or four, pupils must think of three sentences for each illustration, e.g. for illustration a: *El aeropuerto está cerca de la plaza de toros.* The groups then read out their sentences to the other pupils. Ask individual pupils to translate these sentences to reinforce the learning.

Cuaderno A, page 48

1 Completa el crucigrama. (AT4/1) [W1,7]

✳ *Knowing about language*

Writing. Pupils write the numbers in words to complete the crossword.

Answers

Across: CUARENTA, CIEN, DIEZ, SESENTA, VEINTE, TREINTA, NOVENTA
Down: OCHENTA, CINCUENTA, SETENTA, CINCO

2 Elige la frase apropiada para cada lugar. (AT3/2) [W2,5]

✳ *Knowing about language*

Reading. Pupils choose the correct phrase to describe the location of each of the places on the signs.

Answers

1 c	2 a	3 e	4 b	5 d

3 ¿Están cerca o lejos de tu casa? Escribe los lugares en las listas apropiadas. (AT3/1, AT4/1) [W2,5; S9]

módulo 5 — Mi pueblo

✖ *Writing to exchange information and ideas – Level C*

Reading/Writing. Pupils decide whether the places listed are near or far from their own homes and copy the words into the appropriate column.

Cuaderno B, page 48

1 Completa el crucigrama. (AT4/1) [W1,7]

✖ *Knowing about language*

Writing. Pupils write the numbers in words to complete the crossword.

Answers

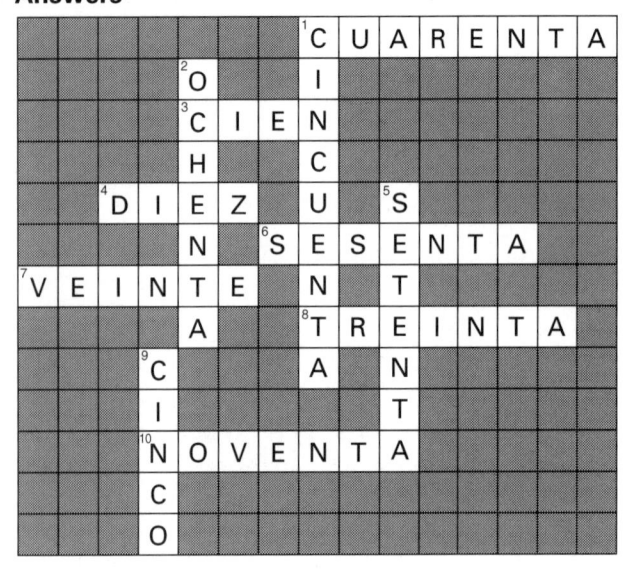

						¹C	U	A	R	E	N	T	A
			²O			I							
			³C	I	E	N							
			H			C							
		⁴D	I	E	Z		U		⁵S				
			N			⁶S	E	S	E	N	T	A	
⁷V	E	I	N	T	E		N		T				
			A			⁸T	R	E	I	N	T	A	
		⁹C				A			N				
		I				T							
		¹⁰N	O	V	E	N	T	A					
		C											
		O											

2 Elige la frase apropiada para cada lugar. (AT3/2) [W2,5]

✖ *Knowing about language*

Reading. Pupils choose the correct phrase to describe the location of each of the places on the signs.

Answers

| 1 c | 2 a | 3 e | 4 b | 5 d |

3 Escribe frases para indicar la distancia entre tu casa y los lugares. (AT4/2) [W2,5; S9]

✖ *Writing to exchange information and ideas – Level D*

Writing. Pupils write sentences to say how far the places illustrated are from their own homes.

Skills, Resource and Assessment File, page 91 [W7]

These activities provide pupils with the opportunity to develop their language-learning skills detailed in paragraph 3 of the Programme of Study, reflecting on patterns to help them to learn and memorise numbers more effectively.

módulo 5

5 ¿Cómo es tu ciudad?

(Pupil's Book pages 88–89)

Main topics
- Talking about what your town is like

Key Framework Objectives
- Compound sentences 7S6 (Reinforcement)
- Geographical facts 7C1 (Reinforcement)
- Contact with native speakers 7C3 (Reinforcement)
- Stories and songs 7C4 (Reinforcement)

Other aims
- Adjective agreement

Key language

¿Cómo es tu ciudad/pueblo/barrio?
Es la capital de (España).
Es …

antiguo/a   industrial
bonito/a   moderno/a
grande   pequeño/a
histórico/a   tranquilo/a
importante

Me gusta (mucho) porque …
¿Qué hay en tu ciudad/pueblo/barrio?
Hay varios monumentos.
Hay mucho tráfico.
Hay muchos turistas.
Hay/Tiene …

un acueducto (romano)	un monumento
un alcázar	un museo
un castillo	un palacio
un edificio	un parque nacional
un equipo de fútbol	un puerto
una fábrica	un quiosco
una iglesia	la sierra
un lugar	la universidad

Resources

Cassette C, side 1
CD 3, track 6
Cuaderno A and B, page 49
Starter 1, Resource and Assessment File, page 93
Hoja de trabajo 2, Resource and Assessment File, page 88

Starter 1: ¿España? [W1,6; L1; C1]

Aims: To build on cultural knowledge of Spanish and South American towns/cities; to develop pupils' knowledge of vowel sounds. (Timing: 10 minutes)

Resources: Resource and Assessment File, page 93 (Starter 1)

Activity: Make an OHT using the master provided. At the start of the lesson, read out the following cities in a random order: *Santiago de Compostela, Córdoba, Burgos, Ronda, Jerez, Cádiz, Medellín, Lima, Guadalajara, Buenos Aires*. Pupils must say *Sí* or *No* as to whether the cities or towns are located in Spain. This response could be physical (stand up/sit down) or verbal: Answers (*Sí*): *Santiago de Compostela, Córdoba, Burgos, Ronda, Jerez, Cádiz*. Then give pupils a copy of the OHT to work on in pairs. Reveal the gapped words one at a time. Pupils must try to complete the missing vowels, with the correct accents, by listening to their pronunciation.

Suggestion: Teaching and learning foundation subjects

This unit could form the basis of a cross-curricular activity with the school's Humanities department, based on the topic of 'Settlements' in the Geography Schemes of Work.

1a Mira el mapa de España y lee. Elige los pueblos o las ciudades apropiados para cada descripción. (AT3/3–4) [W2,5; S6; T1; C1]

Knowing about language

Reading. The level of this activity will be determined by the degree of support given by the teacher.

In order to achieve level 4, pupils should first make sure they understand the key to the map, which will help them to work out the meanings of unfamiliar words in the four texts. The pupils work out which cities on the map are being referred to in the texts.

Teachers may wish to give their pupils more support, but this may mean level 3, since the unpredictable element would be removed.

Answers

a Bilbao	b Pedraza	c Madrid	d Sevilla

1b Escucha y comprueba tus respuestas. (AT1/3–4) [W2,5; S6; T1; L1; C1]

Knowing about language

Listening. Pupils listen to the recording and check their answers to activity 1a. As in activity 1a, the level of this activity will depend on the degree of support given by the teacher.

Tapescript

a Bilbao es una ciudad industrial. Está en el norte del país. Tiene un puerto y muchas fábricas. Pero también tiene un museo muy famoso, el museo Guggenheim.

b Pedraza es un pueblo antiguo y muy histórico. Es pequeño y tranquilo. Tiene iglesias y un castillo. Hay una plaza muy bonita. Está al norte de Madrid.

c Madrid es la capital de España. Está en el centro del país. Es una ciudad antigua y moderna. Es comercial y residencial. Hay museos importantes y el Palacio Real.

módulo 5 — Mi pueblo

Tiene un aeropuerto, el aeropuerto de Barajas. También hay mucho tráfico.

d *Sevilla está en el sur. Es una ciudad muy antigua y bonita. Tiene muchos monumentos, una catedral y muy cerca hay un parque nacional, el parque nacional de Doñana. Hay muchos turistas de todo el mundo.*

2a Escucha y empareja los dibujos con las descripciones. (1–4) (AT1/3) [W5; S4,6; L3]

Listening for information and instructions – Level D

Listening. Pupils listen to the descriptions on the recording and decide which of the four towns pictured is being described in each.

Answers

| 1 d | 2 c | 3 b | 4 a |

Tapescript

1 – ¿Cómo es tu pueblo?
 – Es antiguo y muy bonito. Es tranquilo.
 – ¿Qué hay en tu pueblo?
 – Hay una plaza, un museo y un castillo.
 – ¿Hay tiendas?
 – Sólo hay una tienda, pero hay dos bares. Es un poco aburrido.

2 – ¿Cómo es tu ciudad?
 – Es industrial. Hay mucho tráfico.
 – ¿Qué hay en tu ciudad?
 – Hay un puerto y muchas fábricas. No es tranquilo, pero me gusta.

3 – ¿Cómo es tu barrio?
 – Es residencial. Es moderno y limpio.
 – ¿Qué hay en tu barrio?
 – Hay un parque, un hospital, y muchas tiendas.

4 – ¿Cómo es tu ciudad?
 – Es antigua y muy histórica.
 – ¿Qué hay en tu ciudad?
 – Hay monumentos, museos, una catedral … y muchos turistas. Me gusta mucho.

2b Con tu compañero/a, pregunta y contesta. (AT2/3) [W2,5; S4,6,9; L4]

Speaking and interacting with others – Level D/E

Speaking. Pupils work in pairs to ask and answer questions about where they live, what it is like, and what there is.

R Teachers may wish to practise the structures *es* and *hay* with the new vocabulary encountered in this unit before pupils attempt this activity.

Starter 2: ¿Verdad o mentira? [W1; L2,3,4]

Aims: To revise descriptive language for places; to develop ability to respond to spoken language.
(Timing: 5 minutes)

Activity: Before the lesson, jot down ten statements about the place where your school is located, including some false statements. For example, *Londres no es grande ni industrial / En Londres hay un palacio*, etc. Pupils respond to the sentences you read out by writing down *Verdad* or *Mentira*. Alternatively, pupils could put their thumbs up for *Verdad* and down for *Mentira*. Where there is a discrepancy with the responses, ask pupils to translate the sentence and then justify their response.

R With lower-ability classes, write the sentences on the board or a transparency and revise key language before starting this exercise.

3a Lee la carta de Mateo. Busca las palabras que no conoces en el diccionario. (AT3/4) [S6; T1,4]

Reading for information and instructions – Level D

Reading. Pupils read the letter and look up words that they do not understand in the glossary or a dictionary.

3b ¿Verdad (✓) o mentira (✗)? (AT3/4) [T1]

Reading for information and instructions – Level D

Reading. Pupils decide whether the sentences are true (*verdad*) or false (*mentira*) based on their understanding of the letter in activity 3a.

Answers

| a ✗ | b ✗ | c ✓ | d ✓ | e ✓ | f ✓ | g ✗ |
| h ✗ | i ✗ | | | | | |

3c Escribe una descripción de un barrio/un pueblo/una ciudad. (AT4/2–4) [S6; T5,6]

Writing to establish and maintain personal contact – Level D/E/F

Writing. Pupils write a description of where they live.

ICT activity [T5; C3]

Teachers may wish to use desk-top publishing software such as *Publisher* to produce a brochure about their town or area. This could then be either printed and sent to a partner school in Spain or Latin America, or sent as an attachment to an e-mail, in order to give pupils opportunities to compare their experiences with those of other young people in another country. This could even be incorporated into a Citizenship activity.

4 Escucha y lee la canción. (AT1/3, AT3/3) [S6; L1; C4]

Listening for enjoyment

Listening/Reading. Pupils listen to the song and read the text. Teachers may wish to play the song through

Mi pueblo — módulo 5

once and check that pupils have understood, before encouraging pupils to sing along. Teachers may even wish to organise a class singing contest, dividing the class into three groups and assigning one verse to each group, in order to encourage participation.

Tapescript

Mi ciudad es industrial
También es muy comercial
Hay un aeropuerto
Y también un puerto
Cine, tiendas y hospital.

Mi pueblo es tranquilo
También es muy antiguo
Hay una iglesia
Y una plaza
Bares, parque y museo.

Mi barrio es bonito
También es muy ruidoso
Hay un estadio
Y un mercado
Y un polideportivo.

Plenary

Pupils work in pairs. Using page 88 of the Pupil's Book, ask pupils to cover the map and text so that only the four illustrations are visible at the bottom of the page. Pupils can then use the language grid on page 89, and their exercise books, to produce sentences about each illustration, e.g. *Es muy industrial y hay un puerto*. Their partner must identify the correct picture in Spanish, e.g. *Es 'c'*.

Cuaderno A, page 49

1a and **b** Mira los dibujos y completa las frases con las palabras apropiadas. (AT3/2) [W1,5]

Reading for information and instructions – Level C

Reading. Pupils choose the appropriate word(s) to complete each sentence.

Answers

1a			
a un pueblo	**b** pequeño	**c** tranquilo	**d** histórico
e un castillo			
1b			
a una ciudad	**b** grande	**c** ruidosa	**d** industrial
f un aeropuerto			

2 Completa las frases con los nombres de ciudades y pueblos de tu país. (AT3/2) [W5; S2]

Reading for information and instructions – Level C

Reading. Pupils complete the sentences, giving the names of towns or cities in their own country.

3 Escribe cuatro frases sobre tu ciudad o pueblo. (AT4/2–3) [W5; S9]

Writing to establish and maintain personal contact – Level C/D

Writing. Pupils write four sentences about their own town or city.

✚ Teachers may wish to encourage pupils to practise a particular structure, such as *hay* or *es*, or encourage pupils to write more creatively, including structures practised in this unit, such as describing location.

Cuaderno B, page 49

1 Mira el dibujo y completa las frases con las palabras apropiadas. (AT3/2) [W1,5]

Reading for information and instructions – Level C

Reading. Pupils choose the appropriate word(s) to complete each sentence.

Answers

a una ciudad	**b** grande	**c** ruidosa	**d** industrial
e un puerto	**f** un aeropuerto		

2 Completa las frases con los nombres de ciudades y pueblos de tu país. (AT3/2) [W5; S2,9]

Reading for information and instructions – Level D

Reading. Pupils complete the sentences giving the name of a town or city in their own country.

3 Escribe seis frases sobre tu ciudad o pueblo. (AT4/2–4) [W5; S9]

Writing to establish and maintain personal contact – Level D/E/F

Writing. Pupils write six sentences about their own town or city.

✚ Teachers may wish to encourage pupils to practise a particular structure, such as *hay* or *es*, or encourage pupils to write more creatively, including structures practised in this unit, as well as more varied descriptions, opinions and connectives, incorporating language learnt in different contexts.

Hoja de trabajo 2, page 88 [L4]

Pairwork activity for pupils to practise asking and talking about what there is in their town. Pupils should draw the appropriate symbol for what there is in their partner's town, and they then compare their answers at the end of the activity.

módulo 5

6 ¿Qué tiempo hace?

(Pupil's Book pages 90–91)

Main topics

- Talking about the weather

Key Framework Objectives

- Time and tenses 7S7 (Part-launch. See also 3.4 and 6.5) (see Optional Thinking Skills activity, p.157 of Teacher's Guide)
- Letters and sounds 7W6 (Reinforcement)
- Improving written work 7T7 (Reinforcement)
- Sound patterns 7L1 (Reinforcement)

Key language

¿Qué tiempo hace?
Hace calor.
Hace frío.
Hace sol.
Hace buen tiempo.
Hace fresco.
Hace mal tiempo.
Hace viento.
Hay niebla.
Llueve.
el invierno
el otoño
la primavera
el verano
a veces
Hay tormenta.
Nieva.
en invierno
en otoño
en primavera
en verano

Resources

Cassette C, side 1
CD 3, track 7
Cuaderno A and B, page 50
Starter 1, Resource and Assessment File, page 94
Hoja de trabajo 3, Resource and Assessment File, page 89
OHTs 25 and 26: the weather, the seasons

Suggestion

If satellite TV is available, either through school or home, or a friend or colleague living in Spain, the teacher could try and make a video-recording of the weather forecast at the end of the midday *Telediario* on *TVE*. The language used and pronunciation are generally very clear, as are the graphics. The video-recording could be used in a variety of contexts, including: introducing the symbols for different types of weather; prediction (turning down the volume and seeing if pupils can guess what the presenter is saying); reinforcing the geography of Spain.

Starter 1: Letter strings [W6; L1]

Aims: To introduce weather vocabulary and to make links between the spelling and pronunciation of words. (Timing: 5 minutes)

Resources: Resource and Assessment File, page 94 (Starter 1)

Activity: Make an OHT using the master provided. Quickly revise the alphabet with the whole class, with an oral chant of each letter. Display the OHT and ensure pupils can pronounce each letter string correctly. Read out a list of words describing the weather (*hace, viento, tiempo, llueve, nieva, niebla*). Pupils must try to write down the correct word using the letter strings on the OHT and their knowledge of the Spanish alphabet. Pupils then check their spellings against page 90 of the Pupil's Book, writing the English equivalent next to each word. To extend the length of this activity, progress to other words that pupils write down by listening to how they sound (a few will be familiar), e.g. *sol, mal, hay, tormenta, frío, calor, fresco*.

✚ Higher-ability students can try the exercise without the use of the OHT.

1a Escucha y repite. Pon atención a la pronunciación. (AT1/1, AT2/1) [W5; L1]

✉ *Knowing about language*

Listening/Speaking. Pupils listen to the phrases about the weather and repeat them, paying attention to the pronunciation and, in so doing, the connection between sound and writing.

Teachers may wish to introduce the new vocabulary for the weather before attempting this activity, as well as the symbols which are not always understood by all pupils. Flashcards or an OHT could be used, or video as suggested above.

Tapescript

a – Hace sol.
b – Hace fresco.
c – Hace calor.
d – Hace viento.
e – Hace frío.
f – Hace mal tiempo.
g – Hace buen tiempo.
h – Llueve.
i – Nieva.
j – Hay niebla.
k – Hay tormenta.

1b Empareja las frases con los dibujos. (AT3/1) [W5; S9]

✉ *Knowing about language*

Reading. Pupils match up the phrases with the drawings.

Answers

1 c	2 e	3 a	4 d	5 b	6 g	7 f
8 h	9 i	10 k	11 j			

Mi pueblo — módulo 5

2a Escucha y empareja los dibujos con las descripciones del tiempo. (1–6) (AT1/3) [W2,5; S4; L3]

✠ *Listening for information and instructions – Level D*

Listening. Pupils listen to the conversations about the weather, each of which contain more than one of the phrases from activity 1. They choose the appropriate picture for each conversation.

➕ Teachers may additionally wish to ask pupils to write the letters for the types of weather they hear in each conversation, as this will help with activity 2b.

Answers

| 1 b | 2 e | 3 a | 4 c | 5 f | 6 d |

Tapescript

1 – ¿Qué tiempo hace?
 – Llueve mucho. Hace frío y hace viento. Hace muy mal tiempo.
2 – ¿Qué tiempo hace hoy?
 – Llueve pero no hace frío, hace mucho calor.
3 – ¿Qué tiempo hace?
 – Hace muy buen tiempo. Hace sol y hace mucho calor.
4 – ¿Qué tiempo hace esta mañana?
 – Nieva. Hace mucho frío. Me gusta la nieve, es bonita.
5 – ¿Qué tiempo hace hoy?
 – Hay tormenta. Hace mal tiempo.
6 – Hace frío. Hay niebla. Hace mal tiempo. ¡Brrrrr!

2b Con tu compañero/a, describe el tiempo en cada dibujo. (AT2/2) [W2,5; S4,9; L4]

✠ *Speaking and interacting with others – Level D*

Speaking. In pairs, pupils ask and answer questions about the weather in each of the pictures in activity 2a.

Starter 2: Hangman [W1,6,7; S1,2]

Aims: To revise weather vocabulary and to reinforce spellings (*hace … sol, viento, calor, fresco, frío, mal/buen tiempo, llueve; nieva, hay … niebla, tormenta*). (Timing: 5–10 minutes)

Activity: Choose a weather phrase and represent it with dashes on the board, e.g. _ _ _ _ / _ _ _ _ / _ _ _ _ _ _ (*hace buen tiempo*). Play the hangman game with the class divided into two groups. Start by conducting the game yourself and then ask pupils to come up to the board to choose the word dashes and write in the correct letters. Then pupils can play in pairs, using page 90 of the Pupil's Book to check spellings, if necessary.

3a Copia y completa la descripción del tiempo durante las estaciones del año. (AT4/2) [W2,5; S2,6,9]

✠ *Writing to exchange information and ideas – Level C*

Writing. Pupils copy and complete the description of the weather in the different seasons, replacing the pictures with the appropriate words.

Teachers may wish to introduce and practise the seasons listed in the box at the top of page 91 before attempting this activity.

Answers

En primavera llueve pero a veces hace buen tiempo.
En verano hace sol y hace mucho calor. A veces hay tormenta.
En otoño hace fresco y hace viento. A veces hay niebla.
En invierno nieva. Hace mal tiempo. Hace mucho frío.

3b Escucha y comprueba tus respuestas. (AT1/2–3) [W2,5; S2,6,9; L1]

✠ *Knowing about language*

Listening. Pupils listen to the recording and check their answers to activity 3a.

Tapescript

En primavera llueve pero a veces hace buen tiempo.
En verano hace sol y hace mucho calor. A veces hay tormenta.
En otoño hace fresco y hace viento. A veces hay niebla.
En invierno nieva. Hace mal tiempo. Hace mucho frío.

4a Mira el mapa. ¿Verdad (✓) o mentira (✗)? (AT3/2) [W2,5; S3,6,9]

✠ *Reading for information and instructions – Level D*

Reading. Pupils look at the weather map and decide whether the sentences are true (*verdad*) or false (*mentira*).

➕ Teachers may wish to ask pupils to correct the sentences that are false.

Answers

| 1 ✓ | 2 ✗ | 3 ✗ | 4 ✓ | 5 ✗ | 6 ✗ |

4b Describe el tiempo en cinco ciudades. (AT4/2–3) [W5; S6,9; T5]

✠ *Writing to exchange information and ideas – Level D*

Writing. Pupils write descriptions of the weather in five different cities on the map.

Teachers may prefer pupils to write one sentence for each city, or may prefer to encourage pupils to develop more extended writing techniques, through the use of connectives.

módulo 5 — Mi pueblo

Plenary

Ask pupils to use the *Resumen* section on page 92 in the Pupil's Book to test each other on the language that has been introduced during the module. Pupils can award each other a point for each correct answer. Pupils with the most points after three minutes can take up the challenge of the 'hot seat', where they have to accurately answer questions asked by the teacher and/or other pupils in order to stay in the seat.

Cuaderno A, page 50

1 Mira el mapa y completa las frases. (AT3/2) [W1,5]

Reading for information and instructions – Level C

Reading. Pupils use the map and the key to the symbols to help them complete the sentences about the weather in each city.

Answers

| a Llueve en La Coruña. |
| b Hace mal tiempo en Bilbao. |
| c En Barcelona hay tormenta. |
| d Nieva en Burgos. |
| e En Palma de Mallorca hace buen tiempo. |
| f Hay niebla en Zaragoza. |
| g En Granada hace calor. |
| h Hace sol en Córdoba. |
| i En Huelva y Cádiz hace viento. |

2 ¿Verdad (✓) o mentira (✗)? (AT3/2) [W1,5; S2]

Reading for information and instructions – Level D

Reading. Pupils decide whether the sentences describing the weather on the map in activity 1 are true (*verdad*) or false (*mentira*).

✚ Teachers may wish to ask pupils to correct the sentences that are false.

Answers

| a ✓ | b ✗ | c ✓ | d ✓ | e ✗ | f ✗ |

3 Colorea cinco meses para revelar las cuatro estaciones del año. (AT3/1) [W1,7]

Reading for enjoyment

Reading. Pupils identify and colour in five months of the year in the word snake in order to find the four seasons.

Answers

meses: abril, mayo, septiembre, enero, agosto
estaciones: verano, primavera, otoño, invierno

4 Completa las frases con las estaciones del año. (AT3/2) [W1,5; S9]

Reading for information and instructions – Level C

Reading. Pupils choose the appropriate season to complete each sentence.

Answers

| a verano | b invierno | c primavera | d otoño |

Cuaderno B, page 50

1 Mira el mapa y completa las frases. (AT3/2) [W1,5]

Reading for information and instructions – Level C

Reading. Pupils use the map and the key to the symbols to help them complete the sentences about the weather in each city.

Answers

| a Llueve en La Coruña. |
| b Hace mal tiempo en Bilbao. |
| c En Barcelona hay tormenta. |
| d Nieva en Burgos. |
| e En Palma de Mallorca hace buen tiempo. |
| f Hay niebla en Zaragoza. |
| g En Granada hace calor. |
| h Hace sol en Córdoba. |
| i En Huelva y Cádiz hace viento. |

2 ¿Verdad (✓) o mentira (✗)? (AT3/2) [W1,5; S2]

Reading for information and instructions – Level D

Reading. Pupils decide whether the sentences describing the weather on the map in activity 1 are true (*verdad*) or false (*mentira*).

✚ Teachers may wish to ask pupils to correct the sentences that are false.

Answers

| a ✓ | b ✗ | c ✓ | d ✓ | e ✗ | f ✗ |

3 Colorea cinco meses para revelar las cuatro estaciones del año. (AT3/1) [W1,7]

Reading for enjoyment

Reading. Pupils identify and colour in five months of the year in the word snake in order to find the four seasons.

Answers

meses: abril, mayo, septiembre, enero, agosto
estaciones: verano, primavera, otoño, invierno

Mi pueblo — módulo 5

4 Completa las frases con la estación apropiada. (AT3/2) [W1,5; S9]

Reading for information and instructions – Level D

Reading. Pupils choose the appropriate season to complete each sentence.

Answers

invierno, verano, otoño, verano, otoño, invierno

Hoja de trabajo 3, page 89 [L4]

Pupils take turns to ask their partner what the weather is like in the Spanish cities on the map. Pupils should draw the appropriate symbol by the city to show the weather, and then compare with their partner at the end of the activity.

Optional Thinking Skills lesson

Aims
To develop reading and writing skills; to encourage pupils to think more laterally about the texts that they read. (Timing: 40 minutes)

Resources
Resource and Assessment File, page 94 and 95 (Thinking skills)

Fact or opinion? [W5; S7; T1,3,6,7]

Activity: Read through the letter on Reading Card 6 with the class. The letter includes a small number of verbs in the preterite (as required by the Modern Languages Framework objectives for Year 7), but these are for receptive purposes only and should be treated as lexical items at this point. Ask pupils to work in groups of three or four. Give out a copy of Reading Card 7 and a pair of scissors for pupils to cut out individual statements. Take one of these statements to use as an example and invite the whole class to compare this to the letter. Pupils decide whether the statement is one of fact or opinion. When they decide, they should be aware that there is no right or wrong answer, but that they have to justify their answer. A fact is something they believe is definitely true, while an opinion is something that they may think is true but cannot prove. Pupils then work through each statement from Reading Card 7, establishing its meaning and discussing whether or not it is a statement of fact or an opinion, using the letter to support their decisions. This can be done in English. Emphasise that they should always have a reason for their decision.

módulo 5

Resumen y Prepárate

(Pupil's Book pages 92–93)

Resumen

This is a checklist of language covered in Module 5. There is a comprehensive **Resumen** list for Module 5 in the Pupil's Book (page 92) and a **Resumen** test sheet in Cuaderno A and B (page 54).

Key Framework Objectives

- Simple sentences 7S9 (Reinforcement)
- Gist and detail 7L3 (Reinforcement)
- Classroom talk 7L4 (Reinforcement)

Prepárate

A revision test to give practice for the test itself at the end of the module.

Resources

Cassette C, side 1
CD 3, track 8
Cuaderno A and B, Repaso (previously ¡Extra!), pages 51–52; Gramática, page 53

---

1 ¿Adónde van? Escucha y elige el dibujo apropiado para cada diálogo. (AT1/3) [W2,5; S4; L3]

✉ *Listening for information and instructions – Level C*

Listening. Pupils listen to the short conversations to identify where each person is going.

Answers

| 1 d | 2 e | 3 b | 4 c | 5 a |

Tapescript

1 – ¡Hola, Carlos! ¿Adónde vas?
 – Voy al parque.
2 – Voy al centro comercial.
3 – ¿Adónde vas?
 – Voy al cine.
4 – ¿Adónde va Pablo?
 – Va al polideportivo.
5 – ¿Vais a la playa?
 – No, vamos a la piscina.

2 Escucha y empareja cada dirección con el dibujo apropiado. (AT1/2) [W2,5; L3]

✉ *Listening for information and instructions – Level D*

Listening. Pupils listen to the directions and find the appropriate picture for each one.

Answers

| 1 b | 2 a | 3 c | 4 e | 5 d |

Tapescript

1 – Sigue todo derecho.
2 – Toma la segunda a la derecha.
3 – Cruza la plaza.
4 – Toma la primera a la izquierda. Está cerca.
5 – Sigue todo recto y al final, dobla a la izquierda.

3 Con tu compañero/a, pide y da direcciones para llegar a los lugares en el mapa. (AT2/2–3) [W2,5; S4,9; L4]

✉ *Speaking and interacting with others – Level D*

Speaking. In pairs, pupils ask for and give directions to the places on the map.

4 Empareja cada texto con el dibujo apropiado. (AT3/3) [W2,5; S9; T1]

✉ *Reading for information and instructions – Level D*

Reading. Pupils match up the short descriptions with the appropriate pictures.

Answers

| 1 c | 2 d | 3 b | 4 a |

5 Escribe una frase para cada dibujo. (AT4/1–2) [W5; S9]

✉ *Knowing about language*

Writing. Pupils write a phrase to describe each type of weather depicted.

Answers

| a Hace sol. | b Hace calor. | c Hace viento. | d Llueve. |

6 Escribe sobre tu pueblo o ciudad. Contesta a las preguntas. (AT4/2–4) [W2,5; S9]

✉ *Writing to establish and maintain personal contact – Level D/E*

Writing. Pupils write about their own town or city, using the questions as prompts.

Mi pueblo — módulo 5

Cuaderno A, pages 51–52

Repaso (previously ¡Extra!)

1 Completa el crucigrama con las palabras apropiadas. (AT3/2, AT4/1) [W1,2,5,7; S2]

✗ *Knowing about language*

Reading/Writing. Pupils use the clues to complete the crossword.

Answers

			¹G	²R	A	N	D	E		
³P				E			⁴B			
I		⁵D	E	R	E	C	H	A		
S	⁶O			O			J			
⁷C	A	F	É	⁸P	L	A	Y	A	⁹L	
I	I			U					E	
N	¹⁰C	I	N	E					J	
A	I		¹¹R	U	I	¹²D	O	S	O	
	¹³E	N		T		O			S	
		A	¹⁴V	O	Y		B			
							L			
			¹⁵C	I	U	D	A	D		

2a Mira la carta y elige las palabras apropiadas para describir Sevilla. (AT3/4) [W4; T1]

✗ *Reading for information and instructions – Level D/E*

Reading. Pupils read the letter and choose the adjectives that best describe Sevilla. Teachers may wish to ask pupils to justify their choice of adjective by asking them to pick out the relevant sections from the letter.

Answers

histórica, bonita, grande, tranquila, importante, interesante

2b ¿Verdad (✓) o mentira (✗)? (AT3/4) [W5; T1]

✗ *Reading for information and instructions – Level D*

Reading. Pupils reread the letter in activity 2a to help them decide whether the sentences are true (*verdad*) or false (*mentira*).

➕ Teachers may wish to ask pupils to correct the sentences that are false.

Answers

| a✓ | b✗ | c✓ | d✗ | e✓ | f✗ | g✓ |
| h✓ | | | | | | |

Cuaderno B, pages 51–52

Repaso (previously ¡Extra!)

1 Completa el crucigrama. (AT3/2, AT4/1) [W1,2,5,7; S2]

✗ *Knowing about language*

Reading/Writing. Pupils use the clues to complete the crossword.

Answers

			¹G	²R	A	N	D	E		
³P				E			⁴B			
I		⁵D	E	R	E	C	H	A		
S	⁶O			O			J			
⁷C	A	F	É	⁸P	L	A	Y	A	⁹L	
I	I			U					E	
N	¹⁰C	I	N	E					J	
A	I		¹¹R	U	I	¹²D	O	S	O	
	¹³E	N		T		O			S	
		A	¹⁴V	O	Y		B			
							L			
			¹⁵C	I	U	D	A	D		

2a Mira la carta y elige las palabras apropiadas para describir Sevilla. (AT3/4) [W4; T1]

✗ *Reading for information and instructions – Level D/E*

Reading. Pupils read the letter and choose the adjectives that best describe Sevilla. Teachers may wish to ask pupils to justify their choice of adjective by asking them to pick out the relevant sections from the letter.

Answers

histórica, bonita, grande, tranquila, importante, interesante

2b ¿Verdad (✓) o mentira (✗)? (AT3/4) [W5; T1]

✗ *Reading for information and instructions – Level E*

Reading. Pupils reread the letter in activity 2a and decide whether the sentences are true (*verdad*) or false (*mentira*).

➕ Teachers may wish to ask pupils to correct the sentences that are false.

Answers

| a✓ | b✗ | c✓ | d✗ | e✗ | f✓ | g✗ |
| h✗ | i✓ | j✗ | | | | |

módulo 5 Mi pueblo

Cuaderno A, page 53

Gramática

1 Completa las frases con *al* o *a la*. (AT3/2) [W2]

✉ *Knowing about language*

Reading. Pupils revise the rule for *al* and *a la* and then complete the sentences.

Answers

a al	b a la	c al	d al	e al	f a la

2 Completa las frases con la forma apropiada del verbo *ir*. (AT3/2) [W5]

✉ *Knowing about language*

Reading. Pupils revise the verb *ir* and then complete the sentences with the appropriate form of the verb.

Answers

a vas	b Voy	c vais	d Vamos	e va	f Va	g Vamos

3 Escribe cuatro frases sobre los lugares que visitas. (AT4/2) [W2,5; S9]

✉ *Knowing about language*

Writing. Pupils write four sentences about places they go to, starting each sentence with *voy*.

Cuaderno B, page 53

Gramática

1 Completa las frases con *al* o *a la*. (AT3/2) [W2]

✉ *Knowing about language*

Reading. Pupils revise the rule for *al* and *a la* and then complete the sentences.

Answers

a al	b a la	c al	d al	e a la	f al	g a la	h al

2 Completa las frases con la forma apropiada del verbo. (AT3/2) [W5]

✉ *Knowing about language*

Reading. Pupils revise the verb *ir* and then complete the sentences with the appropriate form of the verb.

Answers

a vas	b Voy	c vais	d Vamos	e va	f Va	g Vamos

3 Escribe cuatro frases sobre los lugares que visitas. (AT4/2) [W2,5; S9]

✉ *Knowing about language*

Writing. Pupils write four sentences about places they go to, starting each sentence with *voy*.

módulo 5

¡Extra! 7 Un paseo por Barcelona

(Pupil's Book pages 94–95)

Main topics

This is an optional unit which reviews some of the key language of the module: it consists of features and activities relating to Barcelona.

Key Framework Objectives

- Finding meanings 7W8 (Reinforcement)
- Everyday culture 7C2 (Reinforcement)

Resources

Cassette C, side 1
CD 3, track 9

Suggestion

At the end of this unit teachers may wish to ask their pupils to undertake a project about Barcelona, or an aspect of Barcelona that interests them, such as *el Barrio Gótico* or *Gaudí*.

Starter 1: Find the Spanish [W8; S2; T1]

Aims: To consolidate learning on the topic; to compare similarities and differences between English and Spanish and to develop pupils' confidence in understanding challenging language. (Timing: 5–10 minutes)

Activity: Write up the following phrases on the board or a transparency: A Mediterranean port; An excellent climate; The Olympic Games; Designed by; It is not finished yet. Give pupils five minutes to look for the Spanish translations of the phrases on page 94 of the Pupil's Book (*Un puerto mediterráneo; Un clima excelente; Los Juegos Olímpicos; Diseñado por; No está terminada todavía*). Ask pupils to feed back the words and explain any differences and similarities in their own words. This can lead to a brief discussion on position of adjectives.

1a Empareja las frases con las fotos. Busca las palabras que no conoces en el diccionario. (AT3/4) [T1,4; C1]

Reading for information and instructions – Level E

Reading. Pupils use a glossary or dictionary to look up any words they do not understand from the text about Barcelona.

Before attempting this activity, teachers may wish to talk to pupils about some of the landmarks listed which will not appear in their dictionaries.

Pupils then show their understanding by matching the sentences 1–8 with the pictures a–h.

Answers

| a 3 | b 6 | c 7 | d 2 | e 5 | f 4 | g 8 | h 1 |

1b ¿Verdad (✓) o mentira (✗)? (AT3/4) [T1; C1]

Reading for information and instructions – Level D

Reading. Pupils reread the text to decide whether the sentences are true (*verdad*) or false (*mentira*).

➕ Teachers may wish to ask pupils to correct the sentences that are false.

Answers

| 1 ✗ | 2 ✓ | 3 ✓ | 4 ✗ | 5 ✓ | 6 ✓ | 7 ✓ |
| 8 ✗ | 9 ✗ | 10 ✓ | | | | |

1c Clara visita Barcelona. Escucha y contesta a las preguntas. (AT1/4) [L3; C1]

Listening for information and instructions – Level D

Listening. Pupils listen to the description of Clara's visit to Barcelona, and then answer the questions in English. Teachers will need to play the recording at least twice, and may need to pause it to give pupils time to work out and write down the answers.

Answers

1 The Barrio Gótico is very old.
2 The cathedral is huge.
3 She visits the port at midday.
4 She eats sardines and salad.
5 The Parque Güell is very pretty and quiet.
6 It has stairs in the shape of a dragon.
7 On Saturday morning she goes to the beach.
8 It's very good weather. It's hot.
9 The Olympic stadium and the Palacio de los Deportes are very modern.
10 On Sunday morning she visits la Sagrada Familia cathedral.
11 She has a lemonade to drink in the café.
12 On Sunday afternoon she goes to a football match at the Camp Nou stadium.

Tapescript

El viernes por la mañana voy al Barrio Gótico. Es muy antiguo. Hay calles estrechas, una catedral enorme y museos interesantes.
Al mediodía como en un restaurante en el puerto. Como sardinas y ensalada. La comida es deliciosa.
Por la tarde voy de paseo al Parque Güell. Es muy bonito y tranquilo. Tiene escaleras en forma de dragón.

módulo 5 — Mi pueblo

El sábado por la mañana lo paso en la playa tomando el sol. Hace muy buen tiempo. Hace calor.
Por la tarde visito el estadio Olímpico y el Palacio de los Deportes. Son instalaciones muy modernas. ¡La piscina es enorme!

El domingo por la mañana visito la catedral de la Sagrada Familia. Es muy extraña. No está terminada.
Después doy un paseo por las Ramblas, una avenida muy larga y ancha. Tomo una limonada en la terraza de un café.
Por la tarde voy a ver un partido de fútbol en el estadio Camp Nou. Juega el Barça contra el Atlético de Madrid. ¡Gana el Atlético de Madrid!

Starter 2: Barcelona memory game [L2,3; C1,2]

Aims: To develop memory skills and to increase cultural knowledge of Spain. (Timing: 10 minutes)

Activity: Ask pupils to indicate, by writing down or with a physical response, if the following phrases are true (*verdad*) or false (*mentira*). Read the phrases aloud and, when correcting the answers, ask for justification in English. 1 *Barcelona es una ciudad española* (V); 2 *La Sagrada Familia es el estadio para el equipo de fútbol 'Barça'* (M); 3 *Hay muchos monumentos históricos en Barcelona* (V); 4 *La avenida principal se llama el Parque Güell* (M). Then give pupils two minutes to look at pages 94 and 95 of the Pupil's Book to prepare for five more difficult true or false statements about Barcelona: 1 *En el año 1992, hubo los Juegos Olímpicos en Barcelona* (V); 2 *No hay muchos lugares para andar en monopatín* (M); 3 *Barcelona es la tercera ciudad más importante de España* (M); 4 *En Barcelona se habla el español y el vasco* (M); 5 *El barrio gótico tiene edificios muy antiguos* (V).

2 Mira el mapa de Barcelona. Escribe direcciones a tres lugares en el mapa. (AT4/2–3) [W2,5; S9]

✂ *Writing to exchange information and ideas – Level D*

Writing. Pupils use the map to help them write directions to three landmarks.

3 ¿Te gustaría visitar Barcelona? ¿Por qué? Escribe cinco frases. (AT4/2–5) [W2,5; S6,9; C1]

✂ *Writing to establish and maintain personal contact – Level D/E/F*

Writing. Pupils write five sentences about which landmarks they would like to visit in Barcelona, and why.

Before attempting this activity teachers may wish to practise the structure *me gustaría* + infinitive. If pupils are able to produce an extended piece of writing containing this conditional structure as well as recycling structures in the present tense, descriptions and opinions that they have learnt in this module, this is evidence that they are working at level 5 on this particular task.

4 Produce un folleto en el ordenador describiendo tu ciudad con fotos y un mapa. (AT4/2–4) [W2,5; T5]

✂ *Writing to exchange information and ideas – Level D/E/F*

Writing. Pupils produce a brochure about their own town, including photos and a map.

🖱 ICT activity [T5; C3]

Pupils could produce their brochure using a desk-top publishing package such as *Publisher*. This could then either be printed and sent to a partner school in Spain or Latin America, or sent as an attachment to an e-mail, in order to give pupils opportunities to compare their experiences with those of other young people in another country. This could even be incorporated into a Citizenship activity.

Plenary

Working in groups of three or four, ask pupils to develop three true or false statements, similar to the ones they heard in Starter 1, on the place where they live. Pupils can use the leaflet they prepared for exercise 4 on page 95 of the Pupil's Book as a basis. These statements can then be presented to the class, who can vote on whether they are true or false, e.g. *Manchester tiene muchos monumentos históricos; En Manchester no hay un puerto grande*, etc. Award points for interesting and original statements in terms of lexis, grammar or content.

módulo 5

Te toca a ti

(Pupil's Book pages 124–125)

- Self-access reading and writing at two levels.

A Reinforcement

1 Empareja las frases con los dibujos apropiados. (AT3/1–2) [W5; S9]

✉ *Knowing about language*

Reading. Pupils match up the words and phrases describing the weather with the symbols.

Answers

| 1 a | 2 e | 3 b | 4 c | 5 d | 6 g | 7 f |

2 Mira el mapa y empareja las frases. (AT3/2) [W2,5; S1,2,9]

✉ *Knowing about language*

Reading. Pupils use the map to help them match up the sentence halves.

Answers

| 1 c | 2 d | 3 a | 4 e | 5 b |

3a ¿Qué son A, B y C? Lee las direcciones. Escribe la letra apropiada. (AT3/3) [W2,5; S2,9]

✉ *Reading for information and instructions – Level D*

Reading. Pupils read the short paragraphs to help them work out which location each is giving directions to, and what each location is.

Answers

| 1 A, la tienda de regalos | 2 C, el museo |
| 3 B, el centro comercial | |

3b Escribe direcciones para llegar a tres lugares en el mapa. (AT4/2–3) [W2,5; S9]

✉ *Writing to exchange information and ideas – Level D*

Writing. Pupils write directions to get to three places on the map.

B Extension

1a Empareja cada descripción con el dibujo apropiado. (AT3/4) [T1]

✉ *Reading for information and instructions – Level E*

Reading. Pupils choose the appropriate picture for each description.

Answers

| 1 d | 2 c | 3 a | 4 b |

1b Elige la descripción apropiada para cada frase. (AT3/4) [T1]

✉ *Reading for information and instructions – Level D*

Reading. Pupils decide which of the four descriptions in activity 1a is being referred to in each of the sentences.

Answers

| a 3 | b 3 | c 2 | d 1 | e 4 | f 1 | g 2 |

2 Escribe una descripción de un pueblo o de una ciudad de tu país. (AT4/3–4) [S6; T5,6]

✉ *Writing to exchange information and ideas – Level D/E/F*

Writing. Pupils write a description of a town or city in their own country.

módulo 6 — *El tiempo libre*

(Pupil's Book pages 98–115)

Unit/topics	Key Framework Objectives	PoS	Key language and Grammar
1 ¿Qué deportes practicas? (pp. 98–99) Talking about sports	7W1 Everyday words (R) 7W5 Verbs present (R) 7S1 Word order (R) 7S2 Sentence gist (R)	1a sounds and writing 1c how to express themselves 2c ask/answer questions	Verbs *jugar* and *practicar* *¿Qué deportes practicas?* *Juego al fútbol.* *Juego al tenis.* *Practico la natación.* *Practico el atletismo.*
2 ¿Qué te gusta hacer en tu tiempo libre? (pp. 100–101) Talking about what you like doing in your free time	7W1 Everyday words (R) 7W4 Gender/plural (R) 7S8 Punctuation (R)	1b grammar and how to apply it 5c express opinions	Expressing likes, dislikes and preferences using *me gusta* (etc.) + infinitive *(No) Me gusta tocar el piano.* *Me encanta escuchar música.* *Odio/Detesto ver la televisión.* *Prefiero mandar mensajes.*
3 ¿Qué haces los fines de semana? (pp. 102–103) Talking about what you do during the week Talking about what you do at weekends	7W5 Verbs present (R) 7S2 Sentence gist (R) 7S5 Basic negatives (R)	1b grammar and how to apply it 2f adapt language for different contexts 5i working in a variety of contexts	Consolidation of present tense (singular) of *ver* and *hacer* Consolidation of present tense of regular -*ar* verbs *mi, tu, su* *¿Qué haces todos los días?* *¿Qué haces los fines de semana?* *Voy a un parque temático.* *Hago los deberes.*
4 Una cita (pp. 104–105) Arranging to go out	7S4 Basic questions (R) 7S7 Time and tenses (R) 7L4 Classroom talk (R)	2d initiate/develop conversations 2f adapt language for different contexts 5h use TL for real purposes	Review of times and days of the week *¿Quieres ir al cine?* *¿Dónde nos encontramos?* *En la plaza/mi casa.* *¿A qué hora?* *A las siete y media.*
5 Este fin de semana (pp. 106–107) Saying what you are going to do at the weekend	7S7 Time and tenses (Part-L) 7W5 Verbs present (R) 7S1 Word order (R) 7T1 Reading using cues (R) 7T2 Reading aloud (R)	1b grammar and how to apply it 2f adapt language for different contexts 2h scan texts	The immediate future using *ir + a +* infinitive Consolidation of *ir* (present tense) *Voy a ver un vídeo.* *Va a dormir.* *Van a montar en bicicleta.*
6 ¿Ayudas en casa? (pp. 108–109) Saying how you help at home Saying how you are going to help at the weekend	7W1 Everyday words (R) 7S5 Basic negatives (R) 7C4 Stories and songs (R)	1c how to express themselves 2a listen for gist/detail 2d initiate/develop conversations 5a communicating in the target language	Consolidation of the immediate future (*ir + a +* infinitive) Vocabulary for household chores *Voy a ir al supermercado el sábado por la mañana.* *El lunes barro el patio.*
Resumen y Prepárate (pp. 110–111) Pupils' checklist and practice test	7S5 Basic negatives (R) 7L3 Gist and detail (R) 7T1 Reading using cues (R) 7T6 Texts as prompts (R)	3a memorising 3e develop their independence	
¡Extra! 7 ¡Hasta luego! (pp. 112–113) Optional unit: Young Spanish people talking about their routines and interests	7T1 Reading using cues (R) 7T3 Checking before reading (R) 7T4 Using resources (R) 7C2 Everyday culture (R)	4a working with authentic materials 4c compare cultures 4d consider experiences in other countries	
Te toca a ti (pp. 126–127) Self-access reading and writing at two levels		1b grammar and how to apply it 2f adapt language for different contexts 5d respond to different types of language	

módulo 6

1 ¿Qué deportes practicas?

(Pupil's Book pages 98–99)

Main topics
- Talking about sports

Key Framework Objectives
- Everyday words 7W1 (Reinforcement)
- Verbs present 7W5 (Reinforcement)
- Word order 7S1 (Reinforcement)
- Sentence gist 7S2 (Reinforcement)

Grammar
- Present tense of *practicar* and *jugar*

Key language

¿Qué deportes practicas?
Practico/Practica/Practican …
el atletismo   el golf
el ciclismo   la natación
la equitación   el patinaje
el esquí   la vela
la gimnasia
Juego/Juega/Juegan …
al bádminton   al rugby
al baloncesto   al squash
al cricket   al tenis
al fútbol   al voleibol
al hockey

Resources

Cassette C, side 1
CD 3, track 10
Cuaderno A and B, page 55
Starter 2, Resource and Assessment File, page 115
Hojas de trabajo 1 and 2, Resource and Assessment File, pages 106 and 107

Starter 1: Categorising sports [W1,4,8]

Aims: To introduce sports, including pronunciation, spelling and meaning. (Timing: 10 minutes)

Pairwork activity: Refer pupils to the illustration of sports (a–k) on page 98 of the Pupil's Book (*el fútbol, el hockey, el voleibol, el baloncesto, el tenis, la vela, la natación, el atletismo, el ciclismo, la equitación, la gimnasia*). Give pupils the following categories, one at a time, writing them on the board or on a transparency and clarifying their meaning if necessary: 1 *Dos deportes olímpicos*; 2 *Cuatro juegos de pelota*; 3 *Cinco deportes de equipo*; 4 *Un deporte acuático*. Ask pupils to identify the appropriate sport(s) by writing down the correct letter(s) for each category. When going over the answers, encourage pupils to say the sports, many of which are cognates, with accurate Spanish pronunciation.

1 Escucha y escribe los deportes en el orden correcto. (1–11) (AT1/2) [W1,2,5; L1]

✱ *Knowing about language*

Listening. Pupils listen to the recording and write the sports in the order they hear them mentioned.

R Before attempting this activity, teachers should introduce the names of the sports and see if pupils can work out the rule for *juego* and *practico*. A good way of practising this new vocabulary is to mime each sport. Teachers may wish to play 'Simon Says' with the whole class.

Teachers may also wish to get pupils to repeat the sports they hear on the recording and find the words in order to reinforce the link between sound and writing.

Answers

1 b, Juego al hockey.
2 f, Practico la natación.
3 g, Practico el atletismo.
4 c, Juego al tenis.
5 h, Practico la gimnasia.
6 e, Juego al voleibol.
7 j, Practico el ciclismo.
8 a, Juego al fútbol.
9 k, Practico la vela.
10 d, Juego al baloncesto.
11 i, Practico la equitación.

Tapescript

1 – Juego al hockey.
2 – Practico la natación.
3 – Practico el atletismo.
4 – Juego al tenis.
5 – Practico la gimnasia.
6 – Juego al voleibol.
7 – Practico el ciclismo.
8 – Juego al fútbol.
9 – Practico la vela.
10 – Juego al baloncesto.
11 – Practico la equitación.

2 Con tu compañero/a, pregunta y contesta. (AT2/2) [W1,2,5; S4,9; L4]

✱ *Speaking and interacting with others – Level D*

Speaking. Working in pairs, pupils ask and answer questions about what sport they do.

Before attempting this activity, teachers may wish to ask pupils to read through the *Gramática* box to familiarise themselves with the parts of the verbs *jugar* and *practicar*.

módulo 6 — El tiempo libre

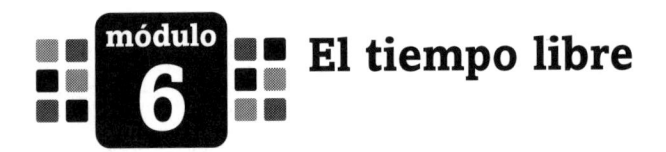

3 Escucha y escribe "j" (*jugar*) o "p" (*practicar*) para cada deporte. (AT1/2) [W2,5]

✂ *Knowing about language*

Listening. Pupils listen to the recording and write "j" for *jugar* and "p" for *practicar* for each activity they hear mentioned.

Before attempting this activity, teachers may wish to ask pupils to predict whether it will be *jugar* or *practicar* for each activity, in order to reinforce the difference between these verbs.

Teachers may also wish to ask pupils to write out the correct sentence for each activity, to check that they remember to put *al* after *jugar*.

Answers

a j	b p	c j	d j	e p	f p

Tapescript

a – Juego al rugby.
b – Practico el esquí.
c – Juego al bádminton.
d – Juego al cricket.
e – Practico el patinaje.
f – Practico el golf.

Starter 2: **Verb revision** [W5; S1,2,3]

Aims: To revise the present tense of the verbs *jugar* and *practicar*. (Timing: 5 minutes)

Resources: Resource and Assessment File, page 115 (Starter 2)

Pairwork activity: Make an OHT using the sheet provided. Give pupils three minutes to write down the Spanish equivalent for each of the English sentences below the grid on the OHT, using the correct person of the verb (*Jugamos al fútbol; No practicas la equitación; Juegan al hockey y al baloncesto; Practico el ciclismo; ¿Practicáis el atletismo?; Nunca practica la vela*). When correcting the exercise, ask pupils to justify their answers.

---

4 Empareja las personas con los deportes y escribe frases. (AT4/2) [W2,5; S3,9]

✂ *Knowing about language*

Writing. Pupils write sentences about what each of the sports stars do. Before attempting this activity, teachers may wish to ask pupils to reread the *Gramática* box on page 98 to familiarise themselves with the 3rd person singular and plural forms of the verbs.

Answers

David Beckham juega al fútbol.
Marion Jones y Maurice Greene practican el atletismo.
Matt Dawson juega al rugby.
Jennifer Capriati juega al tenis.
Darren Gough juega al cricket.
Kobe Bryant juega al baloncesto.
Ellen MacArthur practica la vela.
Tiger Woods y Sergio García practican el golf.

5 Lee el texto y dibuja un símbolo para los deportes que practica Juan. (AT3/3) [W2,5; T1]

✂ *Reading for information and instructions – Level D*

Reading. Pupils read the letter from Juan and draw a symbol for each of the sports he does. If pupils prefer not to draw the sports, they could write the letters of the pictures on page 98.

Answers

Pupils should have produced simple drawings indicating: cycling, swimming, tennis, football, basketball

6 Escribe sobre los deportes que practicas. (AT4/2–3) [W2,5; S9; T5]

✂ *Writing to exchange information and ideas – Level D/E/F*

Writing. Pupils write sentences about the sports they do. Teachers may prefer to ask pupils to adapt Juan's letter to produce a piece of extended writing.

Plenary

Consolidate sports language with a throw-and-catch game, using a soft ball or object. Throw it to a pupil and ask the question: *¿Qué deportes practicas?*. The pupil answers and throws the ball back to you. When you have asked the question a number of times to different pupils, a pupil can replace you and throw the ball and ask the questions. Eventually the ball can be thrown to a pupil who will answer a question and then pose another question while throwing the ball to another pupil.

Cuaderno A, page 55

1 Completa el crucigrama para revelar el nombre de un club español famoso. (AT4/1) [W1,7]

✂ *Knowing about language*

Writing. Pupils use the picture clues to complete the names of the sports in the crossword, and find the name of the famous football club (FC Barcelona).

Answers

1					**F**	Ú	T	B	O	L				
2			H	O	**C**	K	E	Y						
3					**B**	A	L	O	N	C	E	S	T	O
4					**A**	T	L	E	T	I	S	M	O	
5					**R**	U	G	B	Y					
6					**C**	I	C	L	I	S	M	O		
7					**E**	Q	U	I	T	A	C	I	Ó	N
8			V	E	**L**	A								
9				V	**O**	L	E	I	B	O	L			
10					**N**	A	T	A	C	I	Ó	N		
11	G	I	M	N	**A**	S	I	A						

2 Escribe la frase apropiada para cada dibujo. (AT4/2) [W2,5]

Knowing about language

Writing. Pupils write the correct sentence for each picture.

Answers

a Juego al hockey.	**b** Juego al fútbol.
c Practico la natación.	**d** Juego al baloncesto.
e Practico la vela.	**f** Juego al tenis de mesa.
g Practico la gimnasia.	

3 ¿Qué deportes practicas tú? Escribe tres frases. (AT4/2–3) [W2,5; S9]

Writing to establish and maintain personal contact – Level D

Writing. Pupils write three sentences about the sports they do. Teachers may wish to encourage pupils to produce a short paragraph, including a short introduction about themselves.

Cuaderno B, page 55

1 Completa el crucigrama para revelar el nombre de un club español famoso. (AT4/1) [W1,7]

Knowing about language

Writing. Pupils use the picture clues to complete the names of the sports in the crossword, and find the name of the famous football club (FC Barcelona).

Answers

1					**F**	Ú	T	B	O	L				
2			H	O	**C**	K	E	Y						
3					**B**	A	L	O	N	C	E	S	T	O
4					**A**	T	L	E	T	I	S	M	O	
5					**R**	U	G	B	Y					
6					**C**	I	C	L	I	S	M	O		
7					**E**	Q	U	I	T	A	C	I	Ó	N
8			V	E	**L**	A								
9				V	**O**	L	E	I	B	O	L			
10					**N**	A	T	A	C	I	Ó	N		
11	G	I	M	N	**A**	S	I	A						

2 Lee los globos y elige los dibujos apropiados para cada persona. (AT3/3) [W2,5; S6; T1]

Reading for information and instructions – Level D

Reading. Pupils read the descriptions in the speech bubbles and choose the appropriate sports for each person.

Answers

Tania: 3, 5, 2, 7
Ignacio: 1, 4, 2, 6

3 ¿Qué deportes practicas tú? Escribe tres frases. (AT4/2–3) [W2,5; S9]

Writing to establish and maintain personal contact – Level D

Writing. Pupils write three sentences about the sports they do. Teachers may wish to encourage pupils to use the descriptions in activity 2 as a model.

Hojas de trabajo 1–2, pages 106–107 [W1,2,5]

15 picture cards and 15 corresponding labels which can be used for matching activities.

módulo 6

2 ¿Qué te gusta hacer en tu tiempo libre? (Pupil's Book pages 100–101)

Main topics
- Talking about what you like doing in your free time

Key Framework Objectives
- Everyday words 7W1 (Reinforcement)
- Gender/plural 7W4 (Reinforcement)
- Punctuation 7S8 (Reinforcement)

Grammar
- I (don't) like doing …: *(no) me gusta/me encanta/odio* + the infinitive
- I prefer: *prefiero* + infinitive

Key language

¿Te gusta ir al cine?
Me gusta escuchar música.
Me encanta …
No me gusta …
Odio/Detesto …
Prefiero …
bailar
cantar
cocinar
escuchar música
hablar por teléfono
ir a la piscina
ir al cine/al polideportivo
ir de compras
jugar con los videojuegos
jugar con el ordenador
leer
mandar mensajes
navegar por Internet
salir con mis amigos
tocar la guitarra
ver la televisión

Resources

Cassette C, side 2
CD 3, track 11
Cuaderno A and B, page 56
Hojas de trabajo 3, 4 and 5, Resource and Assessment File, pages 108, 109 and 110
OHTs 27 and 28: hobbies, saying what you like and dislike doing

---

Starter 1: **Odd one out** [W1,4]

Aims: To reinforce the understanding and knowledge of gender and meaning with sports, and to use thinking skills. (Timing: 5 minutes)

Pairwork activity: Copy the following words onto a grid with three columns and three rows: (Row 1) 1 *la guitarra* 2 *el amigo* 3 *el libro*; (Row 2) 4 *la música* 5 *la televisión* 6 *el fútbol*; (Row 3) 7 *el ordenador* 8 *la cocina* 9 *la piscina*. Explain to pupils that they have met these words in other topics and/or they are cognates. Pupils must locate the odd one out in each row. Encourage use of the target language by giving an example and putting keywords on the board (*masculino, femenino, diferente, número tres es la excepción porque …*), but allow pupils to communicate in English for more complex ideas. Pairs feed back to the whole class and justify their decision (in English). Accept all valid suggestions. Repeat the process using the columns instead of the rows.

1a Escucha y escribe los pasatiempos en el orden correcto. (1–12) (AT1/2) [W2,5; S4,5; L1]

✄ *Knowing about language*

Listening. Pupils listen to the recording and write down the letters of the hobbies in the order they hear them mentioned.

Before attempting this activity, teachers should introduce the vocabulary for the hobbies, which are all in the infinitive. A good starting point would be to take *jugar* and *practicar* since pupils are already familiar with these verbs.

▣ Teachers may then wish to use an OHT or flashcards to introduce the remaining activities. A number of games could be played to reinforce these activities: take one activity away and ask pupils *¿Qué pasatiempo es?* to see if they can work out which hobby is missing; as for the sports, do mimes for each activity and play 'Simon Says'; give pupils pictures of the hobbies and the captions and get them to play 'Pelmanism' in pairs; play noughts and crosses on the OHP using a 3 x 4 grid with the names of the activities.

Answers

1 c	2 f	3 b	4 g	5 h	6 j	7 e
8 i	9 d	10 a	11 l	12 k		

Tapescript

 – *¿Qué te gusta hacer en tu tiempo libre?*
1 – *Me gusta escuchar música.*
2 – *Me gusta leer.*
3 – *No me gusta jugar con los videojuegos.*
4 – *Me gusta cantar.*
5 – *Me gusta ver la televisión.*
6 – *Me gusta hablar por teléfono.*
7 – *Odio ir de compras.*
8 – *Me gusta navegar por Internet.*
9 – *Me encanta bailar.*
10 – *Me gusta tocar la guitarra.*
11 – *Me gusta salir con mis amigos.*
12 – *Me encanta cocinar.*

1b Escribe una lista de los pasatiempos que te gusta hacer. (AT4/2) [W2,5; S9]

✄ *Writing to establish and maintain personal contact – Level D*

Writing. Pupils write a list of the hobbies that they like doing. Teachers may prefer to ask pupils to draw

El tiempo libre — módulo 6

up four columns headed *me gusta, me encanta, no me gusta, detesto/odio* and to write the hobbies from activity 1a in the appropriate column.

Before attempting this activity, teachers need to introduce the structures *me gusta, me encanta, no me gusta, detesto/odio* which appear in the box on page 100.

1c Con tu compañero/a, pregunta y contesta. (AT2/2) [W2,5; S4,5,9; L4]

✉ *Speaking and interacting with others – Level D*

Speaking. In pairs, pupils ask and answer questions about what hobbies they like doing.

R Before attempting this activity, teachers may wish to ask pupils to read through the *Gramática* box to reinforce the *me gusta* + infinitive structure. Teachers may also wish to suggest that pupils use their answers from activity 1b to help prompt them with this activity.

2 ¿Les gusta o no les gusta hacer estos pasatiempos? Escucha y dibuja un símbolo. (1–10) (AT1/2) [W2,5; S5; L3]

✉ *Listening for information and instructions – Level C*

Listening. Pupils listen to the recording and draw the appropriate symbol from the box on page 100 to indicate whether the people like or dislike doing the activities. Teachers may also wish to ask pupils to write the letter of the activity mentioned, and ask pupils to report back the answers: *¿Qué dice la persona (1)? … Dice 'me gusta leer'.*

Answers

1 ☺ ✓ 2 ☹ ✗ 3 ☺ ✓ 4 ☺ ✓ 5 ☺ ✓✓
6 ☹ ✗✗ 7 ☺ ✓ 8 ☺ ✓✓ 9 ☹ ✗ 10 ☺ ✓

Tapescript

1 – Me gusta leer.
2 – No me gusta cantar.
3 – Me gusta ver la televisión.
4 – Me gusta jugar con los videojuegos.
5 – Me encanta ir de compras.
6 – Detesto cocinar.
7 – Me gusta hablar por teléfono.
8 – Me encanta navegar por Internet.
9 – No me gusta bailar.
10 – Me gusta salir con mis amigos.

3a Escucha a los jóvenes. Copia y rellena el cuadro. (AT1/3) [W2,5; S4,5,9; L3]

✉ *Listening for information and instructions – Level D*

Listening. Pupils copy the grid and listen to the recording, filling in the details of what the teenagers like doing.

Before attempting this activity, teachers may wish to introduce *prefiero* and ask pupils to read through the box on page 101.

Answers

	Susana	Enrique	María Luisa
Me gusta	ir al cine, hablar por teléfono	ir al cine, jugar con el ordenador	practicar la vela
No me gusta	jugar con el ordenador	jugar al fútbol	ir al polideportivo
Prefiero	ir al polideportivo, mandar mensajes	practicar la vela	ir a la piscina

Tapescript

– ¿Cómo te llamas?
– Me llamo Susana.
– ¿Te gusta ir al cine, Susana?
– Sí, me gusta ir al cine.
– ¿Te gusta jugar con el ordenador?
– No, no me gusta. Prefiero ir al polideportivo.
– ¿Te gusta hablar por teléfono?
– Sí, me gusta hablar por teléfono pero prefiero mandar mensajes.

– ¿Cómo te llamas?
– Me llamo Enrique.
– ¿Qué te gusta hacer en tu tiempo libre?
– Me gusta ir al cine y me gusta jugar con el ordenador.
– ¿Te gusta jugar al fútbol?
– No, no me gusta jugar al fútbol. Prefiero practicar la vela.

– ¿Cómo te llamas?
– Me llamo María Luisa.
– ¿Qué te gusta hacer en tu tiempo libre?
– Me gusta practicar la vela.
– ¿Te gusta ir al polideportivo?
– No, no me gusta, prefiero ir a la piscina.

Starter 2: Squashed sentences [S1,8,9; T2, L6]

Aims: To write simple sentences accurately and to reinforce knowledge of punctuation and spelling. (Timing: 10 minutes)

Pairwork activity: Choose five different sentences from the texts on page 101 of the Pupil's Book written by Natalia, Elena or Jaime. Write up the sentences with no punctuation, accents or spacings, e.g. *tambienmegustaescucharmusicayverl atelevision*. Give pupils two minutes to say the sentences to each other. Ask different pupils to read out the sentences to the class. Pupils write down the sentences. Remind them that the sentences contain no punctuation so they must add capital letters, accents and full stops.

módulo 6 — El tiempo libre

3b Haz un sondeo. Pregunta a tus compañeros/as de clase. (AT2/2–3) [W2,5; S4,5,9; L4]

✕ *Speaking and interacting with others – Level D*

Speaking. Pupils conduct a survey of what hobbies their classmates like doing.

Before attempting this activity, teachers may wish to ask pupils to draw a grid with the hobbies and likes/dislikes from page 100.

🖱 **ICT activity**

Pupils could transfer their findings to a spreadsheet such as *Excel* and use the chart wizard to produce a pie chart or bar graph of their classmates' likes and dislikes.

4 Lee el texto y empareja cada persona con el regalo apropiado. (AT3/3) [W2,5; T1]

✕ *Reading for information and instructions – Level D*

Reading. Pupils read the texts and match up the people with the appropriate presents.

Answers

1 d	2 b	3 a

5 Escribe sobre lo que te gusta y no te gusta hacer en tu tiempo libre. (AT4/2–4) [W2,5; S5,6; T5]

✕ *Writing to establish and maintain personal contact – Level D/E*

Writing. Pupils write sentences or a paragraph about what they do and don't like doing in their free time.

✚ Teachers may wish to encourage their pupils to use connectives such as *pero* to extend their writing.

> *Plenary*
>
> Fact or opinion? Read out different sentences that use the language introduced during this unit. Pupils must decide if the sentences are fact (*un hecho*) or opinion (*una opinión*). They can represent this by writing down their answers or by giving a physical reponse such as raising their arms in the air for a fact or folding their arms for an opinion. For example: (Teacher) *Voy a la piscina y practico la natación*; (Pupil) *Hecho*; (Teacher) *Me encanta jugar al bádminton*; (Pupil) *Opinión*. Where there are discrepancies in responses from the pupils, discuss the difference between facts and opinions and how to express them in Spanish. This is also a good way to prepare students for the thinking skills activity, which is best completed after studying Module 6, Units 1–3.

Cuaderno A, page 56

1 Rellena los espacios en blanco con las palabras apropiadas. (AT4/1) [W2,5; S5,9]

✕ *Knowing about language*

Writing. Pupils use the pictures to fill in the blanks in the paragraph.

Answers

escuchar música, tocar la guitarra, cocinar, ver la televisión, ir de compras, salir con mis amigos, bailar

2 Elige las actividades que menciona Enrique y dibuja el símbolo apropiado. (AT3/3) [W5; S2,5]

✕ *Knowing about language*

Reading. Using the text in activity 1, pupils draw the appropriate symbol by each activity Enrique mentions to indicate what he does and doesn't like doing.

Answers

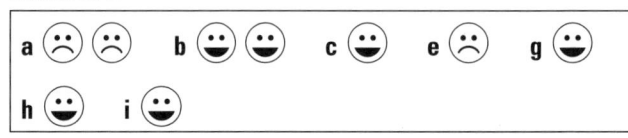

a ☹☹   b ☺☺   c ☺   e ☹   g ☺
h ☺   i ☺

3 Escribe cuatro frases sobre las actividades que te gusta o no te gusta hacer. (AT4/2–3) [W2,5; S5,9]

✕ *Writing to establish and maintain personal contact – Level D*

Writing. Pupils write four sentences about what they do and don't like doing.

Cuaderno B, page 56

1 Rellena los espacios en blanco con las palabras apropiadas. (AT4/1) [W2,5; S5]

✕ *Knowing about language*

Writing. Pupils use the pictures to fill in the blanks in the text.

Answers

escuchar música, tocar la guitarra, cocinar, ver la televisión, ir de compras, salir con mis amigos, bailar

2 Escribe una frase para cada dibujo. (AT4/2) [W2,5; S5,9]

✕ *Knowing about language*

Writing. Pupils write a sentence for each picture, saying what each person does or doesn't like doing.

El tiempo libre

módulo 6

Answers

> a Me gusta leer.
> b Me encanta cantar.
> c No me gusta hablar por teléfono.
> d Odio jugar con los videojuegos.
> e Me gusta jugar con el ordenador.

3 Escribe cuatro frases sobre las actividades que te gusta o no te gusta hacer. (AT4/2–3) [W2,5; S5,9]

✉ *Writing to establish and maintain personal contact – Level D*

Writing. Pupils write four sentences about what they do and don't like doing.

Hojas de trabajo 3–4, pages 108–109 [W1,2,5]

12 picture cards and 12 corresponding labels which can be used for matching activities.

Hoja de trabajo 5, page 110 [L4]

Pairwork activity for pupils to practise asking and answering questions about what freetime activities they do and don't like, using *gustar* + infinitive. Pupils should answer not for themselves, but base their answers on the ticks and crosses on the grid. They should record their partner's answers on the grid, and they then compare answers after completing this activity.

módulo 6

3 ¿Qué haces los fines de semana?

(Pupil's Book pages 102–103)

Main topics

- Talking about what you do during the week
- Talking about what you do at weekends

Key Framework Objectives

- Verbs present 7W5 (Reinforcement)
- Sentence gist 7S2 (Reinforcement)
- Basic negatives 7S5 (Reinforcement)

Grammar

- *ver: veo, ves, ve*
- *hacer: hago, haces, hace*
- Regular *-ar* verbs (*montar, tocar, arreglar*)
- *mi, tu, su*

Key language

¿Qué haces todos los días?
¿Qué haces los fines de semana?
Los fines de semana voy …
a la pista de hielo
a un partido de fútbol
a un parque temático
a casa de mis abuelos
a la playa
al campo
al cine
al instituto
Hago …
deporte
surfing
windsurf(ing)
los deberes
Arreglo mi dormitorio.
Hago la cama.
Juego a las cartas.
Monto en bicicleta.
Monto en monopatín.
Toco la guitarra.
Veo la televisión.
¡Es divertido!

Resources

Cassette C, side 2
CD 3, track 12
Cuaderno A and B, page 57
OHTs 29 and 30: saying what you do in the week and at weekends

---

Starter 1: Find the Spanish [W1,5,8; S2,9]

Aims: To introduce language for talking about what you do at the weekend and during the week; to show pupils that there are many words in Spanish that are very similar to English and build confidence in their learning. (Timing: 5–10 minutes)

Activity: Say the English for one of the following activities: *Voy al instituto, Monto en bicicleta, Toco la guitarra, Arreglo mi dormitorio y hago la cama, Hago deporte, Juego a las cartas, Veo la televisión.* For example: 'I play cards'. Pupils have to locate and write down the Spanish equivalent from the list (a–h) of exercise 1a on page 102 of the Pupil's Book. Correct each sentence by asking one pupil to read out the Spanish and ask other class members to comment on pronunciation.

1a Escucha y repite. (AT1/2) [W2,5; L1]

✉ *Knowing about language*

Listening. Pupils listen to the recording and repeat the expressions they hear, paying attention to their pronunciation. Teachers may wish to ask pupils to follow the words in the book as they listen to the recording in order to reinforce the link between sound and writing.

Teachers may wish to introduce the activities using flashcards or OHT, or using mimes, before attempting this activity.

Tapescript

– *¿Qué haces todos los días?*
a – *Voy al instituto.*
b – *Hago los deberes.*
c – *Monto en bicicleta.*
d – *Toco la guitarra.*
e – *Arreglo mi dormitorio y hago la cama.*
f – *Hago deporte.*
g – *Juego a las cartas.*
h – *Veo la televisión.*

1b Escucha otra vez y empareja cada frase con el dibujo apropiado. (AT1/2, AT3/2) [W2,5]

✉ *Listening for information and instructions – Level C*

Listening/Reading. Pupils listen to the recording again, which follows the same sequence as the phrases in the box, and write the number of the picture for each activity they hear and read.

Answers

a 6	b 5	c 1	d 7	e 8	f 4	g 3
h 2						

Tapescript

As for activity 1a

El tiempo libre — módulo 6

2 Con tu compañero/a, habla sobre las actividades en los dibujos en **1**. (AT2/2–3) [W2,5; S4,5,9; L4]

✠ *Speaking and interacting with others – Level D*

Speaking. Pupils work in pairs to ask and answer questions about the activities they have learnt.

The *¡OJO!* box reminds pupils about *mi, tu* and *su*.

Note There are two types of questions recommended in this activity, an open question and a closed question. Teachers are advised to read through the *Gramática* box with their pupils first in order to consolidate the verb endings: teachers may wish to get pupils to work out the *tú* form of the verbs in activity 1 before attempting the speaking.

Teachers may wish to adapt this activity slightly into a guessing game, where one pupil thinks of an activity, and their partner has five questions to guess correctly, asking *¿Tocas la guitarra?* etc. If they haven't guessed the activity correctly after five questions, their partner asks *¿Qué haces todos los días?*

3 ¿Qué haces todos los días? Escribe cinco frases. Escribe tres frases sobre tu compañero/a. (AT4/2–3) [W2,5; S9]

✠ *Writing to exchange information and ideas – Level D/E*

Writing. Pupils write five sentences about what they do on weekdays, using the phrases from activity 1, and then write three sentences about what their partner does. Teachers will need to make sure that pupils are familiar with the 3rd person form of the verbs before attempting this activity.

Starter 2: Verb revision (changing person) [W5; S3; T5]

Aims: To revise the first- and third-person singular of the present tense of the verbs *hacer, ver, jugar* and regular *-ar* verbs. (Timing: 10 minutes)

Pairwork activity: Explain to pupils that they are going to have to change the verbs from the list of phrases on the language grids on pages 102 and 103 of the Pupil's Book from the first to the third person singular (*va al instituto, hace los deberes, monta en bicicleta, toca la guitarra, arregla su dormitorio, hace la cama, juega a las cartas, ve la televisión*). Draw attention to the *Gramática* section on page 102 for support. Pupils write down five phrases describing the different activities that their family members or friends do at the weekend (you may wish to brainstorm the Spanish for family members first). For example: *Mi padre ve la televisión; Mi madre va a un partido de fútbol; Mi hermana hace la cama; Daniel monta en bicicleta; Sam va al cine.* Pupils then swap books with their partners who check that the verbs and sentences are correct.

---

4 Escucha y elige las actividades apropiadas para Marisol y Manuel. (AT1/3) [W2,5; S4,7; L3]

✠ *Listening for information and instructions – Level D*

Listening. Pupils listen to Marisol and Manuel describing their weekends and write down the letters of the activities mentioned.

Before attempting this activity, teachers may wish to read through the vocabulary in the box with their pupils, and practise these new phrases.

Answers

Marisol: e, c, k
Manuel: h, l, f, g

Tapescript

– ¿Qué haces los fines de semana, Marisol?
– Pues, los fines de semana voy a la playa con mis amigos. A veces voy al campo y monto en bicicleta. ¡Me encanta montar en bicicleta!

– ¿Qué haces los fines de semana, Manuel?
– A veces voy a un parque temático con mis amigos. Es muy divertido. Pues, también monto en monopatín, por ahí. Voy a la pista de hielo o a un partido de fútbol. Lo que sea.

5 Con tu compañero/a, pregunta y contesta. (AT2/2–3) [W2,5; S4,9; L4]

✠ *Speaking and interacting with others – Level D*

Speaking. Working in pairs, pupils ask and answer questions about what they do at the weekend, using the structures from activity 4.

✚ Teachers may wish to extend this activity to a class survey, and compare results with a Spanish-speaking partner school.

6 Completa las frases con las palabras apropiadas. (AT3/3) [W1,2,5; S2]

✠ *Knowing about language – Level D*

Reading. Pupils choose the appropriate words to complete the text about what Juan does during the week and at weekends.

Answers

1 Voy	2 Hago	3 bicicleta	4 veo	5 al	6 playa
7 surfing	8 abuelos				

7 ¿Qué haces los fines de semana? Escribe cinco frases. (AT4/2–4) [W2,5; S9; T6]

✠ *Writing to establish and maintain personal contact – Level D/E/F*

Writing. Pupils write five sentences about what they do at the weekend.

módulo 6 — El tiempo libre

➕ Teachers could encourage pupils to extend their writing by including opinions, details and connectives, as well as adverbs of frequency.

Plenary

Give pupils, in pairs, three minutes to use page 114 of the *Palabras* section in the Pupils' Book to test each other on the language introduced so far during the module. Then divide the group into teams and test their knowledge. Use a dice and pass it to each team, who roll it prior to answering their question. If they answer correctly they win the number of points shown on the dice. Grade the difficulty of the question by the number thrown, e.g. if pupil rolls a 1 ask *¿Cómo se dice* 'I play football' *en español?*; if pupil rolls a 6 ask *¿Cómo se dice* 'My sister tidies her bedroom' *en español?*.

Cuaderno A, page 57

1 Elige las actividades apropiadas para Carlos, María y Elisa. (AT3/3) [W2,5; T1]

✄ *Reading for information and instructions – Level D*

Reading. Pupils read the texts and choose the appropriate activities for the three people.

Answers

| Carlos: d, a, b, e, f |
| María: c, i, g, l |
| Elisa: k, h, j |

2 Escribe la frase apropiada para cada dibujo. (AT3/2) [W2,5; S9]

✄ *Knowing about language*

Reading. Pupils choose the appropriate phrase for each picture.

Answers

| a 3 | b 2 | c 1 | d 6 | e 4 | f 5 |

Cuaderno B, page 57

1 Completa las frases con los verbos apropiados. (AT3/2) [W2,5]

✄ *Knowing about language*

Reading. Pupils choose the appropriate word to complete the sentences.

Answers

| voy, toco, juego, hago, veo, monto, arreglo, hago |

2 Completa las frases con los verbos apropiados. (AT3/2) [W5]

✄ *Knowing about language*

Reading. Pupils write in the correct verbs to complete the phrases.

Answers

| a va | b monta | c va | d va | e hace | f practica |

3 Lee el correo electrónico y contesta a las preguntas. (AT3/4) [T1]

✄ *Reading for information and instructions – Level D*

Reading. Pupils read the e-mail and answer the questions in English.

Answers

1 He goes to school in the morning.
2 In the afternoon and evening he does his homework, plays football and watches television.
3 At weekends he goes to the cinema with his friends.
4 On Sundays he goes to his grandparents' house.

Optional Thinking Skills lesson

Aims
To encourage pupils to look at a longer piece of text and to select relevant information; to begin to appraise a text for gist and purpose. Use the sport and leisure vocabulary from Module 6, Units 1–3 with some verbs in the preterite as lexical items. (Timing: 40 minutes)

Resources
Resource and Assessment File, page 116 (Thinking Skills)

Living graph: El fin de semana de Superman [S2,7; T1,3,5]

Activity: Working in groups of three or four, pupils read an account of Superman's weekend and have to sequence the story and decide how Superman feels at different times.

The text uses some examples of the preterite, which are used as lexical items only at this point. Pupils read the statements on Worksheet 3 and discuss them. They must place them in the right place on the graph on Worksheet 2, both in terms of what happened and Superman's mood. They may discuss in English, but are expected to give the order of the sentences in Spanish. Give the groups 15–20 minutes to sequence the story and plot the graph. Emphasise that discussion is important and that they must

El tiempo libre   módulo 6

justify their decisions. Your role is to observe the discussions and organisation of the task, and to ensure that pupils are making enough sense of the story to consider Superman's feelings. Stop the class after 10 minutes to ensure that the students are on the right track. Ask groups to feed back their decisions to the class and invite other groups to agree or disagree, justifying their thoughts.

Story sequence: 2, 7, 6, 3, 1, 4, 5.

módulo 6

4 Una cita

(Pupil's Book pages 104–105)

Main topics

- Arranging to go out

Key Framework Objectives

- Basic questions 7S4 (Reinforcement)
- Time and tenses 7S7 (Reinforcement)
- Classroom talk 7L4 (Reinforcement)

Key language

¿Quieres ir al cine?
¿Quieres jugar al fútbol?
¿Dónde nos encontramos?
En la plaza/En mi casa/En la entrada/En la estación.
¿Cuándo?
Mañana.
El sábado.
Esta mañana/tarde/noche.
¿A qué hora?
A las siete y media.
Bueno/Vale/De acuerdo/(Está) bien.
un mensaje   un abrazo
un beso   besos
saludos

Resources

Cassette C, side 2
CD 3, track 13
Cuaderno A and B, page 58
Starters 1 and 2, Resource and Assessment File, page 117
Hoja de trabajo 6, Resource and Assessment File, page 111

Starter 1: **Time sequencing** [W1,2; S2,7]

Aims: To revise time and hobbies and to develop memory skills and thinking skills. (Timing: 10 minutes)

Resources: Resource and Assessment File, page 117 (Starter 1)

Activity: Make an OHT using the master provided. Pupils work in pairs or groups of three. Reveal the first set of four options on the OHT. Ask pupils to play the 'fastest finger first' game and to write the letters in the correct time order, beginning with the earliest time in the day. One member of each pair/group brings the paper/whiteboard to the front when finished and pupils stand in finishing order. When all groups are represented at the front, they reveal their answers and the correct solution is ascertained. Repeat with the other sets of times and activities.

---

1 Escucha y lee. Contesta a las preguntas. (AT1/3, AT3/3) [W2,5; S4; T3; L3]

✳ *Knowing about language*

Listening/Reading. Pupils read and listen to the dialogues and answer the questions to check they have understood.

✚ There are a variety of ways in which teachers could approach the activity. For example, more-able pupils could listen to the recording without seeing the text, and then use the text to check their answers. Alternatively, teachers could pause the recording randomly as pupils follow the text, and see if pupils can say which word comes next.

Before attempting this activity, teachers may wish to introduce the core structures, inviting someone on a date, arranging a meeting place and time.

Answers

1
a Los amigos van a jugar al fútbol.
b Mañana.
c Se encuentran en el polideportivo.
d A las once.

2
a Los amigos van al cine.
b El sábado.
c Se encuentran en la plaza.
d A las seis.

Tapescript

1 – ¿Dígame?
– Hola, Pedro. Soy Juan. ¿Quieres jugar al fútbol?
– ¿Cuándo?
– Mañana.
– Vale. ¿Dónde nos encontramos?
– En el polideportivo.
– ¿A qué hora?
– A las 11.
– Está bien.
– Hasta mañana.

2 – ¿Diga?
– Hola, Eduard. Soy Neus. ¿Quieres ir al cine?
– ¿Cuándo?
– El sábado.
– Bueno. ¿Dónde nos encontramos?
– ¿En la plaza?
– De acuerdo. ¿A qué hora?
– A las 6.
– Vale.
– Hasta luego.

2a ¿Adónde van las personas? Escucha y elige el dibujo apropiado. (1–4) (AT1/3) [W2,5; S4; L3]

✳ *Listening for information and instructions – Level C*

El tiempo libre — módulo 6

Listening. Pupils listen to the recording and pick the correct picture to match each dialogue.

Answers

| 1 a | 2 a | 3 a | 4 b |

Tapescript

1 – ¿Diga?
 – ¡Hola, Luis! ¿Quieres ir al parque?
 – ¿Cuándo?
 – ¿Esta tarde?
 – Vale.
2 – ¿Dígame?
 – ¡Hola, Tere! ¿Quieres jugar al baloncesto?
 – ¿Cuándo?
 – ¿El sábado?
 – De acuerdo.
3 – ¿Diga?
 – ¡Hola, Esteban! ¿Quieres ir de compras?
 – ¿Cuándo?
 – ¿El lunes?
 – Está bien.
4 – ¿Dígame?
 – ¡Hola, Esther! ¿Quieres ir a la playa?
 – ¿Cuándo?
 – ¿Mañana?
 – Está bien.

2b Escucha otra vez. ¿Cuándo van a hacer las actividades? (AT1/3) [W2,5; S4,7; L3]

✖ *Listening for information and instructions – Level C*

Listening. Pupils listen to the recording a second time and write down when the people are going to meet to do the activities. Before attempting this activity, teachers may wish to revise days of the week and the expressions *mañana* and *esta tarde*.

Answers

| 1 esta tarde | 2 el sábado | 3 el lunes | 4 mañana |

Tapescript

As for activity 2a

2c Invita a tu compañero/a a salir. (AT2/3) [W2,5; S4,9; L4]

✖ *Speaking and interacting with others – Level D*

Speaking. Pupils work in pairs to make up a phone conversation arranging to go out, agreeing when and where. Teachers may wish to suggest that pupils add the time and meeting place, using structures from activity 1. This could be combined with speaking activity 3b opposite.

Starter 2: Re-ordering text [T1,2,5; L6]

Aims: To develop reading and prediction skills; to revise and practise transactional language. (Timing: 10 minutes)

Resources: Resource and Assessment File, page 117 (Starter 2)

Pairwork activity: Make a copy of the worksheet for each pair of pupils. Each pair will need a pair of scissors. Explain that pupils must cut out each part of the conversation and then put all the parts in the correct order. Pupils can practise the conversation when they have finished. If there is time, encourage pupils to change different details in the conversation and to practise this with their partners.

3a Escucha y empareja los lugares con las horas. (1–4) (AT1/3) [W1,2; S4,7; L3]

✖ *Listening for information and instructions – Level C/D*

Listening. Pupils listen to the recording and match up the places with the meeting times. Before attempting this activity, teachers may wish to revise the time with their pupils.

Answers

| 1 2, c | 2 4, e | 3 1, a | 4 5, b |

Tapescript

1 – ¿Dónde nos encontramos?
 – En la plaza.
 – ¿A qué hora?
 – A las 10.45.
 – De acuerdo.
2 – ¿Dónde nos encontramos?
 – En el polideportivo.
 – ¿A qué hora?
 – A las 5.30.
 – Vale.
3 – ¿Dónde nos encontramos?
 – ¿En el café?
 – ¿A qué hora?
 – A las 4.15.
 – Está bien.
4 – ¿Dónde nos encontramos?
 – En mi casa.
 – ¿A qué hora?
 – A las 11.00.
 – Bueno.

3b Con tu compañero/a, arregla la hora y el lugar de tu encuentro. (AT2/3) [W1,2; S4,9; L4]

✖ *Speaking and interacting with others – Level D/E*

módulo 6 — El tiempo libre

Speaking. Pupils work in pairs to arrange the time and place that they will meet up. This could be combined with the speaking activity 2c overleaf.

4a Lee los mensajes de Inés. Contesta a las preguntas. (AT3/3) [W2,5; S4,7,9; T3]

✠ *Reading for information and instructions – Level D*

Reading. Pupils read the four messages from Inés and answer the questions to check they have understood the key information.

Answers

1 Las amigas van a ir de compras.
2 El sábado por la tarde.
3 Se encuentran en la entrada del centro comercial.
4 A las dos y media.

4b Con tu compañero/a, escribe unos mensajes similares. (AT4/3) [W2,5; S4,9; T6]

✠ *Writing to exchange information and ideas – Level D*

Writing. In pairs, pupils write similar messages asking and agreeing to meet up, including the activity, time and place.

> **Plenary**
> At the beginning of the lesson explain to two students (of similar ability) that you will be asking them to summarise the main points of the lesson at the end of the class. They take it in turns to cover what has been learned, using the board or projector. The rest of the class discusses the summary and corrects any mistakes and adds any information that may have been omitted.

Cuaderno A, page 58

1 Completa los diálogos con las palabras apropiadas. (AT3/3) [W2,5; T1]

✠ *Knowing about language*

Reading. Pupils use the picture prompts to help them choose the appropriate words to complete the dialogue.

Answers

fútbol, parque, cuatro y media

2 Escribe las frases en el orden apropiado. (AT3/3) [W2,5; T1]

✠ *Knowing about language*

Reading. Pupils rearrange the sentences into the correct order to complete the dialogues.

Answers

a	b
Esta tarde.	Mañana.
En la estación.	En la plaza.
A las siete y media.	A las once.
Hasta luego.	Hasta mañana.

3 Escribe un diálogo similar. (AT4/2) [W2,5; T6]

✠ *Knowing about language*

Writing. Pupils use the writing frame to help them write a similar dialogue.

Cuaderno B, page 58

1 Completa los diálogos con las palabras apropiadas. (AT3/3) [W2,5; T1]

✠ *Knowing about language*

Reading. Pupils use the picture prompts to help them choose the appropriate words to complete the dialogues.

Answers

a baloncesto, polideportivo, seis
b fútbol, parque, cuatro y media

2 Escribe las frases en el orden apropiado para completar el diálogo. (AT3/3) [W2,5; T1]

✠ *Knowing about language*

Reading. Pupils rearrange the sentences into the correct order to complete the dialogue.

Answers

El sábado por la tarde.
En la estación.
A las siete y media.
Hasta luego.

3 Escribe un diálogo similar. (AT4/3) [W2,5; T6]

✠ *Writing to exchange information and ideas – Level D*

Writing. Pupils make up a similar dialogue of their own.

Hoja de trabajo 6, page 111 [T1,2]

1a Pupils work in pairs to work out the correct order of the phrases to make a conversation, inviting a friend to go out. Once they have agreed on the sequence, they should write out the phrases in order and practise the resulting dialogue.

1b Pupils then adapt the underlined words in activity 1a to make up their own dialogue. They may wish to write the script.

módulo 6

5 Este fin de semana
(Pupil's Book pages 106–107)

Main topics
- Saying what you are going to do at the weekend

Key Framework Objectives
- Time and tenses 7S7 (Part-launch. See also 3.4 and 5.6)
- Verbs present 7W5 (Reinforcement)
- Word order 7S1 (Reinforcement)
- Reading using cues 7T1 (Reinforcement)
- Reading aloud 7T2 (Reinforcement)

Grammar
- I am going to …: *ir* + *a* + infinitive
- Present tense of *ir*

Key language
¿Qué vas a hacer este fin de semana?
Voy a ver un vídeo.
Va a dormir.
Vamos a hacer muchas cosas.
Van a montar en bicicleta.
Voy a jugar al tenis con mis amigos.
Voy a levantarme pronto.
Voy a acostarme a las once.
Salgo con mis amigos.
por la mañana
por la noche
por la tarde

Resources
Cassette C, side 2
CD 3, track 14
Cuaderno A and B, page 59

Starter 1: Back-to-front sentences
[W3,5; S1,9; T2; L1,6]

Aims: To develop reading skills by focusing closely on the text. (Timing: 5 minutes)

Pairwork activity: Write the following sentences on a transparency: *Voy a ir de compras; Voy a hacer mis deberes; Voy a ver un vídeo; Voy a jugar con mi Playstation.* Display this transparency with the text back-to-front and ask pupils to read the sentences in pairs. One person reads the sentence while the other listens, and corrects any errors in pronunciation. Then select some pupils to read the sentences to the class and comment on pronunciation.

1a Empareja los dibujos con las frases. (AT1/2) [W2,5; S4]

✄ *Knowing about language*

Reading. Pupils match up the pictures with the phrases. Most of the vocabulary has already been encountered in this module, and pupils should be able to attempt this activity without too much intervention from the teacher.

Answers

1 c	2 d	3 f	4 j	5 b	6 i	7 h
8 g	9 a	10 k	11 e			

1b Escucha y comprueba tus respuestas. (AT1/2) [W2,5; S4; L1]

✄ *Knowing about language*

Listening. Pupils listen to the recording and check their answers to activity 1a.

After completing this activity, teachers may wish to see if pupils have understood that *voy a* + infinitive refers to actions in the future.

R Teachers may wish to revise the verb *ir*, and explain to pupils that they need to add *a* to all parts of the verb (as detailed in the *Gramática* box) in order to form the immediate future.

Pupils should be reminded that they have already encountered the infinitive form when learning to express likes and dislikes on pages 100–101.

Tapescript
1 – ¿Qué vas a hacer este fin de semana?
 – Voy a jugar al fútbol.
2 – ¿Qué vas a hacer este fin de semana?
 – Voy a jugar al tenis. ¿Y tú?
3 – Voy a hacer mis deberes.
4 – ¿Qué vas a hacer este fin de semana?
 – Voy a ir de compras.
5 – Voy a jugar con mi Playstation.
6 – Voy a dormir.
7 – ¿Qué vas a hacer este fin de semana?
 – Voy a ver un vídeo.
8 – Voy a ver la televisión. ¿Y tú?
9 – Voy a escuchar música.
10 – ¿Qué vas a hacer este fin de semana?
 – Voy a salir con mis amigos.
11 – Voy a montar en bicicleta.

2a Haz un sondeo. ¿Qué vas a hacer este fin de semana? Pregunta a tus compañeros/as de clase. (AT2/2–3) [W2,5; S4,9; L4]

✄ *Speaking and interacting with others – Level D*

Speaking. Pupils carry out a survey of what their classmates are going to do this weekend.

módulo 6 — El tiempo libre

Before attempting this activity, teachers may wish to practise the question and answer with the whole class, and ask pupils to write down their own answer, which will help them in the survey.

Pupils will need to draw a grid for the survey, to include the activities and space for their classmates' names and responses.

ICT activity

By using a spreadsheet such as *Excel*, pupils can save time as they can enter their results directly on to the computer, instead of drawing a grid in their books. Pupils can also use the chart wizard to produce pie charts or bar graphs which can be used to summarise the results, providing an opportunity to practise the third-person form of the immediate future (see activity 2b below).

2b ¿Cuáles son las actividades más populares en tu clase? Escribe las actividades en orden. (AT4/2) [W2,5; S9]

Writing to exchange information and ideas – Level D

Writing. Pupils use their data from the survey to write sentences about the most popular activities in the class, following the model in the example.

Starter 2: Text scanning [W1,2; S7; T1,3]

Aims: To develop pupils' confidence in reading longer texts in Spanish; to build on reading skills by getting pupils to focus on specific aspects of a text; to revise knowledge of time indicators (*este fin de semana, el sábado por la mañana, a las diez, después, por la noche, el domingo por la mañana*). (Timing: 5 minutes)

Activity: Ask pupils to look briefly (ten seconds maximum) at the text on page 107 of the Pupil's Book and to tell you, in English, what they can about it. Ask pupils questions to elicit an assessment of the text. For example: What kind of text is this? Is this a formal or informal letter? How do we know? What is the objective of the letter? What is the main verb tense used by María? Then give pupils 90 seconds to scan the text for time indicators. Give them one example to start them off. Ask pupils how many they have found. Compile a list on the board which pupils can then refer to when they write their own letter in exercise 3c.

3a Lee la carta y pon los dibujos en el orden en que se mencionan. (AT3/4) [W5; T1,3]

Reading for information and instructions – Level D

Reading. Pupils read the letter from María and use the information to put the pictures into the order in which the activities are mentioned.

Answers

c, g, b, h, a, f, d, e

3b Contesta a las preguntas. (AT3/4) [T1,3]

Reading for information and instructions – Level E

Reading. Pupils reread the letter in activity 3a and answer the questions in English.

Answers

1. At 10 o'clock on Saturday, she is going to go to her piano lesson.
2. Afterwards she is going to play tennis with her friends.
3. In the afternoon she and her cousin are going shopping.
4. María is going to buy a CD.
5. They are going out to eat in a restaurant.
6. On Sunday morning, María is going to get up late, at 11 o'clock.
7. She is going with her parents to visit her grandmother.
8. In the afternoon she is going to go to the cinema with her friends.
9. In the evening she is going to do her homework and watch a bit of television.
10. She is going to go to bed at 10 o'clock.

3c Contesta a la carta de María. (AT4/3–5) [T6]

Writing to establish and maintain personal contact – Level D/E/F

Writing. Pupils use the writing frame to write a reply to María. Teachers may wish their pupils to include some reference to the present tense, such as their name and age, which will fulfil the criteria for writing at level 5.

Plenary

Divide the class into groups of three or four and assign each group a picture from page 107 of the Pupil's Book (a–h). The groups have three minutes to invent as many sentences as they can about their picture. Ask each group how many sentences they have written. Discuss briefly with pupils strategies for inventing sentences, such as changing the verbs, negatives and adding adjectives. For example: for picture 'a' you could say: *Me gusta salir con mi familia; No me gusta salir con mi familia; Voy a ir a un restaurante con mi familia; Voy a ir a un restaurante con mi familia grande.* Then give pupils another three minutes to add to their list of sentences.

El tiempo libre — módulo 6

Cuaderno A, page 59

1 Elige la frase apropiada para cada dibujo. (AT3/2) [W2,5]

✖ *Knowing about language*

Reading. Pupils choose the correct sentence for each picture.

Answers

| a 1 | b 7 | c 4 | d 5 | e 3 | f 2 | g 6 |

2 Mira los dibujos y completa las frases. (AT3/2) [W5; S2]

✖ *Knowing about language*

Reading. Pupils use the pictures to help them complete the appropriate infinitive form of the verbs in each sentence.

Answers

| a ir | b salir | c hacer | d jugar | e escuchar | f jugar |

3 ¿Qué vas a hacer este fin de semana? Escribe cuatro frases. (AT4/2–3) [W2,5; S9]

✖ *Writing to establish and maintain personal contact – Level D*

Writing. Pupils write four sentences about what they are going to do this weekend.

Cuaderno B, page 59

1 Mira el cuadro y lee las frases. ¿Quién(es) habla(n)? (AT3/2) [W2,5]

✖ *Reading for information and instructions – Level C*

Reading. Pupils use the information in the grid to help them decide which person (or persons) is saying each sentence.

Answers

a	Montse, Andrés
b	Miriam, Oriol
c	Miriam
d	Montse, Miriam, Oriol
e	Montse, Andrés, Miriam, Oriol
f	Montse, Andrés
g	Andrés, Miriam, Oriol

2 Lee el texto. Subraya y corrige las frases falsas. (AT3/3) [W5; S3; T1]

✖ *Reading for information and instructions – Level D*

Reading. Pupils read the text and underline the sentences that give incorrect information about the people in activity 1. They then correct these sentences.

Answers

Montse y Miriam van a jugar al fútbol – Andrés, Miriam y Oriol …
Oriol va a jugar en su Playstation y va a dormir – Oriol va a jugar al fútbol, escuchar música e ir de compras.
Andrés va a ir de compras – Miriam y Oriol van …

3 ¿Qué vas a hacer este fin de semana? Escribe cinco frases. (AT4/2–5) [W2,5; S9]

✖ *Writing to establish and maintain personal contact – Level D/E/F*

Writing. Pupils write five sentences about what they are going to do this weekend.

✚ Teachers may wish to set this as an extended writing task, to include descriptions, opinions, connectives and at least one reference to the present tense in order to fulfil the criteria for level 5 writing.

módulo 6

6 ¿Ayudas en casa?

(Pupil's Book pages 108–109)

Main topics

- Saying how you help at home
- Saying how you are going to help at the weekend

Key Framework Objectives

- Everyday words 7W1 (Reinforcement)
- Basic negatives 7S5 (Reinforcement)
- Stories and songs 7C4 (Reinforcement)

Grammar

- The immediate future: *ir + a + infinitive*

Key language

¿Ayudas en casa?
Arreglo mi dormitorio.
Friego los platos.
Lavo el coche.
El lunes barro el patio.
Cocino.
Hago la compra.
Paso la aspiradora.
Plancho mi uniforme.
Preparo la cena.
Saco la basura.
No hago nada.
Pongo la mesa.
Quito la mesa.
Ayudo un poco.
¿Cómo vas a ayudar?
Voy a preparar la cena el domingo.
Voy a ir al supermercado el sábado por la mañana.

Resources

Cassette C, side 2
CD 3, track 15
Cuaderno A and B, page 60
Starter 1, Resource and Assessment File, page 118
Hoja de trabajo 7, Resource and Assessment File, page 112
Grammar 1 and 2, Resource and Assessment File, pages 113 and 114
OHTs 30 and 31: household chores

Starter 1: Letter strings [W1,6; T2; L1,6]

Aims: To revise phonetic alphabet pronunciation by introducing the different pronunciation of *rro, cho, go, rre, che, ge* and to introduce household chores vocabulary. (Timing: 10 minutes)

Resources: Resource and Assessment File, page 118 (Starter 1)

Activity: Make an OHT using the master provided. Display the top part of the OHT with the letter strings. Ask pupils to pronounce individual letters with the Spanish alphabet, e.g. *rr* (erre), *o* (oh), *g* (heh), *ch* (cheh), etc. Pupils then attempt to pronounce the letter strings. Then say the letter strings for pupils to repeat. Discuss the properties of the letter *g* (hard sound before u, a and o). Display the words on the OHT (some will be familiar and some unfamiliar) and give pupils two minutes with their partner to try to pronounce them correctly. Go through the correct pronunciation and reward pupil accuracy. Display the gapped words and read out the complete version: *Barro el patio; Arreglo mi dormitorio; Hago la compra; Pongo la mesa; Lavo el coche; Plancho mi uniforme; No hago nada; Friego los platos.* Pupils write down the full version by listening. Then display the tongue-twisters. Pupils work in pairs to try to say them. End with a competition of who can say the tongue-twisters in the shortest time.

1 Escucha y repite. Pon atención a la pronunciación. (AT1/2) [W2,5; L1]

✣ *Knowing about language*

Listening. Pupils listen to the recording and repeat, paying attention to their pronunciation. Teachers may wish to ask pupils to follow the phrases at the same time as listening to the recording, to reinforce the link between sounds and writing.

Before attempting this activity, teachers may wish to introduce the new structures using an OHT or flashcards, or mime.

Teachers should also make it clear that the phrases in this activity are in the present tense, not the immediate future. It is important to reinforce the difference between the two tenses at this early stage in pupils' learning.

Tapescript

a – Cocino. Preparo la cena.
b – Barro el patio.
c – Arreglo mi dormitorio.
d – Hago la compra.
e – Paso la aspiradora.
f – Saco la basura.
g – Pongo la mesa.
h – Quito la mesa.
i – Friego los platos.
j – Lavo el coche.
k – No hago nada.
l – Plancho mi uniforme.

2 Haz un sondeo. Pregunta a tus compañeros/as de clase si ayudan en casa y cuándo. (AT2/3) [W2,5; S4,9; L4]

✣ *Speaking and interacting with others – Level D*

Speaking. Pupils conduct a survey to find out what their classmates do to help out at home, and when.

3a Escucha y lee la canción. ¿Verdad (✓) o mentira (✗)? (AT1/3, AT3/3) [W2,5; T1; L1; C4]

✣ *Listening for enjoyment*

El tiempo libre — módulo 6

Listening/Reading. Pupils read and listen to the song, and decide whether the statements are true (*verdad*) or false (*mentira*) to show they understand.

✚ Depending on the ability of the pupils, teachers may prefer to ask them to cover up the text of the song and attempt the comprehension activity by listening, and then read the text to check their answers.

Answers

| 1 ✓ | 2 ✗ | 3 ✓ | 4 ✓ | 5 ✗ | 6 ✓ |

Tapescript

Ayudo en casa
El lunes saco la basura,
Saco la basura
Y paso la aspiradora.
Ayudo en casa,
Ayudo en casa.

El martes pongo la mesa,
Pongo la mesa
Y quito la mesa.
Ayudo en casa,
Ayudo en casa.

El miércoles hago la compra,
Hago la compra
Y saco la basura.
Ayudo en casa,
Ayudo en casa.
El jueves barro el patio,
Barro el patio
Y arreglo mi cuarto.
Ayudo en casa,
Ayudo en casa.

El viernes lavo el coche,
Lavo el coche
Y plancho mi uniforme.
Ayudo en casa,
Ayudo en casa.

El fin de semana, sábado y domingo
Sábado y domingo
No hago nada.
No ayudo en casa,
No ayudo en casa.

3b Escribe una lista de las tareas domésticas que haces todos los días. (AT4/2–4) [W2,5; S9; T5]

✉ *Writing to exchange information and ideas – Level D/E*

Writing. Pupils write a list of the chores they have to do each day. They may need to invent their answers if they are not very helpful! Teachers may wish to encourage their pupils to produce paragraphs including connectives and opinions.

Starter 2: Opposites [W1,5; S3,5,9]

Aims: To revise household chores and the third-person singular of the present tense of regular -*ar* verbs and *hacer*; to reinforce knowledge of forming negative sentences. (Timing: 5–10 minutes)

Activity: Pupils look at the statements (1–6) for exercise 3a on page 108 of the Pupil's Book. Ask pupils to read out each statement and check their understanding in English. Pupils work in pairs to make the statements the opposite of what is written: (*El lunes el chico no saca la basura; El martes no pasa la aspiradora; El miércoles barra el patio; El jueves no arregla su dormitorio; El viernes no lava su uniforme; El fin de semana hace mucho*). Pupils then read out their sentences and the other members of the class indicate if the word order of the sentences is correct. NB: the last one is slightly more difficult as it requires pupils to substitute the word *nada* with an appropriate opposite word.

✚ Higher-ability groups, or pupils who have completed this quickly, could then change the sentences to the immediate future, using the *Gramática* box on page 109 for support.

4a ¿Cómo van a ayudar en casa este fin de semana? Lee y empareja los jóvenes con los dibujos. (AT3/3) [W2,5; S9; T1]

✉ *Reading for information and instructions – Level D*

Reading. Pupils match up the texts with the pictures to show what the young people are going to do to help at the weekend.

Answers

| Leonora 2, Agustín 3, Enrique 1, Eva 4 |

4b Escucha y comprueba tus respuestas. (AT1/3) [W2,5; S4; L1]

✉ *Listening for information and instructions – Level D*

Listening. Pupils listen to the recording and check their answers to activity 4a.

R Teachers may wish to use this opportunity to consolidate the immediate future tense, and ask pupils to read through the *Gramática* box.

Tapescript

1 – ¿Cómo vas a ayudar en casa este fin de semana, Leonora?
  – Pues el sábado por la tarde voy a arreglar mi dormitorio. Está muy desorganizado.
2 – ¿Cómo vas a ayudar en casa este fin de semana, Agustín?
  – Voy a hacer la compra.
  – ¿Cuándo?

módulo 6 El tiempo libre

– Voy a ir al supermercado el sábado por la mañana con mi madre.
3 – ¿Cómo vas a ayudar en casa este fin de semana, Eva?
– Voy a pasar la aspiradora.
– ¿Cuándo?
– El domingo por la tarde.
4 – Y tú, Enrique. ¿Cómo vas a ayudar en casa este fin de semana?
– Voy a cocinar. Me gusta mucho cocinar.
– ¿Cuándo?
– Voy a preparar la cena el domingo.

4c Con tu compañero/a, pregunta y contesta. (AT2/3) [W2,5; S4,9; L4]

✉ *Speaking and interacting with others – Level D/E*

Speaking. In pairs, pupils take turns to ask and answer questions about what they are going to do to help at the weekend, and when.

4d Escribe cómo y cuándo vas a ayudar en casa este fin de semana. (AT4/3–5) [W2,5; S6,9]

✉ *Writing to exchange information and ideas – Level D/E/F*

Writing. Pupils write about how and when they are going to help at home this weekend.

➕ Teachers may wish to ask pupils to contrast how they normally help out, using the present tense, with how they are going to help out this weekend, using the immediate future tense, to practise the contrast between these tenses and fulfil the criteria for writing at level 5.

Plenary
Using the *Resumen* section on page 110 of the Pupil's Book, pupils test each other on the language that has been introduced during the module. Pupils can award each other a point for each correct answer. Pupils with the most points after three minutes can take up the challenge of the 'hot seat', where they have to accurately answer questions asked by the teacher and/or other students to stay in the seat.

Cuaderno A, page 60

1 Mira los dibujos y completa las frases con las letras que faltan. (AT3/2) [W1,5,7]

✉ *Knowing about language*

Reading. Pupils fill in the missing letter in each gap to complete the sentences, using the pictures to help them.

Answers

a Saco	b Paso	c dormitorio	d Pongo	e los
f Barro	g Lavo	h Hago		

2 ¿Qué hace Sergio para ayudar en casa? Mira los dibujos y escribe frases con los verbos apropiados. (AT4/2) [W1,5,9]

✉ *Knowing about language*

Writing. Pupils write sentences, using the third-person form of the verbs, to say what Sergio does to help around the house.

Answers

a Pone la mesa.	d Hace la compra.
b Saca la basura.	e Arregla su dormitorio.
c Barre el patio.	f Friega los platos.

3 ¿Qué haces para ayudar en casa? Escribe cuatro frases. (AT4/2–5) [W2,5; S9]

✉ *Writing to exchange information and ideas – Level D*

Writing. Pupils write four sentences saying what they do to help at home.

Cuaderno B, page 60

1 Empareja las frases y elige el dibujo apropiado. (AT3/2) [W2,5; S1]

✉ *Knowing about language*

Reading. Pupils match up the sentence halves and choose the appropriate picture for each completed sentence.

Answers

Arreglo mi dormitorio. c	Pongo la mesa. d
Hago la compra. h	Lavo el coche. g
Paso la aspiradora. b	Friego los platos. e
Saco la basura. a	Barro el patio. f

2 ¿Qué hace Sergio para ayudar en casa? Mira los dibujos y escribe frases con los verbos apropiados. (AT4/2) [W1,5; S9]

✉ *Knowing about language*

Writing. Pupils write sentences, using the third-person form of the verbs, to say what Sergio does to help around the house, following the picture cues.

Answers

a Pone la mesa.	d Hace la compra.
b Saca la basura.	e Arregla su dormitorio.
c Barre el patio.	f Friega los platos.

El tiempo libre — módulo 6

3 ¿Qué vas a hacer para ayudar en casa este fin de semana? Escribe cuatro frases. (AT4/2–5) [W2,5; S9]

Writing to exchange information and ideas – Level D

Writing. Pupils write four sentences saying what they are going to do to help at home this weekend. Teachers may wish to encourage pupils to contrast what they usually do with what they are going to do.

Hoja de trabajo 7, page 112

Pairwork activity for pupils to practise asking and answering about what they do to help out at home. Pupils should answer not for themselves, but base their answers on the ticks and crosses on the grid. Pupils should record their partner's answers on the grid and they then compare answers after completing this activity.

Grammar 1, Resource and Assessment File, page 113 [W5]

Activities to practise adapting the infinitive forms of verbs to produce phrases in the present and immediate future tenses.

1 Answers

Infinitive	Present	Immediate future
practicar la natación (to do / go swimming)	practico la natación (I do / go swimming)	voy a practicar la natación (I am going to do / go swimming)
escuchar música (to listen to music)	escucho música (I listen to music)	voy a escuchar la música (I am going to listen to music)
jugar al baloncesto (to play basketball)	juego al baloncesto (I play basketball)	Voy a jugar al baloncesto (I'm going to play basketball)
pasar la aspiradora (to vacuum clean)	paso la aspiradora (I vacuum clean)	voy a pasar la aspiradora (I am going to vacuum clean)
montar a caballo (to go horseriding)	monto a caballo (I go horseriding)	voy a montar a caballo (I'm going to go horseriding)
mandar un mensaje (to send a message)	mando un mensaje (I send a message)	voy a mandar un mensaje (I'm going to send a message)
poner la mesa (to lay the table)	pongo la mesa (I lay the table)	voy a poner la mesa (I'm going to lay the table)
hacer la cama (to make the bed)	hago la cama (I make the bed)	voy a hacer la cama (I'm going to make the bed)
arreglar el dormitorio (to tidy the bedroom)	arreglo el dormitorio (I tidy the bedroom)	voy a arreglar la dormitorio (I'm going to tidy the bedroom)
cocinar (to cook)	cocino (I cook)	voy a cocina (I'm going to cook)

Grammar 2, Resource and Assessment File, page 114 [W5; S9; T1]

Further practice of verbs in different forms.

2 Answers

Me llamo, tengo, me gustan, practico, juego, practican, vamos, me gusta, leer, tocar, ayudamos, arreglo, pasa, prepana, friega, ayudas

3 Answers

Me gustan los deportes, me gusta leer. The verb 'gustar' agrees with the object. If the object is singular then gusta is used. If it is plural, use gustan.

4 Answers

Se llama Miguel. Tiene 12 años. Le gusta la equitación y le gusta al tenis. Los fines de semana, con su hermana va de compras. Con su hermana, ayudan en casa. Arregla su dormitorio …

módulo 6

Resumen y Prepárate

(Pupil's Book pages 110–111)

Resumen

This is a checklist of language covered in Module 6. There is a comprehensive **Resumen** list for Module 6 in the Pupil's Book (page 110) and a **Resumen** test sheet in Cuaderno A and B (page 63).

Key Framework Objectives

- Basic negatives 7S5 (Reinforcement)
- Gist and detail 7L3 (Reinforcement)
- Reading using cues 7T1 (Reinforcement)
- Texts as prompts 7T6 (Reinforcement)

Prepárate

A revision test to give practice for the test itself at the end of the module.

Resources

Cassette C, side 2
CD 3, track 16
Cuaderno A and B, Repaso (previously ¡Extra!), page 61; Gramática, page 62

---

1 Escucha y elige las actividades que se mencionan. (AT1/3) [W1,2,5; L3]

✉ *Listening for information and instructions – Level C*

Listening. Pupils listen to the recording and note down the letters of the activities that are mentioned.

Answers

a, b, e, g, i, j

Tapescript

– ¿Qué deportes practicas?
– Juego al fútbol.
– Practico el atletismo.
– ¿Qué te gusta hacer en tu tiempo libre?
– Me gusta escuchar música.
– Me gusta leer.
– ¿Qué haces todos los días?
– Voy al instituto.
– Veo la televisión.

2a Escucha los diálogos y elige las actividades que se mencionan. (1–3) (AT1/3) [W2,5; S4; L3]

✉ *Listening for information and instructions – Level D*

Listening. Pupils listen to the recording and note down the letter of the activity that is mentioned in each dialogue.

Answers

1 c	2 d	3 a

Tapescript

1 – Hola, Eli. Soy Carina. ¿Quieres ir de compras?
– ¿Cuándo?
– El sábado.
– Vale. ¿A qué hora?
– ¿A las cinco y media?
– El sábado a las cinco y media. De acuerdo.
2 – Hola, Jaime. Soy Luis. ¿Quieres jugar al baloncesto?
– ¿Cuándo?
– El miércoles.
– ¿A qué hora?
– A las siete.

– Está bien.
– Fenomenal. Nos vemos el miércoles.
3 – Hola, Neus. Soy Eduard. ¿Quieres ir al cine?
– ¿Cuándo?
– El viernes.
– ¿A qué hora?
– ¿A las seis y media?
– Sí, de acuerdo. El viernes a las seis y media.
– Eso es. Hasta entonces.

2b Escucha otra vez y escribe el día y la hora. (AT1/3) [W1,2; S4,7; L3]

✉ *Listening for information and instructions – Level D*

Listening. Pupils listen to the recording again and note down the day and the time for each dialogue.

Answers

1	el sábado a las cinco y media
2	el miércoles a las siete
3	el viernes a las seis y media

Tapescript

As for activity 2a

3 Con tu compañero/a, di si haces o no haces las tareas en los dibujos. (AT2/2) [W5; S5,9]

✉ *Speaking and interacting with others – Level D*

Speaking. In pairs, pupils use the picture prompts to tell their partner what they do and don't do to help at home.

4a Completa las frases de la carta con las palabras apropiadas. (AT3/4) [W5; S1; T1]

✉ *Knowing about language*

Reading. Pupils choose the appropriate words from the list to fill in the blanks in the letter.

Answers

tiempo, gusta, ir, juego, hago, leer, dormitorio, voy

El tiempo libre — módulo 6

4b Escribe una carta similar. Cambia las palabras subrayadas. (AT4/5) [W2,5; T6]

✉ *Writing to establish and maintain personal contact – Level D*

Writing. Pupils adapt the letter by changing the words that are underlined.

Cuaderno A, page 61

Repaso (previously ¡Extra!)

1a Lee la entrevista y empareja los dibujos con seis actividades que Virginia menciona. Escribe una frase de la entrevista para cada dibujo. (AT3/4) [W2,5; S9; T1]

✉ *Reading for information and instructions – Level D*

Reading. Pupils read the interview with Virginia and choose the six activities that she mentions. Under the pictures of the six activities that she mentions, pupils write the appropriate sentence from the interview.

Answers

| a Practico el atletismo. |
| b Juego al tenis. |
| c Me gusta salir con mis amigos. |
| d Odio los videojuegos. |
| e Voy al cine con mis amigos. |
| f Pongo y quito la mesa. |

1b ¿Verdad (✓) o mentira (✗)? (AT3/4) [T1]

✉ *Reading for information and instructions – Level D*

Pupils decide whether the statements are true (*verdad*) or false (*mentira*).

Answers

| a ✓ | b ✓ | c ✗ | d ✓ | e ✗ | f ✓ | g ✗ |
| h ✓ | | | | | | |

Cuaderno B, page 61

Repaso (previously ¡Extra!)

1 Lee la entrevista y subraya. (AT3/4) [W1,2,5; T1]

✉ *Reading for information and instructions – Level D*

Reading. Pupils read the interview and underline information which comes under the categories a–d (**a** six sports, **b** four things Virginia likes doing, **c** two things she doesn't like doing, **d** four things Virginia does to help at home).

Answers

| a el atletismo, la natación, el ciclismo, el tenis, el surfing, esquiar |
| b escuchar música, leer, salir con sus amigos, ir a la playa |
| c ir de compras, jugar con los videojuegos |
| d arreglar su dormitorio, pasar la aspiradora, poner la mesa, quitar la mesa |

2 ¿Verdad (✓) o mentira (✗)? (AT3/4) [T1]

✉ *Reading for information and instructions – Level D*

Reading. Pupils reread the interview and decide whether the statements are true (*verdad*) or false (*mentira*).

Answers

| a ✓ | b ✗ | c ✗ | d ✓ | e ✓ | f ✗ | g ✓ |
| h ✗ | | | | | | |

3 Escribe respuestas a las preguntas de la entrevista sobre ti. (AT4/2–4) [W2,5; S9; T6]

✉ *Writing to establish and maintain personal contact – Level D/E/F*

Writing. Pupils write answers to the interview questions for themselves.

Cuaderno A, page 62

Gramática

1 Escribe *el* o *la* en los espacios. (AT3/1) [W2,4]

✉ *Knowing about language*

Reading. Pupils write *el* or *la* for each noun as appropriate in the spaces.

Answers

| a el | b el | c la | d el | e el | f la | g el |
| h el | i la | j el | | | | |

2 Completa las frases con la forma apropiada del verbo. (AT3/3) [W5]

✉ *Knowing about language*

Reading. Pupils revise the parts of the verbs *jugar* and *practicar* and then complete the sentences with the appropriate verb, correctly conjugated.

Answers

| a juega | b juegan | c juega | d juegan | e practican |
| f practica | g practica | | | |

módulo 6 — El tiempo libre

3 Completa las frases con las palabras apropiadas. (AT3/4) [W5]

✉ *Knowing about language*

Reading. Pupils fill in the correct words in the sentences.

Answers

a escuchar	**b** jugar	**c** ir	**d** arreglar	**e** ver
f dormir	**g** lavar	**h** salir	**i** bailar	**j** planchar

Cuaderno B, page 62

Gramática

1 Escribe *el* o *la*. (AT3/1) [W2,4]

✉ *Knowing about language*

Reading. Pupils write *el* or *la* for each noun.

Answers

a el	**b** el	**c** la	**d** el	**e** el	**f** la	**g** el
h el	**i** la	**j** el				

2 Completa las frases con el verbo apropiado. (AT3/3) [W5]

✉ *Knowing about language*

Reading. Pupils revise the parts of the verbs *jugar* and *practicar* and then complete the sentences with the appropriate verb, correctly conjugated.

Answers

juegan, practican, practica, juega, practica, juego

3 Completa las frases con las palabras apropiadas. (AT3/4) [W5]

✉ *Knowing about language*

Reading. Pupils choose the correct word from the list to complete each sentence.

Answers

a prefiero	**b** voy	**c** ir	**d** jugar	**e** Quieres
f Detesto	**g** hacer			

módulo 6

¡Extra! 7 ¡Hasta luego!

(Pupil's Book pages 112–113)

Main topics

This is an optional unit which reviews some of the key language of the module: it features young Spanish people talking about their routines and interests and an activity on the sport of *pelota*.

Key Framework Objectives

- Reading using cues 7T1 (Reinforcement)
- Checking before reading 7T3 (Reinforcement)
- Using resources 7T4 (Reinforcement)
- Everyday culture 7C2 (Reinforcement)

Resources

Cassette C, side 2
CD 3, track 17

Starter 1: **Summarising texts [T1,3,5]**

Aims: To reinforce pupils' knowledge of scanning text for specific details and gist; to develop pupils' confidence in reading longer, more complex Spanish texts and to build on dictionary skills. (Timing: 10 minutes)

Pairwork activity: Before the exercise, write up the following headings on the board or on a transparency, laid out as a form to complete: *Nombre, Edad, Ciudad, Deportes, Otros Pasatiempos, Familia, Mascotas*. Divide the class into two: one side will study the texts on page 112 of the Pupil's Book by *José Manuel* and *Patricia*, the other will look at those by *David* and *María*. Working in pairs, pupils complete the form for the two people they have been assigned. Explain to pupils that they may use dictionaries. However, there is a time limit (seven minutes) and so they must decide how and when to use their dictionaries. When pupils have finished, ask them to feed back the answers and also to discuss the difficulties associated with reading long texts and the advantages and disadvantages of dictionary use.

1a Lee las cartas y elige un/a compañero/a de intercambio ideal para cada joven. (AT4/4) [T1,3,4]

✉ *Reading for information and instructions – Level E*

Reading. Pupils read the letter and choose an ideal exchange partner for each teenager.

Answers

José Manuel – Saleh, Patricia – Zara, David – Alex, María – Erica

1b Escucha y lee las cartas otra vez. Elige un/a amigo/a para tus compañeros/as. (AT1/4, AT3/4) [T1,3; L1]

✉ *Listening for information and instructions – Level D/E*

Listening/Reading. Pupils listen to the recording and reread the letters from page 112. They should choose an exchange partner for their classmates.

➕ Teachers may wish to ask pupils to justify their choice. For example *David es un compañero de intercambio ideal para Hassan porque le gusta la música.*

Tapescript

– *¡Hola! Me llamo José Manuel. Tengo 14 años. Vivo en Altafulla. Es un pueblo bastante pequeño al lado del mar. En mi tiempo libre me gusta montar en bicicleta o en monopatín. Los fines de semana a veces voy al cine con mis amigos. Juego al fútbol y al baloncesto. También practico el windsurf. Tengo un hermano y un perro. Cuando estoy en casa, me gusta ver la televisión, jugar con la Playstation y descansar.*

– *Me llamo Patricia. Tengo 13 años. Vivo en Pamplona. Es una ciudad bastante grande. Voy al instituto en autobús pero no está lejos. Las clases empiezan a las ocho y media y terminan a las dos. Luego voy a casa a comer. Ayudo un poco en casa: pongo y quito la mesa y arreglo mi dormitorio. Después, hago los deberes. Luego salgo un rato con mis amigos. Los fines de semana, me gusta ir de compras o a la piscina. Tengo dos hermanas. Me encanta jugar con mi gato. ¡Odio el fútbol!*

– *Me llamo David. Tengo 14 años. Vivo en un pueblo cerca de Granada en el sur de España. En verano me gusta practicar el ciclismo. Tengo una bicicleta todoterreno. En invierno, vamos a Sol y Nieve. Es una estación de esquí en las montañas de Sierra Nevada. Me gusta esquiar pero prefiero hacer snowboarding. ¡Es mega! Tengo tres hermanos. Me gusta la música y me gusta jugar con el ordenador.*

– *¡Hola! ¿Qué tal? Soy María. Vivo en Barcelona. Me gusta la música, el cine y bailar. También me gusta montar a caballo. No tengo hermanos, soy hija única. ¡Pero tengo un hámster y tengo muchos amigos!*

1c ¿Cuál de los jóvenes eliges para hacer un intercambio? Mira las cartas otra vez y escribe una respuesta similar. (AT4/4) [T5]

✉ *Writing to establish and maintain personal contact – Level D/E/F*

Writing. Pupils choose an exchange partner from the young people on page 112 and write a reply for themselves.

189

módulo 6 — El tiempo libre

Starter 2: Matching sentence halves [S1,3; T1,5]

Aims: To reinforce the understanding of gender, verbs and basic sentence structure. (Timing: 5–10 minutes)

Activity: Write up the following sentences on the board or on a transparency, but jumble up the two halves: *Me gustan los deportes; Es un pueblo bastante grande y moderno; Jugamos al fútbol los sábados; Prefiero la natación porque es muy divertida; Practico el windsurf y me gusta esquiar.* Pupils match up the correct sentence halves. Correct the sentences and ask for justification of pupils' answers. Pupils then have three minutes to change one detail in each sentence. This could be a grammatical detail (i.e. from singular to plural), or a meaning. Pupils then read out their sentences to the class.

2 Haz una entrevista con dos compañeros/as de clase. Copia y rellena la ficha para ellos. (AT2/4) [W2,5; S4,9]

Speaking and interacting with others – Level D

Speaking. Pupils interview two classmates and fill in their answers on the form.

3 Lee el texto y completa las frases. (AT4/4) [T1,4; C2]

Knowing about language

Reading. Pupils read the text about the sport *pelota* and look up any new words, before completing the sentences using the words supplied.

Answers

a rápido	b España	c cesta	d paredes	e va
f pelota				

Plenary

Grammar focus: Ask pupils to write a list of four words that they have learned in the module for each of the following categories:

- Nouns – masculine
- Nouns – feminine
- Verbs – infinitive
- Verbs – present tense (first person)
- Verbs – present tense (third-person singular)
- Verbs – immediate future (first person)

Individuals reveal their answers and the rest of the class decides if the words they have chosen are correct by giving the thumbs up or down.

módulo 6 — *Te toca a ti*

(Pupil's Book pages 126–127)

- Self-access reading and writing at two levels.

A Reinforcement

1 ¿Qué deportes practica Luis? Copia y completa las frases. (AT3/3) [W2,5; T1]

✉ *Knowing about language*

Reading. Pupils copy the text and complete the sentences saying what sports Luis does.

Answers

fútbol, baloncesto, rugby, bicicleta, esquí, surfing, voleibol

2 ¿Qué pasatiempos mencionan Sandra, Jaime, Bea y Juan Pablo? Empareja los dibujos con las personas apropiadas y dibuja los símbolos. (AT3/3) [W2,5; S5; T1,3]

✉ *Reading for information and instructions – Level D*

Reading. Pupils read the texts about Sandra, Jaime, Bea and Juan Pablo, and decide which pictures go with which people. They also draw an appropriate symbol to show if the people like the activity.

Answers

Sandra: e ☺, k ☺, b ☺, l ☺, j ☹

Jaime: n ☺, h ☺, a ☺, g ☹

Bea: d ☺, i ☺, f ☺, c ☺, m ☹

Juan Pablo: e ☺, k ☺, f ☺, i ☺, c ☹

3 Escribe seis frases para describir los dibujos en **2**. (AT4/2–4) [W2,5; S9]

✉ *Writing to establish and maintain personal contact – Level D/E*

Writing. Pupils use the pictures in activity 2 to write six sentences about what they do and don't like doing. Teachers may wish to encourage pupils to produce a piece of extended writing, including connectives and reasons.

B Extension

1 Pon las frases del diálogo en el orden correcto. (AT3/3) [W1; S9; T1]

✉ *Knowing about language*

Reading. Pupils put the phrases in the correct order to make a dialogue.

Answers

g, a, d, h, b, e, f, c

2a Lee la carta y pon los dibujos en el orden en que se mencionan. (AT3/5) [S7; T1,3]

✉ *Reading for information and instructions – Level D*

Reading. Pupils put the pictures in order to match the sequence in which they are mentioned in the letter.

Answers

c, f, i, a, e, d, g, h, b

2b Escribe una carta similar a Enrique. (AT4/4–5) [W2,5; S6,7; T6]

✉ *Writing to establish and maintain personal contact – level D/E/F*

Writing. Pupils write a similar letter to reply to Enrique.

Resource and Assessment File – Skills Sheet Answers

Module 1, Resource and Assessment File, page 8

1a Answers
1 c 2 e 3 b 4 g 5 a 6 d 7 f

1b Answers
1 Open the books
2 Listen to the tape
3 Silence, please!
4 Look at the page
5 Write in the notebooks
6 Look at the blackboard
7 Put the chewing gum in the bin

2 Answers
la silla   el libro   la puerta   el cuaderno   la pizarra   el ordenador

3 Answers
Pupils make their own list of words.

Module 2, Resource and Assessment File, page 24

1a Answers (please set answers in grid)

Orden alfabético	m/f	English
alumno	m.	pupil (male)
bolígrafo	m.	pen
cuaderno	m.	notebook
cumpleaños	m.	birthday
ejercicio	m.	exercise
estuche	m.	pencil case
jueves	m.	Thursday
lápiz	m.	pencil
mal	–	bad
marzo	m.	March
mochila	f.	ruck sack
pluma	f.	fountain pen
profesor	m.	teacher (male)
puerta	f.	door
regla	f.	ruler
sacapuntas	m.	pencil sharpener

2 Answers
¿Cómo?   español   escocés   inglés   pequeño   página   miércoles   sábado

3 Answers

	category
una agenda	c
un profesor	b
una carpeta	c
diciembre	a
un ratón	c
micrófono	a
octubre	a

Module 3, Resource and Assessment File, page 45

1 Answers
All of these words have accents.

3 Answers
1 e 2 c 3 a 4 b 5 d

4 Answers
1 e 2 d 3 a 4 f 5 c 6 b

5 Answers
1 Me llamo …
2 Tengo … el lunes.
3 Las clases empiezan a las …
4 Tengo español a las …
5 Me gusta el profesor de matemáticas porque …

Module 4, Resource and Assessment File, page 61

Answers

English	Español
in a town/village	en un pueblo
the mountains	las montañas
old	antiguo
I get up	me levanto
big	grande
toast	pan tostado
stairs	la escalera
bedroom	el dormitorio
dining room/hall	comedor
first	primero
room	la habitación
downstairs	la planta baja
curtains	las cortinas
office	el despacho
toilets	los servicios
to go horseriding	practicar la equitación
bookcase	la librería
you go to bed	te acuestas
television	la televisión
washbasin	el lávabo
opposite	enfrente
early	pronto
in the afternoon	por la tarde

Module 5, Resource and Assessment File, page 77

1 Answers
They all end in ce

2 Answers
In English: ten and six/ten and seven/etc. In Spanish then: dieciséis/diecisiete/etc.

3a Answers
In English: twenty and one/twenty and two/etc.
In Spanish then: veintiuno/veintidós/etc.

3b Answers
You must add an accent

4 Answers
They all end in a

5 Answers
41	cuarenta y uno	71	setenta y uno
51	cincuenta y uno	81	ochenta y uno
61	sesenta y uno	91	noventa y uno

6 Answers
25	veinticinco	16	dieciséis
78	setenta y ocho	99	noventa y nueve
37	treinta y siete	12	doce
4	cuatro	83	ochenta y tres
65	sesenta y cinco	44	cuarenta y cuatro
15	quince	19	diecinueve
36	treinta y seis		